George Hugh Smith

Elements of Right and of the Law

To which is added a historical and critical essay upon the several theories of

jurisprudence

George Hugh Smith

Elements of Right and of the Law
To which is added a historical and critical essay upon the several theories of jurisprudence

ISBN/EAN: 9783337319694

Printed in Europe, USA, Canada, Australia, Japan

Cover: Foto ©Suzi / pixelio.de

More available books at **www.hansebooks.com**

ELEMENTS OF RIGHT

AND

OF THE LAW.

TO WHICH IS ADDED

A HISTORICAL AND CRITICAL ESSAY UPON THE
SEVERAL THEORIES OF JURISPRUDENCE.

By GEORGE H. SMITH.

*Ante omnia videndum est quid sit justitia, quid jus, quid juris-
prudentia.*—PANDECTS.

SECOND EDITION.

CHICAGO:
CALLAGHAN AND COMPANY.
1887.

PREFACE.

In submitting this little work upon jurisprudence to the public, the author is conscious that the subject is one not likely to attract at first sight either the professional or the general reader; as the latter will probably regard it as belonging exclusively to the province of the former; while the former will be apt to consider any work on general principles as unworthy the attention of the practical lawyer. It will not be out of place, therefore, to explain at some length the object and scope of the work, with a view of showing that the subject at least is one pre-eminently worthy of the attention of all intelligent readers.

The subject is expressed in the title of the work, and will be readily understood by reference to the table of contents. The first book treats of the nature of rights, and of their several kinds, and of the principles by which they are determined; and the second of the nature and general principles of the law, and of its relation to right; the remaining book consists of a historical and critical review of the several theories of jurisprudence.

Of the supreme importance and dignity of the subject there can be no room for doubt; for the term "rights" includes every claim which men can have to personal liberty and security, to the acquisition and use of property, to the enjoyment of the family relations, and even to life itself; and it is therefore obvious that the subject of rights, and of the means by which they are practically protected and enforced, is, of all others, the one in which they are most vitally interested.

It is also, of all branches of human philosophy, the most susceptible of scientific treatment, the most readily understood by readers of ordinary intelligence, and the most interesting. Hence, in all periods distinguished by literary genius, it has attracted the attention of the greatest minds,[1] and has thus given rise to a literature which—whether we regard its utility or the ability displayed in it—is one of the most remarkable achievements of human genius; and to which, also, it may be added, is due the establishment of principles which constitute the very foundation of our modern civilization.

Unfortunately, this literature has in England and America fallen into neglect—in the latter country principally from a general lack of interest in philosophical subjects; in the former from the prevalence of a false theory, which, originating with Bentham, has usurped complete possession of the English mind.

This theory—which we regard as poisoning the very sources of jurisprudence—is to the effect that the law is merely an expression of the will of the state, and that consequently men's rights are

[1] As for example, Socrates, Plato, Aristotle, Grotius, Hobbes, Leibnitz, Kant, Cousin, and others too numerous to mention—besides professional writers.

mere creatures of legislation—a theory which owes
its origin to an accidental blunder of Blackstone in
defining the law, and its general acceptance to the
unfortunate ambiguity of that term; and which also
is as absurd and pernicious in its consequences as it
is ridiculous in its origin—being, in fact, subversive
of human rights and liberty, and of the very foundations of justice and morality.[1]

Nor in making this assertion should the author
be charged with presumption; for, though the
theory referred to is generally regarded by English
jurists as having been so completely demonstrated
by Bentham and Austin[2] as to place it beyond the
pale of legitimate discussion, it stands opposed, not
only to the most deeply seated convictions of mankind generally, but also to the views of jurists and
philosophers of all ages and countries, with the exception of those of England and America; and to
those of English jurists also prior to the advent of
Bentham.

We are supported, also, by the high, but perhaps
unconscious, authority of Sir Henry Maine, one of
the most distinguished advocates of the theory, who
in effect admits that it is in fact untrue of any system of law which exists or ever has existed, and

[1] For a full discussion of this theory, see book 3.

See also, for an interesting discussion and thorough refutations
of the theory, the late work of Mr. Bliss on Sovereignty—published after my own was in print. The identity of the views
taken in the two works, and the coincidence of the arguments
used, furnishes a striking confirmation of the correctness of the
conclusion thus independently reached by the authors.

[2] "One who has led captive a whole English speaking generation:" Bliss on Sovereignty, Preface, viii.

also that it is peculiar to English jurispudence; "there being," as he says, "no signs of its being known on the continent at all." (See observations of Maine, cited *infra*, §§ 573–4,) and we have also in one remarkable passage of his writings, the express admission of its unsatisfactory character.[1]

With regard to the state of English literature upon the subject, one favorable remark may be made that unfortunately is not true of that of America, viz., that there is in fact such a literature; and though the works lately published in that country, owing to the false theory upon which they are based, have served to retard rather than advance the progress of the science, they at least furnish gratifying evidence of a growing interest in jurisprudence, which it is hoped may be communicated to this country.

In conclusion, it must not be inferred from these remarks that our work is addressed exclusively, or even principally, to students of philosophy. It is in fact a law book, written by a lawyer in the intervals of an active practice, and primarily designed for professional lawyers and students of the law—being, indeed, a mere attempt to express in scientific form

---

[1] "There is," he says, "such wide-spread dissatisfaction with existing theories of jurisprudence, and so general a conviction that they do not really solve the question they pretend to dispose of, as to justify the suspicion that some line of inquiry necessary to a perfect result has been incompletely followed, or altogether omitted, by their authors:" Ancient Law, c. 5. We may cite also the authority of Mr. Holland, who, though failing to emancipate himself from Bentham and Austin, has adopted a definition inconsistent with their theory: *Infra*, § 201 a.

the fundamental and general principles of the existing law.

When the author began the study of the law, he was, like other students, bewildered by the confusion reigning in Blackstone and other text-books with regard to the nature and general principles of private right; and he then formed the design that, if he should ever come to understand the subject himself, he would write a plain elementary treatise on the law, which a student could understand, and which should at least be free from logical inconsistency.

In attempting, however, in after years, to carry out this plan, he found it impracticable to proceed without first ascertaining the nature of the law and of its fundamental principles; and he therefore temporarily abandoned his original design and devoted his studies to this problem. The result, after the patient and persevering meditations of a quarter of a century (exceeding by five years the *lucubrationes viginti annorum* of Coke), is contained in this volume; which is therefore to be regarded principally as preparatory to the study of the law.

The work is eminently practical in design; and treats only of subjects to which the attention of the student should be directed at the very outset of his studies, and without attention to which he can acquire only an imperfect knowledge of the law, and that only at a great and unnecessary expense of time and labor. It is also believed that a knowledge of the principles here developed and explained will remove the chief difficulties that beset the path of the student, and—though there be no royal road to knowledge of the law—that it will at least put it into his power to acquire a competent knowledge of it within the compass of a reasonable time.

In its general scope, the work includes the ground covered by the works of Austin, Amos, Holland, and Markby, but takes a fundamentally different view of the subject, and includes much that they do not touch upon. Especially, it refers more constantly to the law in its existing state; and the conclusions arrived at, though demonstrated as far as possible from principle, are supported by a copious citation of authorities.

PREFACE TO SECOND EDITION.

LOS ANGELES, CAL., July 29, 1886.

The destruction of nearly the whole of the first edition of this work by the burning of the premises of Messrs. A. L. Bancroft & Co., the publishers, renders necessary the issue of a new edition, and I avail myself of the opportunity to thoroughly revise the work, and to add some authorities to those originally cited.

Among these is the late able work of Mr. Bliss on "Sovereignty," which I did not have the opportunity of consulting before the issue of the first edition; in reference to which, I may be permitted to say, in view of the general neglect of jurisprudence in this country, that I have been much encouraged to find another devoting himself to the same subject, and reaching with regard to some of its principal topics, the same conclusions. Thus supported I need no longer fear to be charged with presumption in asserting the absurdity of the prevailing theory of jurisprudence.

(ix)

CONTENTS.

BOOK I.—ELEMENTS OF RIGHT.

CHAPTER I.

OF THE FUNCTION OF GOVERNMENT WITH REFERENCE TO THE ADMINISTRATION OF JUSTICE.

CHAPTER II.

CLASSIFICATION OF RIGHTS.

(xi)

CHAPTER III.

DEFINITION OF RIGHTS.

CHAPTER IV.

THE DEFINITION OF RIGHTS CONTINUED ; AND HEREIN OF MORALITY AND ITS RELATION TO RIGHT.

CHAPTER V.

OF THE METHOD AND PRINCIPLES OF RIGHT.

CHAPTER VI.

OF THE RIGHTS OF THE STATE, OR PUBLIC RIGHTS.

CHAPTER VII.

OF PRIVATE RIGHTS; AND HEREIN FIRST OF RIGHTS OF OWNERSHIP, OR RIGHTS IN REM.

CHAPTER VIII.

OF RIGHTS OF OBLIGATION, OR RIGHTS IN PERSONAM.

BOOK II.—ELEMENTS OF THE LAW.

CHAPTER I.

ANALYTICAL OUTLINE OF THE LAW.

CHAPTER II.

DEFINITION OF THE LAW AND OF COGNATE TERMS.

CHAPTER III.

OF THE JUS GENTIUM AND JUS CIVILE.

CHAPTER IV.

OF LAWS AND JUDICIAL PRECEDENTS AS ELEMENTS OF JUS.

CHAPTER V.

OF THE PRACTICAL IMPORTANCE OF THE DISTINCTION
BETWEEN ACTIONS AND RIGHTS, AND BETWEEN JUS
AND RIGHT.

CHAPTER VI.

HISTORICAL DEVELOPMENT OF THE ENGLISH LAW.

BOOK III.—HISTORICAL AND CRITICAL REVIEW OF
THE SEVERAL THEORIES OF JURISPRUDENCE.

CHAPTER I.

STATEMENT OF THE SEVERAL THEORIES OF THE LAW.

CHAPTER II.

HISTORICAL SKETCH OF THE JURAL THEORY.

CHAPTER III.

EXPLICATION OF THE LEGAL THEORY.

CHAPTER IV.

OF THE SUPPOSED DISTINCTION BETWEEN LEGAL AND
MORAL RIGHT, OR JUSTICE, AND LEGAL AND MORAL
RIGHTS.

CHAPTER V.

OF THE PROPOSITION THAT THE POWER OF THE GOVERNMENT IS ABSOLUTE OR UNLIMITED.

CHAPTER VI.

OF THE PROPOSITION THAT THE POWER OF THE SOV-
EREIGN IS UNSUSCEPTIBLE OF LEGAL OR STATUTORY
LIMITATION.

CHAPTER VII.

HISTORICAL REVIEW OF THE LEGAL THEORY.

CHAPTER VIII.

OF THE THEORY OF UTILITY.

OF

RIGHT AND OF THE LAW.

BOOK I.
ELEMENTS OF RIGHT.[1]

CHAPTER I.

OF THE FUNCTION OF GOVERNMENT WITH REFERENCE TO THE ADMINISTRATION OF JUSTICE.

§ 1. The principal end of government is to act as judge, or umpire, in the controversies which arise between men as to their mutual claims and demands upon each other.[2]

[1] For reasons hereafter to be explained, we use the term "right," or " theoretical jurisprudence," to denote the science or doctrine of rights; and to this subject our first book is devoted.

[2] " Man, born in a family, is compelled to maintain society, from necessity, from mutual inclination, and from habit. The same creature, in his further progress, is engaged to establish political society, in order to administer justice; without which there can be no peace among them, nor safety, nor mutual intercourse. We are therefore to look upon all the vast apparatus of our government as having ultimately no other object or purpose but the distribution of justice, or in other words, the support of the twelve judges. Kings and parliaments, fleets and armies, officers of the

2   (17)

.

§ 2. This end involves the performance of two functions; viz., 1. That of deciding actual controversies as they arise; and 2. As preliminary to this, that of providing in advance for the decision of such controversies, by such legislation as may be necessary for that purpose.

§ 3. The function of hearing and determining actual controversies between men is called *jurisdiction*,[1] and in all well-organized governments is vested in courts of justice charged exclusively with its performance.

§ 4. . The function of providing by legislation for the determination of such controversies is in this country vested in the legislative department of the government; and this species of legislation, to distinguish it from other kinds—from which it differs essentially in object and nature—may be termed *jural*[2] legislation.

§ 5. The laws that relate to the administration of the government, other than those which relate to the performance of its judicial functions—as, for instance, laws that provide for the support of the government

court and revenue, ambassadors, ministers and privy counselors, are all subordinate in their end to this part of administration:" Hume's Essays.

[1] "Jurisdiction is the power to hear and determine the subject in controversy between parties to the suit:" *Rhode Island* v. *Massachusetts*, 12 Pet. 657, 717. It has also been defined as "an authority or power which a man hath *to do justice* in causes of complaint brought before him:" Jacob's Law Dict., tit. Jurisdiction. But obviously the power to decide implies the power to decide erroneously, and therefore *to do injustice*.

[2] For justification of the use of this term, see Whewell's Elements of Morality, art. 90.

and its defense at home and abroad, the administration of its finances, education, the support of the poor, etc.—may all be included under the term "*administrative* legislation."

§ 6. *Jural* legislation differs essentially in its nature from *administrative;* for, with regard to the latter, the state is vested, within certain limits, with power or right to adopt any means which it may deem most conducive to the efficient administration of the government, or the general welfare of the people; while as to the former, it is, or ought to be, governed solely by the consideration of what is just and equal between men.[1] In other words, the object of administrative legislation extends to the promotion of the welfare of the people generally; while that of jural legislation extends only to the promotion of its welfare in a particular way; viz., by causing justice to be observed.

§ 7. Jural legislation is of two kinds; viz., such as provides for the establishment of a jurisdiction and the regulation of its procedure, and such as establishes rules of decision for the determination of controversies. The latter species of legislation may, with propriety, be termed *judicial* legislation.[2]

§ 8. The function of judicial legislation is closely akin in its nature to that of jurisdiction. In the

[1] This obvious distinction is wholly ignored by the prevailing theory of jurisprudence; which is based merely upon the general formula that it is the function of the government to promote the welfare of its subjects.

[2] This term is commonly used to denote "legislation by judges," and generally in a reproachful sense, as implying that they have gone beyond their proper functions. The propriety of its use as in the text is, however, obvious.

one case, the state is called upon to decide by its courts particular controversies; in the other, by its legislature, to decide in advance questions which it anticipates will occur, by establishing rules for their decision.

§ 9. In either case, its function is essentially that of judge or umpire; and whether deciding particular cases or classes of cases, justice constitutes the only admissible rule of decision. For it would be a monstrous proposition to assert that it is the function of the state to establish and enforce in the comparatively few cases that are presented to it for decision a set of principles different from those principles of justice by which honest men, and indeed men in general, hold themselves to be bound, and by which, in fact, their mutual claims and demands upon each other are habitually regulated.[1]

§ 10. The term *justice* is used in two senses. In its wider sense it denotes the observance of all the duties which men owe to each other; but in its strict and proper sense it denotes only the observance of those duties which correspond to rights in others to exact them.[2] Justice may therefore be defined as consisting in the observance of the rights

---

[1] The great majority of men seldom or never have occasion to come into court; and probably not one of a million of transactions between men ever results in a lawsuit. In this respect, judging from the comparatively small number of judges in England, that country seems to have greatly the advantage over America.

[2] Justice is accordingly distinguished by Aristotle into universal and particular; the former of which he regarded as co-extensive with virtue: Ethics, b. 5, c. 1, pp. 12 *et seq.* (Our references are to the translation of the Nicomachean Ethics, by R. W. Browne, published in Bohn's Classical Library.)

of others; or in other words, in rendering to every man his right.[1]

§ 11. There is, however, an ambiguity in the term "rights," corresponding to that presented by the term "justice," against which it is necessary to guard. For the term "rights" is sometimes used to denote all the moral claims which men have against each other; and rights are accordingly divided into perfect and imperfect; the former being those which are susceptible of being and which may rightfully be enforced; as, for instance, the right to life, liberty, or property, or to compensation for an injury, or to the return of a deposit or the payment of a debt; and the latter, those which are not susceptible of being or which ought not to be enforced; as, for instance, the so-called right to the affection or active assistance of a friend, or to the charity of a stranger in case of need, or to the return of a benefit, or, in general, to the exercise of benevolence on the part of others in all cases where it is right that it should be exercised. This use of language is, however, clearly inadmissible; for the term "a right" implies, as part of its essential meaning, the idea that its observance may be rightfully enforced.[2]

---

[1] *Justitia est constans et perpetua voluntas jus suum cuique tribuendi:* Just. Inst., 1, 1. This is a definition of justice considered as a habit or virtue; which is to be distinguished from what Aristotle calls *the abstract or political just;* which, as he says, is "the just of which we are in search:" Ethics, b. 5, c. 6, p. 3. The propriety of the emendation in the text is therefore obvious.

[2] "There is, however, another virtue, of which the observance is not left to the freedom of our wills, which may be extorted by force, and of which the violation exposes to resentment, and conse-

Hence most of the moral claims included under the head of imperfect rights, such, for instance, as those enumerated above, are not rights at all, in the proper sense of the term; and with them the government, at least in its judicial capacity, is not concerned. We are to be understood, therefore, as using the term "justice" as denoting merely the observance of rights properly so called, and not as including the

quently to punishment; this virtue is justice; the violation of justice is injury; it does real and positive hurt to some particular persons, from motives which are naturally disapproved of. It is therefore the proper object of resentment, and of punishment, which is the natural consequence of resentment. As mankind go along with and approve of the violence employed to avenge the hurt which is done by injustice, so they much more go along with and approve of that which is employed to prevent and beat off the injury, and to restrain the offender from hurting his neighbors. The person himself who meditates injustice is sensible of this, and feels that force may, with the utmost propriety, be made use of, both by the person whom he is about to injure and by others, either to obstruct the execution of the crime or to punish him when he has executed it. And upon this is founded that remarkable distinction between justice and all the other social virtues, which has of late been particularly insisted upon by an author of very great and original genius—that we feel ourselves to be under a stricter obligation to act according to justice than agreeably to friendship, charity, or generosity; that the practice of these last-mentioned virtues seems to be left in some measure to our own choice, but that, somehow or other, we feel ourselves to be in a peculiar manner tied, bound, and obliged to the observation of justice; we feel, that is to say, that force may, with the utmost propriety, and with the approbation of mankind, be made use of to constrain us to observe the rules of the one, but not to follow the precepts of the other:" Smith's Moral Sentiments, pt. 2, § 2, c. 1.

Judge Story, in his work on equity, strangely ignores this obvious distinction: 1 Eq. Jur., § 2.

duties of gratitude, charity, or any other kind of mere benevolence.

§ 12. Our first proposition may therefore be varied in form without changing its effect, by saying that it is the function of government to administer justice, or in other words, to protect and enforce rights; and that the performance of this function constitutes the principal end of its existence.[1]

[1] "We hold these truths to be self-evident: that all men are created equal; that they are endowed by their creator with certain inalienable rights; that among these are life, liberty, and the pursuit of happiness; that to secure these rights, governments are instituted among men, deriving their just powers from the consent of the governed:" Declaration of Independence. "We, the people of the United States, in order to form a more perfect union *establish justice*, ... and secure the blessings of liberty to ourselves and our posterity, do ordain and establish this constitution for the United States of America:" Const. U. S., preamble. "The principal aim of society is to protect individuals in the enjoyment of those absolute rights which were vested in them by the immutable laws of nature. . . . Hence it follows that the first and primary end of human laws is to maintain and regulate those absolute rights of individuals:" 1 Bla. Com. 124. "The protection of the rights of each one demands an impartial and disinterested force that may be superior to all particular forces. This disinterested party, armed with the power to secure and defend the liberty of all, is called government. The right of government expresses the rights of all [and each. It is the right of personal defense, transferred to a public force, to the profit of the common liberty. . . . Government, in principle at least, is precisely what Pascal desired—justice armed with force. . . . The mission, the end of government, is to make justice, the protector of the common liberty, reign—whence it follows that as long as the liberty of one citizen does not injure the liberty of another, it escapes all repression:" Cousin's the True, the Beautiful, and the Good, lect. 15. "The idea of a perfect right presupposes that he on whom it is conferred must be enabled to maintain it by force. But this force can not be exercised by himself; because the question

whether a right had been violated can not be left to the decision
of him who pretended to have suffered a violation of right; and
because he who really has suffered a violation of right would not
always possess the power required to enforce his right against the
offender. The compulsion, therefore, can be exercised only by the
supreme power of a state, which has been constituted for the purpose of maintaining the rights and liberties of individual members
of the community against the violations and aggressions of others: "
Mackeldy's Modern Civil Law, Introd., 1, 8, 13. "And further,
States, Confederacies, Federal Unions, must live if life be enduring, by submitting to the dictates of justice, by securing its
supremacy. Justice is their chief end, especially in regulating
private, personal, and property relations:" Bliss on Sovereignty,
Preface viii. "So the State must establish justice; to systematically fail to do so will dissolve society:" Id. 17. Indeed,
properly speaking, the term civilization itself expresses nothing
more than a people's capacity of realizing justice; for etymolog-
ically, the term denotes simply the capacity of a people for the
social state, and justice is but the aggregate of the conditions
essential to that state. See definition of Kant, *infra*, § 35. Hence,
properly speaking, Athens was more civilized from the time of
Themitocles to the beginning of the Peloponnesian war than in
the time of Socrates, Plato, and Aristotle; and Rome in the ruder
ages of the Republic, than in the times of Cicero and Cæsar.

CHAPTER II.

CLASSIFICATION OF RIGHTS.

§ 13. Rights are of two kinds, differing essentially in their nature; namely, rights of *ownership*—such as the right which one has in his horse, land, or other property; and rights of *obligation*—such as the right to the payment of a debt or the performance of any other obligation. A right of the former class is generally called a right *in rem;* and a right of the latter a right *in personam,* or *in personam certam;* that is to say, against a specific person.[1] The two

[1] "The terms *jus in rem* and *jus in personam* were devised by the civilians of the middle ages, or arose in times still more recent. I adopt them without hesitation, though at the risk of offending your ears. For of all the numerous terms by which the distinction is expressed, they denote it the most adequately and the least ambiguously:" Austin's Jur. 380. "Rights *in rem* may be defined in the following manner: rights residing in persons and availing against other persons generally; or . . . . answering to duties incumbent upon other persons generally. . . . . The following definition will apply to personal rights: rights residing in persons, and availing exclusively against persons specifically determinate; or . . . . answering to duties which are incumbent exclusively on persons specifically determinate:" Id. 381. The term "exclusively" should be omitted: *Vide infra,* § 19. The terms "rights *in rem*" and "*in personam*" were derived from the names of the corresponding actions; and accordingly the former are defined by Thibaut as rights which can be enforced by an action *in rem,* and the latter as those enforced by an action *in personam:* Lindley's Introd. to Jur. 57. The classical Roman jurists divided rights into those of *ownership* (*dominium*) and those of *obligation* (*obligationes*), the latter term including not only obligations, but the corresponding rights: Austin's Jur. 956.

classes of rights are also respectively called *real* and *personal* rights, and also *absolute* and *relative* rights. The terms most commonly used, however, are "rights *in rem*" and "rights *in personam;*" and we will generally follow this usage.

§ 14.　The most common and familiar of the rights *in rem*, or rights of ownership, is the right of property; and an analysis of this right will disclose to us the nature of this class of rights generally.

§ 15.　To say that one has a right to a horse, or other thing, that it is his, or his own, or that it belongs to him, or is his property, are all equivalent expressions, and signify that the thing specified is or rightly should be appropriated to him; that is (in the sense of the Latin *proprius*), proper or peculiar to him, and not common to others. The term "property," or "right of property," therefore, signifies rightful appropriation by the owner of the thing owned; and there is implied in it the following propositions, viz.:

1.　Actual appropriation is not sufficient·to constitute the right, nor is it necessary to its existence; for a man may appropriate that which is another's and the owner be thereby deprived of the enjoyment of his right;

2.　The owner of the thing may, to the extent of his right, act freely with regard to the thing owned, according to the dictates of his own will; and

3.　The power of free action with regard to the thing owned is taken from the rest of the world, and a corresponding moral restraint or duty imposed upon them.

§ 16. All other rights *in rem* are of essentially the same nature as the right of property. Thus, a man's right in his own person consists in its being, like his horse or land, appropriated (*proprius*) to himself, and free from the power or control of others. So also a husband's right in his wife, or a wife's right in her husband, or a parent's right in a child, or *vi e versa*, consists in the wife, husband, child or parent, as the case may be, being, for certain purposes and to a certain extent, appropriated or exclusively devoted to the husband, wife, parent, or child, respectively, and free from the power, control, or interference of others.[1] These rights, therefore, to the extent indicated, are of the same essential nature, and in each case we may say of the object of the right, whether property, wife, husband, or child, that it belongs to the one having the right, or that it is his, or his own (*proprius*), or in other words, that it is or should be appropriated or exclusively devoted to him.

§ 17. An obligation is a duty owing from one person to another, the performance of which may be rightfully exacted by the obligee or person to whom it is owed. A mere duty, without such corresponding right to exact its performance, is not, properly speaking, an obligation. Thus there is an

---

[1] " Considered as the subject of the real right (right *in rem*) which resides in the child, the parent is placed in a position analogous to that of a thing. In short, whoever is the subject of a right which resides in another person, and which avails or obtains against a third person or persons, is placed in a position analogous to that of a thing, and might be styled (in respect to that analogy) a thing:" Austin's Jur. 398.

obligation on the part of a bailee to restore the property intrusted to him, and the bailor may rightfully exact the performance of this obligation; but there may be a duty upon the part of a man to perform a charitable act without any right upon the part of another to exact it, or obligation on his part to perform it.[1] This right to exact the performance of an obligation is called a right *in personam*.

§ 18. Obligations and the corresponding rights *in personam* originate either from contract, or from delict or from mere right (*ex mero jure*), without the intervention of contract or delict.[2]

---

[1] " The term ' obligation ' has two senses: in its more extensive signification it is synonymous to duty, and comprises imperfect as well as perfect obligations. Those obligations are called imperfect for which we are accountable to God only, and of which no person has the right to require performance. Such are the duties of charity and gratitude . . . . . The term ' obligation,' in a more proper and confined sense, comprises only perfect obligations, which are also called personal engagements, and which give the person with whom they are contracted a right to demand their performance. . . . . Jurists define these obligations to be a jural tie which binds us to another, either to give him something, or to do or to abstain from doing some act. *Vinculum juris quo necessitate adstringimur alicujus rei solvendæ, obligationum substantia consistit ut alium nobis obstringat ad dandum aliquid vel faciendum, vel præstandum:*" Pothier on Obligations, p. 1. " By the classical jurist, ' obligation ' is never employed in that large generic sense which it has acquired in subsequent times:" Austin's Jur. 956; *i.e.*, as synonymous with " duty."

[2] In the Institutes, obligations are divided into *obligationes ex contractu, ex maleficio, quasi ex contractu,* and *quasi ex maleficio:* Just. Inst. 3, 14, 2; the last two together constituting the class of obligations *ex mero jure*. Gaius, however, divides them as in the text: " *Obligationes aut ex contractu nascuntur, aut ex maleficio, aut proprio quodam jure ex variis causarum figuris:* " Dig. 44, 7, 1, cited 2 Austin's Jur. 1017—the last being again sub-

To the first class belong all obligations arising out of contracts or agreements; to the second, all obligations arising from invasions or violations of rights *in rem;* and to the third, all other obligations.

§ 19. The three propositions implied in the nature of a right *in rem* are equally true, *mutatis mutandis,* with reference to a right *in personam;* that is to say: 1. Actual power to enforce the obligation is not necessary, nor is actual power to compel another to do an act sufficient to constitute a right; 2. The owner of the right has the liberty to exercise it or not, as he pleases; 3. There is a duty or moral restraint on all the rest of mankind not to interfere with the exercise of the right, or the performance of the obligation. But in the case of a right *in personam* there is an additional element, viz., an obligation or duty upon a specific person—namely, the obligor—toward the owner of the right. The characteristic distinction between a right *in rem* and a right *in personam,* therefore, is, that in the former case the object of the right is the thing owned, and in the latter it is an obligation due from another.

§ 20. This distinction between rights *in rem* and rights *in personam*—which is taken from the Roman lawyers—seems to correspond precisely with the distinction made by Aristotle between *distributive* and

divided into *obligationes quasi ex contractu* and *quasi ex maleficio.* In the common law, according to the most ordinary division, obligations are divided into those which arise from contract and those which arise from tort (*ex contractu* and *ex delicto*)—obligations *ex mero jure* being called implied contracts, and classed under the first head.

corrective, or (as it may, perhaps, be more properly called) *commutative,* justice; the former being that branch of justice which determines the distribution or relative appropriation of things and also of persons, where the latter are the objects of ownership —as, for instance, where they are parties to the family relation; and the latter, that is, corrective or commutative justice, being that which relates to obligations.[1]

[1] "But of the particular justice, and of the particular just which is according to it, one species is that which is concerned *in the distribution* of honor, or of wealth, or of any of those things which can possibly be distributed among the members of a political community; . . . . . the other is that which is *corrective* in transactions between man and man; and of this there are two divisions, for some transactions are voluntary and others involuntary. The voluntary are such as follow: selling, buying, lending, pledging transactions, borrowing, depositing of trusts, hiring; and they are so called because the origin of such transactions is voluntary. Of involuntary transactions some are secret, as theft, adultery, poisoning, pandering, enticing away slaves, assassination, false witness; others accompanied with violence, as assault, imprisonment, death, robbery, mutilation, evil speaking, contumelious language:" Ethics, b. 5, c. 3, pp. 8, 9. " Voluntary " transactions correspond precisely to obligations *ex contractu;* " involuntary," to obligations *ex delicto* and *ex mero jure.*

CHAPTER III.

DEFINITION OF RIGHTS.

§ 21. There is implied in every right the liberty or power of acting freely with reference to the object of the right, and it is this which constitutes the essence of the right.

§ 22. This liberty or power, however, is not to be understood as actual liberty or power, for whatever theory of rights we adopt, it is clear that a man may be prevented from exercising his right without losing the right itself.[1] Thus a man has a right to

---

[1] "We must not, therefore, confound a simple power with right. A simple power is a physical quality; it is a power of acting to the full extent of our natural strength and liberty; but the idea of right is more confined. This includes a relation of agreeableness to a rule which modifies the physical power, and directs its operations in a manner proper to conduct man to a certain end. It is for this reason we say that right is a moral quality. . . . . In short, the use of our faculties becomes a right only so far as it is approved by reason, and is found agreeable to the primitive rule of human action:" Burlamaqui, b. 1, c. 7, § 3. "A man's natural power extends to everything which his strength enables him to perform, whether the law allows of it or not; but his moral power, to such things only as his strength enables him to perform consistently with law. For in a moral sense, or in reference to such rules as a man is strictly bound to observe in his behavior, he is not supposed to have any more power than what the law allows him:" Rutherford's Nat. Law, b. 1, c. 2, § 3. It will be observed that under the term "law" the author includes natural as well as positive law. "Laws are divided into two sorts, natural and voluntary. Natural laws are those which mankind are obliged to

his liberty though unjustly imprisoned, and to his property though unjustly deprived of it. · The liberty or power in which a right consists is therefore to be understood according to one theory as *legal*, and according to another as *jural*, liberty or power; that is to say, according to the former a right consists in the liberty or power which it is the will of the state a man shall have, or in other words, which, according to the will of the state, he ought to have; and according to the other, in the liberty or power · which it is right for him to have, or which, according to right, he ought to have.

§ 23. Indeed, according to the most logical and consistent of the supporters of the former theory, the will of the state is itself the paramount standard of right and wrong.[1] The latter definition will therefore equally apply to both theories; for upon this hypothesis, whatever the state wills is *ipso facto* right. Hence the issue between the two theories

observe from their nature and constitution. Voluntary laws, or, as they are sometimes called, positive laws, are those which mankind are obliged to observe by the will and appointment of a superior:" Id., b. 1, c. 1, § 5. "There seems to be this difference between the terms 'power' and 'right,' that the first does more expressly import the presence of the said quality, and does but obscurely denote the manner how any one acquired it, whereas the word 'right' does properly and clearly show that the quality was fairly got and is now fairly possessed:" Puffendorf, b. 1, c. 1, § 20.

[1] This was the view of Hobbes, and in effect that of Bentham, and has been expressly adopted by Austin and his followers generally. The proposition rests upon the assumption that there is no natural standard of right; from which it follows that an artificial one must be invented. As to the argument used to sustain the proposition, see *infra*, book iii.

resolves itself, not into the question of the definition of rights, but into the question as to whether
the will of the state is in fact the true moral standard.

§ 24. We may therefore define a right without
regard to the theory adopted, as the jural or rightful liberty or power to act in a particular case or
class of cases.

§ 25. The terms "liberty" and "power," in this
connection, though not strictly synonymous, have
substantially the same meaning—the difference between them corresponding to that between the
terms "may" and "can." In logical phrase, the
former denotes the absence of restraint, and connotes[1] ability to act; while the latter denotes the latter quality, and connotes the former; for one can
not be said to have the liberty to act without also
having the power, or to have the power without the
liberty. The two terms, therefore, may be indifferently used in the definition.

§ 26. In certain cases, the term "power" implies
control over others; as in the case where the act
which one has the power to do is to coerce another;
and in common language this is perhaps the idea
most prominently suggested by the term; but the
term nevertheless, in its proper sense, denotes merely
a quality in the person having the power, namely,
ability to act, and implies control over others only
in those cases where the act which one has the
ability to perform is the coercion of another. In

---

[1] As to the use of this term, see Austin's Jur. 94, and Mill's
Logic, c. 1.

3

many cases, however, the power to act can be exercised without controlling or in any way interfering with others; and the idea of such control is therefore not an essential part of the signification of the term. In all cases where the term "power" implies control over others, the term "liberty" equally implies it; but the idea is not so obviously suggested by the latter term, and we are therefore not in danger of mistaking it, as in the case of the term "power," for an essential part of the definition. The term "liberty" is therefore the more appropriate term to use in the definition; and we will accordingly generally make use of it.

§ 27. The term "liberty," in its general sense, denotes the absence of any impediment to the performance of that which a man wills to do, and implies the absence of physical or natural impediments, as well as those which are interposed by man. Jurisprudence is not, however, concerned with impediments of the former class, but with the latter only; and the term "liberty," as used in jurisprudence, therefore denotes merely the absence of restraint by others upon the free performance of volition; and *jural liberty*, the absence of rightful restraint, or right to restrain in others. *Jural* liberty is therefore to be distinguished from *actual* liberty, which consists in the absence of actual restraint, and from *moral* liberty, which consists in the absence of moral restraint or duty.

§ 28. There is implied in the term "jural liberty," or *right*, a corresponding duty upon others toward the owner of the right; that is to say, upon all others the general negative duty of not interfering with the exercise of the right ; and in the case of a right *in personam*, also a specific duty or obligation upon some particular person.[1] In either case, however, the right consists in a quality of the owner, namely, his liberty or power to act, and the corresponding duty upon others is a mere consequence of this quality in the owner.

§ 29. In the case of a right *in personam*, the act which the owner of the right has the liberty or power to perform is to compel the obligor either to act or to forbear from acting; and there is, therefore, necessarily implied, as we have seen, a power or control over the obligor. Hence certain jurists, taking their notion from this class of rights, define a right as consisting in control or power over others.

Thus Austin says: "A person has a right when the law authorizes him to exact an act or forbearance ;" and accordingly he defines a right to be "the capacity or power of exacting from another acts or forbearances:" Austin's Jur. 410.

And to the same effect is Amos, who defines a right to be: "A measure of control, delegated by the supreme political authority of a state to persons thereby said to be vested with a right, over the actions of other persons, said to be made thereby liable to the performance of a duty:" Amos's Jur. 79.

And also Holland, who defines a right (or, as he calls it, a legal right) as "a capacity residing in one

---

[1] It is therefore as impossible for rights to conflict as for two bodies to occupy the same space at the same time. Hence the absurdity of Hobbes' notion, that in a state of nature all men have a right to all things, including the persons of their neighbors.

man of controlling, with the assent or assistance of the state, the actions of others;" and he accordingly asserts that "that which gives validity to a legal right is in every case the force which is lent to it by the state:" Holland's Jur. 62.

So also Thibaut says: "A right is neither more nor less than a legal power to compel:" Lindley's Study of Jur. *52.

§ 30. The most serious defect of these definitions is that they regard rights as consisting, not in *jural* power, or power which it is right for one to have, but in *legal* power, or power which it is the will of the state that he should have, and consequently as mere creatures of the legislative will. But independently of this, it is evident that these definitions are inapplicable to rights *in rem;* for it is irrational to say that one's right in himself, or in his wife, or child, or property, consists in control or power over the billion of people, more or less, who inhabit the globe. The non-interference of others with the exercise of the right is indeed essential to its enjoyment, but this non-interference is secured with regard to the mass of mankind by distance or other physical obstacles, and would be more perfect if there were no one in the world to interfere with the exercise of the right.[1] Hence these definitions are inadequate as definitions of rights in general.

§ 31. Accordingly both Austin and Amos elsewhere define rights as consisting in liberty.

---

[1] Man, however, is a social being—πολιτικον ζωον: Aristotle, Pol. (Bohn's edition), b. 1, c. 2; and the term "right" denotes a relation between men, viz., the power to act without restraint from others.

" Liberty or freedom to deal with an external sub-ject," says the former, "seems to be equivalent to right to deal with it. On the whole, right and liberty seem to be synonymous, either meaning, first, permission on the part of the sovereign to dispose of one's person or of any external subject, ... secondly, security against others for the exercise of such liberty:" Austin's Jur. 367.

"The generic expression," says Amos, " which denotes, for any given age or country, the exact measure of personal liberty for every man, which implies the most favorable condition for the highest possible development of the moral existence of all, is rights:" The Science of Law, p. 91.

§ 32. This conception of the nature of rights seems to have originated with Hobbes; and is thus expressed by him in language worthy at once both of his genius and of the subject:

" The names *jus* and *lex*," he says, " that is, *right* and *law*, are often confounded, yet scarcely are there two words of more contrary effect; for right is that liberty which the law leaveth us, and law is that restraint by which we mutually agree to abridge one another's liberty. Law and right, therefore, are no less different than restraint and liberty, which are contrary. . . . . For nothing is signified by the word ' right,' than that liberty which every man has to use his natural faculties according to right reason."

Or, as he elsewhere expresses it: " Though they that speak of this subject use to confound *jus* and *lex*, *right* and *law*, yet they ought to be distinguished;

because right consisteth in liberty to do or forbear; whereas the law determineth and bindeth to one of them, so that *law* and *right* differ as much as obligation and liberty, which in one and the same matter are inconsistent:" De Corpore Politico, b. 2, c. 10, § 5; Leviathan, b. 1, c. 14.[1]

§ 33. To the same effect is Burlamaqui, who defines a right, " as a power that man hath to make use of his liberty and his natural strength in a particular manner, either in regard to himself or in regard to other men, so far as this exercise of his strength and liberty is approved by reason. Thus when we say that a father has a right to bring up his children, all that is meant hereby is, that reason allows the father to make use of his liberty and natural force in a manner suitable to the preservation of his children, and proper to cultivate their understandings, and to train them up in the princi-. ples of virtue:" Burlamaqui, b. 1, c. 7, § 2.

[1] Hobbes rightly conceived this definition of rights to be the fundamental principle of jurisprudence; and accordingly adopted it as the foundation of his system. To him, therefore, is due the credit of pointing out the true method of the science. We quote, with reference to him, an interesting passage from McIntosh's Dissertation on the Progress of Ethical Philosophy: " When Leibnitz, in the beginning of the eighteenth century, reviewed the moral writers of modern times, his penetrating eye saw only two who were capable of reducing morals and jurisprudence to a science. 'So great an enterprise,' says he, 'might have been executed by the deep, searching genius of Hobbes, if he had not set out from evil principles, or by the judgment and learning of the incomparable Grotius, if his powers had not been scattered over many subjects, and his mind distracted by the cares of an agitated life.' "

§ 34. To the same effect is also Puffendorf: "As for the term 'right,' it imports a power of acting granted or left free by the law. . . . . Since a man has the power of doing all such things as can proceed from his natural abilities, except those which are forbidden by some law;[1] right, therefore, in this sense, denotes a liberty:" Puffendorf, b. 1, c. 6, § 3.

§ 35. In like manner, Kant defines rights "as the sum total of the conditions under which the external freedom of the individual can be maintained, in common with the freedom of all."

§ 36. This conception of the nature of rights is strikingly developed by Herbert Spencer, in his Social Statics, in which work he holds that all rights are derived from a single first principle, which he calls "the law of equal freedom." This principle is, "that every man may claim the fullest liberty to exercise his faculties compatible with the exercise of like liberty by every other man:" Social Statics, c. 4, § 3; or, as he elsewhere expresses it,

[1] The term "law" is here used in the same sense as by Rutherford: *Vide supra*, § 22, note. Blackstone also seems to have arrived at a partial perception of this view of the nature of rights: "The absolute rights of man," he says (under which term he includes "the right of personal security, the right of personal liberty, and right of private property"), "are usually summed up in one general appellation, and denominated the natural liberty of mankind:" 1 Bla. Com. 125. "The rights themselves, thus defined by these several statutes, consist in a number of private immunities; which will appear, from what has been premised, to be indeed no other than either that residuum of natural liberty which is not required by the laws of society to be sacrificed to public convenience; or else those civil privileges which society hath engaged to provide in lieu of the natural liberties so given up by individuals:" Id. *129.

"every man has freedom to do all that he wills,
provided that he infringes not the equal freedom of
any other man:" Id., c. 6, § 1. Accordingly he
says: "Rights are nothing but artificial divisions of
the general claim to exercise the faculties, applications of that general claim to particular cases; and
each of them is proved in the same way, by showing that the particular exercise of the faculties
referred to is possible•without preventing the like
exercise of faculties by other persons:" Id., c. 15.[1]

§ 37.   This is also substantially the view of Cousin,
who says: "The limit of liberty is in liberty itself.
Liberty is to be respected, provided that it injure
not the.liberty of another.   I ought to let you do
what you will, but on condition that nothing which
you do shall injure my liberty.   For then, by virtue
of my right of liberty, I should feel myself obliged
to repress the aberrations of your will, in order to
protect my own and that of others. . . . . The
right of government expresses the right of all and
of each.   It is the right of personal defense transferred into public force to the profit of common
liberty:" The True, the Beautiful, and the Good,
lect. 15.

§ 38.   Rights have also been defined by Leibnitz

[1] We know of no other works in which the principle of liberty,
and the derivation of rights from it, are so strikingly illustrated
as in this.   Some startling conclusions are arrived at, but these
result mainly from the assumption that the principle of equal
liberty constitutes the sole first principle of right.   We may
therefore regard the views maintained in the work referred to (as
the author himself seems now to regard them) as inadequate,
ratuer than incorrect: See Social Statics, preface.

and by Grotius and others as consisting in moral power;[1] but by the term, "moral power," nothing more is meant by them than what we have denoted by the term "jural power;" *i. e.*, power which may not rightly be resisted; which is the same thing as to say, power which one ought to have. But as we have seen, power to act or power over one's self is the same thing as liberty,[2] and these definitions therefore substantially agree with ours.

§ 39. It will be observed that in the definitions quoted, Spencer assumes that the only rightful limit to the liberty of the individual is in the equal liberty of others; while Hobbes and Austin place this limit in the will of the government. The former of these propositions may be true, but certainly can not be assumed as self-evident; the latter is certainly false. In the definition we have given, therefore, we adopt neither the one nor the other of these limits, but define rights in the aggregate as consisting simply in the liberty which one ought to have, or which it is right that he should have—leaving for the future the investigation of what its precise extent may be; which is, in fact, as we shall see, the ultimate problem presented by jurisprudence.

[1] "*Est autem jus quædam potentia moralis, et obligatio necessitas moralis. Moralem autem intelligo, quæ apud virum bonum æquipollet naturali; nam ut præclare jurisconsultus Romanus ait, quæ contra bonos mores sunt ea nec facere nos posse credendum est:*" Leibn., Opera., 4, 3, 294, cited Mackintosh, Dissertation on the Progress of Ethical Philosophy. "Right and moral power are expressions of like import:" Rutherford's Institutes of Nat. Law, b. 1, c. 1, § 3.

[2] " A power over our own persons and actions is called liberty:" Puffendorf, b. 1, c. 1, § 19.

CHAPTER IV..

THE DEFINITION OF RIGHTS CONTINUED; AND HEREIN OF MORALITY AND ITS RELATION TO RIGHT.

§ 40. As the term "a right" includes in its signification, or connotes, the idea of rightness, it would be necessary, in order to render our definition of rights complete, to define *the adjective* "right," or the term "right," as used to denote a quality; but to do this would involve the solution of a problem which, in the present state of ethical science, perhaps can not be solved; namely, the metaphysical problem as to the nature of right and duty—a question about which the theories of philosophers widely differ.

§ 41. This problem, indeed—together with the psychological problem as to the nature of the faculty by which men perceive the right, and recognize the duty of conforming to it—belongs rather to the *philosophy of morality* than to morality itself; the province of which is confined to determining the practical problem as to what things are right and what wrong; or in other words, to determining the presence or absence of the quality—a problem which evidently may be solved without defining the nature of the quality, or explaining how we perceive it; and which to some extent must be solved before these questions can even be considered. For in this, as in other branches of science, the perception of the facts to be accounted for must precede the consideration of their nature, and of the manner in which they are perceived; for had not men first perceived right and wrong, and felt the force of duty, obviously no questions ever could have risen upon these points.

§ 42. It has been well observed, therefore, that morality and the philosophy of morality bear the same relations to each other as geometry and the philosophy of geometry; and that, as it was necessary that a body of geometric truth should be developed before the metaphysical and psychological problems as to the nature of geometric truth, and of the faculty by which it is perceived, could be considered, so morality comes before moral philosophy in the order of investigation.[1]

[1] "Morality and the philosophy of morality differ in the same manner and in the same degree as geometry and the philosophy of geometry. Of these two subjects, geometry consists of a series of positive and definite proportions, deduced one from another in succession by rigorous reasoning, and all resting upon certain definitions and self-evident axioms. The philosophy of geometry is quite a different subject; it includes such inquiries as these: Whence is the cogency of geometrical proof? What is the evidence of the axioms and definitions? What are the faculties by which we become aware of their truth? and the like. The two kinds of speculation have been pursued for the most part by two different classes of persons, the geometers and metaphysicians; for it has been far more the occupation of metaphysicians than of geometers to discover such questions as I have stated, the nature of geometrical proofs, geometrical axioms, the geometrical faculty. And if we construct a complete system of geometry, it will be almost exactly the same, whatever may be the views we take on these metaphysical questions. . . . . It has long appeared to me that the relation which thus subsists between geometry and the philosophy of geometry must subsist also between

§ 43. Hence it is, that while moral philosophy has furnished a battle-ground for conflicting theories since the dawn of philosophy, there has always been, at least among civilized nations, a substantial agreement as to the principles of morality.[1] Thus no one can contemplate the crime of murder without disapprobation; or, to refer to less extreme cases, there are none who will deny the obligation of returning a deposit,[2] or of compensating for an injury, or of

morality and the philosophy of morality. If we had a view of morality in which moral propositions were deduced from axioms by successive steps of reasoning, so far as to form a connected system of morality, we should then have before us definite problems, if we proceed to inquire, what is the nature and evidence of moral axioms, and what are the faculties by which we know them to be true? On this account it seemed to me that the construction of elements of morality ought to precede any attempt to settle the disputed and doubtful questions which are regarded as belonging to the philosophy of morality:" Whewell's Elements of Morality, preface.

[1] It is one of the most serious errors of the theory of utility, as asserted by Bentham and Austin, that it denies all authority to the common moral convictions of mankind. "As for the moral sense," says the latter, "innate practical principles, conscience, they are merely convenient cloaks for ignorance or sinister interest:" 1 Austin's Jur. 221. The opinion of Burke was wiser, that the world would fall into ruin "if the practice of all moral duties and the foundations of society rested upon having their reasons made clear and demonstrative to every individual:" Morley's Life of Burke, 17.

[2] Thus we find this principle assumed without hesitation by the little judge in the story of Ali Cogia, in the Arabian Nights; and the youngest hearer to whom the story is related never requires to have it explained to him that such was the law.
"The obligation to return a deposit faithfully was in very early times holden sacred by the Greeks, as we learn from the story of Glaucus, who on consulting the oracle received this answer:

repaying a loan. For these propositions arc universally admitted, and indeed, by common consent furnish the crucial test by which all theories of moral philosophy are judged—the partisans of all striving to show that their respective theories account for the common moral convictions of mankind.

§ 44. The jurist, therefore, is not concerned with the conflicting theories of moral philosophy, but with morality only, and with that only so far as it treats of rights. It is therefore immaterial to the validity of our reasoning what theory we may adopt on this point, provided only we assume the reality of moral distinctions and the possibility of perceiving them; the former of which is attested by the

'that it was criminal to harbor a thought of withholding deposited goods from the owners who claimed them.' And a fine application of the universal law is made by an Arabian poet contemporary with Justinian, who remarks 'that life and wealth are only deposited with us by our Creator, and, like other deposits, must in due time be returned:'" Jones on Bailments, 59, 60, citing Herod, 6, 62; Juv. Sat. 13, 199.

"Moral truths, considered in themselves, have no less certainty than mathematical truths. The idea of a deposit being given, I ask whether the idea of faithfully keeping it is not necessarily attached to it, as to the idea of a triangle is attached the idea that its three angles are equal to two right angles. You may withhold a deposit, but in withholding it do not believe that you change the nature of things, nor that you make it possible for a deposit to become property. These two ideas exclude each other. You have only a false semblance of property, and all the effects of passion, all the sophisms of interest, will not reverse the essential difference. This is the reason why moral truth is so troublesome; it is because, like all truths, it is what it is, and does not bend to any caprice:" Cousin's The True, the Beautiful, and the Good, lect. 14.

common consciousness, and the latter by the common experience of mankind, and both of which are necessarily assumed in all theories of morality, properly so called.

§ 45. We will therefore not attempt to define the term "right," otherwise than by saying we use it in its ordinary acceptation, as denoting a universal and apparently necessary conception of the human mind—leaving to the reader to adopt a more specific definition, according to the theory he may adopt as to the abstract nature of right—as, for instance, that it consists in conformity to the will of God, or to nature, or to universal order, or to the end or destiny of sentient beings, or to utility or tendency to promote the happiness or welfare of human beings.

§ 46. But while it may not be practicable at this time to give a perfect, or essential, definition of the term, some observations may be made which will tend to render the notion of right more definite, and which will at the same time serve to illustrate the nature of the method and principles of morality. The term "right," in one sense, denotes that which is imperatively required by the rule of right, whatever it may be; and it is in this sense we use the term in our definition of jural liberty, as being the liberty which it is right one should have; meaning thereby that it is imperatively required by the will of God, or by universal order, or by utility, or by such other principle of right as we may adopt, that men should have such liberty. As applied to the moral character of human acts or conduct, however, the term "right" does not in general denote a positive, but a mere negative, quality; i. e., the absence of wrong, or violation of duty. For, according to the ordinary use of the term, every act is said to be right that is not contrary to some duty. Thus where the question is as to how one shall enjoy a holiday--whether, for instance, he shall go a-hunting, or a-fishing, or shall otherwise amuse himself— though he should adopt the course least calculated to afford him amusement his act would nevertheless be morally right. And so in questions of greater concern, as, for instance, in questions relating to marriage, or to the choice of a profession, or to other points of vital importance to the individual concerned, though one choose the least advantageous course, we may still affirm of his act that it is morally right. And this is in accordance with our definition of moral liberty, according to which every man, within the limits imposed by duty, may rightfully act according to the dictates of his own will: *Supra*, sec. 27; or in other words, the moral liberty or power of every man is limited only by the duties he owes to God, to others, or himself.

§ 47. Of these duties, some are coupled with a right in others to exact their observance, and others are not. The jural liberty of the individual is therefore more extensive than his moral liberty. Accordingly two very different, though not altogether distinct, problems are presented in morality, namely, the one to determine the *moral*, and the other to determine the *jural*, liberty of mankind; the latter of which belongs to theoretical jurisprudence, or right;

and the former to the science of general duty, or, as, it has been called by Bentham, Deontology.

§ 48. In either case, it is evident that there is always a presumption in favor of liberty, which can only be overcome in the one case by showing the existence of a duty, and in the other by showing the existence of a duty coupled with a right in another.

§ 49. The immediate problem, therefore, is to determine in what cases duties may exist; and hence the first question that presents itself is to determine the principle, or rule, or standard, by which the existence or non-existence of duties is to be determined; and to this the answer may be given in three propositions, viz.:

1. The practical test or standard of right and wrong, to every man, is his own conscience.

2. The common moral convictions, or concurring consciences, of the people, or in other words, *positive* morality, is the common test or standard by which questions of right and wrong are practically to be determined.

3. The ultimate test or standard is *scientific* morality, by which the principles of positive morality are in the main demonstrated to be true, and at the same time its errors and defects corrected.

It will be necessary, therefore, to explain the nature of conscience, and of positive or practical, and of scientific or theoretic, morality; and for this purpose an extended discussion will be necessary.

§ 50. There is in some way generated in every man, as it were, a code of moral convictions or principles, by which in ordinary cases he instantaneously, and without reflection, judges his own actions and those of others to be right or wrong. There is also in every man a faculty—whether innate or acquired it is unnecessary here to inquire—by which he perceives the duty or moral necessity of conforming to the right. This perception is also accompanied by certain sentiments, as, for instance, the sentiment of approbation or disapprobation, with regard to his own actions or those of others, and with regard to the former, the sentiment of conscious rectitude or of remorse. The combination of these moral convictions with the faculty of perceiving the duty of conforming to them, and the accompanying sentiments, together constitute what is called conscience, the existence of which, whatever controversies there may be as to its nature, can not be denied; and it is this which constitutes to every man the practical standard of right, or test of right and wrong, by which his conduct is or ought to be governed.

§ 51. Men, however, acquire their moral convictions, to a great extent, from education and association with others; or in other words (as is indicated by the etymology of the term "morality," and kindred terms), from custom. Hence, every aggregation of people brought together by any principle of association—as, for instance, by common locality, nationality, profession, social intercourse, or otherwise—have a morality to some extent peculiar to themselves. Thus the moral principles of one age or nation are somewhat different from those of another, and the same is true of different neighborhoods, professions, and classes of society, in the

4

same age and nation, and even of different families. In addition to this, the morality of each individual is to some. extent modified by his own peculiar character, moral and intellectual. Under all this diversity, however, there is a substantial conformity in respect to fundamentals; and especially in every nation or people there is always a body of moral principles covering the whole field of practical duties, and universally, or almost universally, recognized, which becomes embodied in the language and habitual thought of the people, and wrought, as it were, into the conscience of nearly every individual.[1] It is this which constitutes the positive or

[1] "This aggregate of beliefs and predispositions to believe, ethical, religious, æsthetical, social, respecting what is true or false, probable or improbable, just or unjust, holy or unholy, honorable or base, respectable or contemptible, pure or impure, beautiful or ugly, decent or indecent,. obligatory to do or obligatory to avoid, respecting the statutes and relations of each individual in the society, respecting even the admissible fashions of amusement and recreation—this is an established fact and condition of things, the real origin of which is for the most part unknown, but which each new member of the society is born to and finds subsisting. It is transmitted by tradition from parents to children, and is imbibed by the latter almost unconsciously from what they see and hear around, without any special season of teaching, or special persons to teach. It becomes a part of each person's nature—a standing habit of mind, or fixed set of mental tendencies, according to which particular experience is interpreted and particular persons appreciated. . . . . 'Nomos (Law and Custom), King of All' (to borrow the phrase which Herodotus cites from Pindar). exercises plenary power, spiritual as well as temporal, over individual minds, molding the emotions as well as the intellect according to the local type, determining the sentiments, the belief, and the predisposition in regard to new matters tendered for belief, of every one; fashioning thought,

received morality (*mores*, or, as the Greeks called it, *Nomos*) of a nation or people; and it can not be doubted that in all questions of common concern this should be held to be of paramount authority; for, as no reason can be given why one man's conscience should be forced upon another, it follows that, in all questions between men, we must resort to the common conscience as the practical test of right and wrong. Accordingly, in this we have a common standard, or test, by which the question of right or wrong is habitually judged, and to which men, by a spontaneous impulse of their nature, involuntarily submit; for those moral principles which are common to all, or nearly all, have in general an authority and power over the conscience of each individual, infinitely superior to those convictions which are peculiar to himself alone;[1] for the

speech, and points of view, no less than action, and reigning under the appearance of habitual, self-suggested tendencies. Plato, when he assumes the function of constructor, establishes special officers for enforcing in detail the authority of King Nomos in his own Platonic variety. But even where no such special officers exist, we find Plato himself describing forcibly (in the speech assigned to Protagoras) the working of that spontaneous ever-present police by whom the authority of King Nomos is enforced in detail—a police not the less omnipotent because they wear no uniform, and carry no recognized title." I, Grote's Plato, 378–382.

See also the numerous authorities and illustrations cited in the notes to the passages quoted; also Mr. Carpenter's work on Mental Physiology, where the above passages are quoted, and the facts stated physiologically explained.

[1] "The customary morality, that which education and opinion have consecrated, is the only one that presents itself to the mind with the feeling of being *in itself* obligatory:" Mill on Utilitarianism, Ch. 3, pp. 38–9.

conscience is made up, not only of intellectual convictions, but also of moral sentiments, which, though to some extent natural, yet (as the etymology of the term "conscience" would seem to indicate) derive their chief force from sympathy and general acceptation.[1] Hence the positive morality of a people not only enters into and forms part of the conscience· of each individual, but generally carries with it an unquestioned supremacy.

§ 52. It is also to be observed, not only that the consciences of individuals concur in the general conscience of the nation or people to which they belong, but also that there is a substantial agreement as to fundamentals in the positive morality of all civilized nations, ancient and modern, and a considerable degree of conformity even among uncivilized and barbarous peoples; and this indicates that positive morality is not accidental, either in its nature or development, but that it is in the main the natural outgrowth of human nature, under the varying circumstances in which it may be placed; and that though modified by accidental causes, it is founded upon the nature and natural relations of men and things.

[1] According to Hobbes, it is this that constitutes conscience. "Two or more men," he says, "are conscious of a thing when they know it together (*conscire*). Hence arises the proper meaning of conscience; and the evil of speaking against one's conscience in this sense is to be allowed. Two other meanings are metaphysical; when it is put for a man's knowledge of his own secret *facts* and thoughts, and when men give their own new opinions, however absurd, the reverenced name of conscience:" Bain, Moral Science, 132. It may be said of this derivation of the term, that if not true it is at least *ben trovato*.

§ 53. On the other hand, in view of the difference in morality of different peoples and ages, and
of different classes of individuals in the same age
and country, it is evident that positive morality can
not be accepted as infallible. Hence the ultimate
standard of right is to be sought in reason, or scientific morality.[1]

§ 54. With regard to scientific morality, two processes are obviously involved; namely, to determine
the first principles of the science, and to deduce from
them their legitimate logical consequences.[2] With
regard to the former, it is perhaps impossible in the
present state of ethical science to lay down the ultimate first principles of morality; but we may, by a
process of induction, ascertain what are the fundamental principles upon which the common moral
convictions of mankind in fact rest; and these, having been determined and accurately defined, may at
least provisionally be accepted as the first principles
of morality. As to the nature and sufficiency of the
proofs upon which these principles rest, it does not

[1] " What appears, as it were, prelusively, unconsciously, and
imperfectly in the one (the historical development) is in the other
(the philosophical development) modified and expanded under the
dominating principle of the *begriff*, by a reflective and self-con-
scious process:" British Quart. Rev., July, 1878, p. 81.

[2] As to the possibility of a moral science, see Locke on the Understanding, b. 4, c. 3, §§ 18-20, from which we extract the following: " Confident I am that if men would in the same method,
and with the same indifferency, search after moral as they do
mathematical truths, they would find them to have a stronger connection one with another, and a more necessary consequence from
our clear and distinct ideas, and to come nearer perfect demonstration than is commonly imagined."

fall within the scope of our work to inquire; but our task will be sufficiently accomplished if we show that the principles of morality, or rather of that branch of morality which treats of rights—with which alone we are at present concerned—are in fact derived from certain fundamental principles, or notions of right, established in the common moral convictions of mankind.

§ 55. According to this conception of the two subjects, positive in the main coincides with scientific morality, but differs from it in two important particulars:

1. It lacks scientific precision in the formulation of its principles, and hence does not admit of an equally rigorous logic; for where premises are only approximately, and not accurately, true, often the deductions from them must be absurd, and the deductions from different principles conflicting. Hence it often becomes necessary to limit the effect of its principles by exceptions; and in this way a result approximately correct is reached. Thus it is generally assumed as a principle that promises give rise to obligations to perform them, or duties coupled with rights in others to enforce them—a proposition which, as will be explained more fully hereafter, is by no means universally true, and to which it has therefore become necessary to establish numerous exceptions; but taking the rule with its exceptions, the result will be found to coincide very nearly with the conclusions of theoretical right: *Vide infra,* §§ 181 *et seq.*

2. The rules of positive morality are not deduced

by accurate logical deductions from its principles, but are in part arrived at by a rough kind of in-duction or experiment; and hence arises another source of inaccuracy.

§ 56. Scientific morality, on the other hand, accepts no principle except as universally true, both immediately and in all its logical results; and ad-mits no conclusions except such as can be rigorously demonstrated from the principles assumed. It is therefore a true deductive science, as certain in its method and in its results as that of geometry, or, to take a more nearly related instance, that of political economy; that is to say, it can not, in the present stage of its development, assert the absolute truth of its conclusions, but it may at least assert with absolute certainty that those conclusions follow nec-essarily from its assumed first principles.

§ 57. As we have observed, however, the prin-ciples of scientific morality can not become practi-cally operative as a common rule or standard of right and wrong, until they meet with a general acceptance and become established in the common moral convictions of the people. The practical end of scientific jurisprudence is therefore to enlighten the general conscience, and to correct and reform the moral convictions of mankind.

CHAPTER V.

OF THE METHOD AND PRINCIPLES OF RIGHT.

§ 58. According to our definition, a right consists in the jural or rightful liberty to act (*facultas agendi*) in a particular case or class of cases. Rights, therefore, are but particular parts or divisions of the general liberty to which a man is rightfully entitled, and in the aggregate constitute such liberty: *Vide supra*, § 36. The ultimate problem presented by right or theoretical jurisprudence is therefore to determine, in view of all existing facts, including laws and customs, the extent of the rightful liberty of the individual.

§ 59. But, obviously, this liberty exists in every case in which one may not rightfully be restrained by other individuals or the state; and as in general this liberty exists, and there is always a presumption in its favor, the immediate problem is to determine the exceptional cases in which it may be rightfully restrained; and in determining this problem, the following propositions may be assumed:[1]

§ 60. [1.] The rightful power to coerce or restrain the free action of another, where it exists, like the power to do any other act, is *ex vi termini* a right; and it follows, therefore, that the rightful liberty of the individual is limited, and limited only,

---

[1] These, to distinguish them from explanatory matter, are indicated by the numerals in brackets.

by the rights of other individuals or of the state; the former of which are called *private* and the latter *public* rights.

§ 61. [2.] The presumption in favor of liberty can be overcome, therefore, only by proof of the existence of some right, private or public, derogating from it; and the burden of proof is always on him who asserts the existence of such a right.[1] In this respect no distinction can be made between public and private rights; but where a right is asserted, either in an individual or the state, which derogates from the liberty of others, it can not be admitted unless a sufficient reason can be given for its existence.

§ 62. [3.] In determining whether such a right exists, or in other words, whether restraint may in any case be rightfully imposed, an obvious principle suggests itself for our guidance; namely, that an unequal or extraordinary restraint can not be imposed unless the case presents some fact or facts which distinguish it from ordinary cases; or in other words, the existence of a right in any one derogating from the liberty of another can not be affirmed unless it can be equally affirmed of all others standing in the same jural relations; for the burden of proof lies on him who asserts the existence of such a right, and according to the hypothesis, it

[1] " There is always a reason against every coercive law—a reason which, in default of any opposing reason, will always be sufficient in itself; and that reason is, that such a law is an attack upon liberty: " Bentham's Theory of Legislation, pt. 1, c. 1.

" The laws of England in all cases favor liberty: " Jacob's Law Dict., tit. Liberty.

is i.npossible to assign any reason why such a right should exist in one which would not in a like case exist in another.

The proposition therefore resolves itself into this: that the jural liberty of all men in the same case is equal; which is the same thing as to say that restraint can not be rightly imposed upon any one unless it may be equally imposed on others *in the same case*—meaning by the term " the same case " a similarity of circumstances material to the question of right. Thus the circumstances of infancy or mental unsoundness clearly distinguishes the case of the infant or *non compos* from that of the ordinary man. So the circumstance that one has manufactured an article of personal property clearly distinguishes the owner from others.

§ 63. [4.] Restraint may be rightly imposed upon the individual either for his own benefit—as in the case of mental incompetency resulting from infancy, old age, or insanity—or for the benefit of others—as in the case of ordinary obligations.

§ 64. [5.] Whether restraint upon the former grounds should be limited to cases where absolute necessity requires it, or, if not, what are the limits to be assigned to it, are questions indeterminate in their character, and, within certain limits, must therefore be determined by custom or by legislation. Such right is, however, obviously limited by the principle itself to cases where such interference is for the benefit of the party restrained; and cases of this kind, as they rest upon the fact that the individuals to which they apply are distinguished from men in general by personal peculiarities, are exceptional in their character.

§ 65. [6.] The liberty to exercise the faculties necessarily implies the acquisition of unequal powers or rights—as, for instance, by the acquisition of property; and it can not therefore be affirmed that the jural liberty or aggregate of rights of all men is equal. We may, however, distinguish between the original rights of mankind, or those resulting from the mere event of birth, and those acquired by labor or personal exertion; and, having the former in view only, it may be affirmed that the original jural liberty of all men of *normal status* is equal.

§ 66. [7.] It is an obvious consequence, from the nature of a right, that one who has been unjustly deprived of its exercise should be restored to its enjoyment; and it seems equally obvious that where restitution in kind is impracticable, restitution in value, or compensation should be made.

§ 67. [8.] Every right originates in the happening of some event, or series of events, and a right can be varied, or terminated, only by the same means.[1]

---

[1] Right has to deal with three principal facts or notions, which together constitute its subject-matter; viz., persons, things, and events. The term " things, " in its widest sense, would include persons, and also events. But in jurisprudence, it is important to distinguish between events, or things that happen, and objects which exist, and of the latter, to distinguish between human creatures and other things; and, in ordinary language, the terms are generally used with regard to this distinction. By a person, therefore, we will denote simply a human creature, and by a thing any other existing object, and by an event that which happens. The relation of these elements to each other and to the science may be

This will clearly appear by the following examples: The right of self-ownership, or property in one's person, originates upon the mere event of one's birth, is varied by the event of his reaching maturity, and terminates with his death. For this right, though at first restricted by the necessary conditions of infancy, is born with every human creature, and upon his reaching maturity becomes unrestricted except by the necessary conditions imposed by the rights of others; and finally, at the end of his life, dies with him. The rights of parent and child originate with the birth of the child, concurring with other events, such as marriage, etc., and are varied by the event of the child's reaching maturity, and terminate by the death of either party. The rights of husband and wife originate in the event of marriage, and such rights are terminated by the death of either party, or by divorce. The original title to personal property may originate either in the event of its manufacture by the owner, or, in some cases, in the event of its mere appropriation. Derived titles may be acquired by conveyances from former owners or by prescription, which is a series of events. The right to property terminates upon its destruction, or may terminate by abandonment. Rights arising from contracts, and also those arising from delicts, are illustrations of the same principle; the former originating in the

stated in the following proposition: " All rights are vested *in persons;* are *in or over persons or things;* are originated, terminated, or varied only *by events;* and are determined by principles deduced *from the nature of persons and things, and the relations between them.*"

execution of contracts and the latter in the commission of injuries, and each terminating in satisfaction, or release, or some other event.

§ 68. Events, upon the happening of which rights
are immediately originated, varied, or terminated,
are called *investitive* or *divestitive* events, accordingly
as they confer upon any one a right, or take it away
from him; as, for instance, an absolute conveyance,
or promise to pay money, or an injury, or a release.

§ 69. Events are of two classes; namely, *acts*, or
events occurring by human agency; and *accidents*,
or events occurring without such agency.

Acts are divided into acts of private persons and
acts of government, or political acts.

Private acts are again divided into *transactions*, or
acts which operate either to transfer a right or to
create an obligation, such as grants, contracts, injuries, etc.; and acts which do not so operate; as, for
instance, the manufacture of personal property, or
the appropriation of unappropriated property.

Political acts are either executive, judicial, or
legislative—the last named being otherwise called
laws or statutes.

§ 70. Under the term "contracts" we include
not only promises, but also conveyances or transfers
of rights—the latter being merely executed contracts. Rights originate or cease upon the execution
of a contract, either immediately, (in which case the
contract is an investitive or divestitive event), or
upon the concurrence of some subsequent events.
In some cases contracts have only the one or the
other of these operations; as, for instance, on the

one hand an absolute grant of property, and on the other that of a promise or grant, conditional upon the happening of some future event. In the first case, the right is originated at once, and the contract has no ulterior effect; and in the latter, no right at all is originated until the happening of the event. In general, however, a contract may have both of these operations—that is to say, a right may be immediately originated, and afterward, upon the concurrence of a subsequent event, an alternative right. In the case of a promise to pay money, and, as a general rule, in the case of an agreement to convey land, and in some other cases, the right immediately originated may be specifically enforced; but in general, the immediate right can not be directly enforced, but only indirectly, by the enforcement of the corresponding alternative right arising upon its violation. Thus, in the case of contracts to sell ordinary commodities, such as wheat or corn, it is obvious that the obligee is fully compensated by giving him the money value, and therefore it would be a vain and useless thing to compel the delivery to him of the article in kind; and it is a reasonable maxim of the law that "the law will not enforce any one to do a thing which will be vain and fruitless." In general, therefore, the immediate effect of a contract is to establish a principle or rule of conduct for the contracting parties, in the nature of a law, upon the violation of which a right arises; and contracts may, therefore, without impropriety, be called private laws. .

[9.] It is obvious that a contract can create a

right only by virtue of some precedent right existing in the contractor.

§ 71. [10.] It is universally, or almost universally, assumed that men may be rightfully compelled to perform their promises; but, in view of
the numerous exceptions to this proposition, it is
evident that this can not be asserted as universally
true, and therefore can not be admitted as a principle of scientific jurisprudence. It is clear, however,
that where one, by means of a promise, has obtained property of another, or induced him to perform services in a way to change his condition for
the worse, the latter is entitled to compensation as
much as though he had been deprived of his property, or otherwise injured by force or fraud.

§ 72. Laws, or legislative acts, are of two kinds:
namely, general or public laws, and private laws.
The former establish general rules applicable to
classes of cases, and the latter apply to particular
cases only. In either case, rights may be immediately originated or divested, in which case the law
is an investitive or divestitive event, or it may be
necessary that other events concur.

§ 73. Laws, or legislative acts, are generally
classed as principles or rules by which rights are
determined rather than as events in which they
originate. This, however, is obviously incorrect
with reference to private laws, and especially with
regard to those which confer rights immediately;
for these are not principles or rules at all, and
therefore do not come within the common definition of law, as a rule of civil conduct. It is also

equally obvious that those public laws which immediately confer rights can not be considered as principles. Nor do other laws stand in any different case; for the efficacy of all laws consist in their being expressions of the will of the sovereign; and, manifestly, if the will of the sovereign is efficacious in the one case, it must be also in the other. It is therefore immaterial whether its will is declared with reference to a particular case, or a class of cases, or whether it is declared to the effect that a right shall immediately exist, or that it shall exist only upon the happening of certain events.

§ 74. A law may, indeed, establish a principle or rule of conduct, but in itself it is neither the one nor the other, but a mere act of the persons vested with legislative powers; and in order to affirm from it the existence of a principle or rule of conduct, another proposition is necessary, to wit, the assertion of the power or right of the legislature to establish the principle or rule, and the obligation of people to conform to it.

§ 75. [11.] Laws or statutes' are mere acts of men, differing from other men only in being vested with the right of legislation; and obviously, therefore, they derive whatever validity they may have from the right vested in the legislature over the matters to which they relate. Whenever, therefore, it is within the right of the legislature to determine any matter, the expression of its will with regard to such matter is conclusive; and rights may therefore originate in legislation, as in contract, or delict, which the moralist as well as the lawyer must recognize. But if a law is in excess of the rightful power, or right, of the legislature, or, to use a technical expression, is *ultra vires*, it has no more force or validity in determining rights than the act of a private individual. The existence or non-existence of rights, therefore, can not be predicated from the mere enactment of laws, but their validity must depend upon the existence of a precedent right in the state to determine the matters to which they relate.

§ 76. With reference to the extent of the right of the state over the rights of individuals, one of two hypotheses must be adopted; either it is limited (which we shall see is in fact the case), or it is unlimited. If we assume the former hypothesis, our proposition is clear; nor is it less clear upon the latter. For even if we assume that the state has the unlimited right to create or destroy rights in private individuals, this itself, if true, would be a principle of natural reason, and equally entitled to recognition by the moralist as by the lawyer. It would follow, therefore, upon this hypothesis, that in all cases where the state has expressed its will that a right shall exist or cease to exist, that will, upon principles of natural right, would be conclusive; and the right in question would exist or not accordingly as the legislature had determined; but in all cases where the will of the legislature did not intervene— and in fact it is only to a limited extent that it does so—the rights of men would necessarily have to be otherwise determined.

§ 77. Laws in this respect are therefore analogous to contracts, grants, and other expressions of

5

the will of private individuals; which, like laws, are valid or otherwise according to the right of the party making them; or in other words, laws, contracts, and grants are all species of one genus, namely, expressions of human will; all of which, so far as they affect the question of rights, are efficacious or otherwise, according to the precedent rights of their respective authors. Thus one can not by his contract or grant confer a right upon any one to the property of another, or create an obligation to another in any one but himself or some one whose liberty he has the right to dispose of; nor can the state transfer the right of one to another, or subject any one to an obligation in favor of another, unless by virtue of some precedent right in the state to do so; it being immaterial to the present question whether such right exists in all or only in a limited number of cases; for, in the absence of such a right, the will of no individual or individuals, whether vested with political power or not, can be binding upon others.

§ 78. Whichever theory we adopt, therefore, laws or statutes, like other expressions of human will, enter into the determination of rights only as elements of the problem; and they are therefore no more inconsistent with the scientific character of right than are contracts or grants. It indeed devolves upon the jurist, with reference to either, to ascertain the will of the party expressed in the instrument, whether that be of the state or a private individual; and thus far right includes the art of hermeneutics, or interpretation; but after the instrument is construed, its effect upon rights is still to be determined; and this must, at least ultimately, be determined by some principle of natural reason, even though it should be none other than the principle sometimes asserted, but manifestly absurd, that the right of the state to dispose of the lives, liberties, and fortunes of its citizens is absolute and unlimited.

§ 79. A custom is merely a series of acts of the same kind; or we may consider the concurrence of a sufficient number of such acts to establish a custom as itself an event. Customs are either general or particular, the latter being those which obtain in particular localities or with particular trades or professions, and the former those which obtain generally throughout the realm or state. Under our law, the term, unless qualified, generally refers to particular customs only; for if a custom is general, "it is common law:" Jacob's Law Dict., tit. Common Law. A custom may or may not give rise to a right, and whether it does so or not is in each case a question for jurisprudence to determine, as will appear from the following considerations:

§ 80. [12.] Where men enter into a contract, it is obvious that they generally have regard to any existing custom relating to the matter about which they are dealing; and to arrive at the intention of the parties, the contract must be construed with reference to the custom. In such cases, customs enter into and form part of contracts, not on account of any particular virtue in them, but because of the presumed intention of the parties. Hence, if the express terms of the contract are inconsistent with the custom, the latter is rejected. Thus where it is the custom of the community that the tenant at the end of his lease shall be entitled to the crops growing on the leased premises, and to enter after the termination of the lease for the purpose of removing them, it is evident, where the lease does not refer to the matter at all, that it is the intention of the parties that the tenant shall have that right. But if the lease expressly states that the lessor is to have the crops growing on the land at the expiration of the lease, the presumption that the parties intended conformity to it is rebutted, and the custom is accordingly rejected.

§ 81. So, also, custom may become an important element in the determination of rights arising from delict or injury. Thus where it is the custom for vehicles meeting each other on the road to pass each other to the right,[1] obviously a party disregarding the custom is responsible for any collision that may occur—not because of the mere disregard of the custom, but because such disregard indicates either gross negligence or willful intention to injure. So, too, with regard to collisions at sea, "there are settled nautical rules by which, in most cases, the want of skill, or care, or duty, may be ascertained. Thus

---

[1] "In England the law of the road is 'that horses and carriages should pass each other on the whip-hand.' . . . . The action in which this rule is applied, viz., for negligently driving a carriage by which any one is injured, is as ancient as the common law; but the uniform determination of the judges, that the non-observance of this rule is negligence, is of modern date:" 1 Bla. Com. *74, note 14.

the vessel that has the wind free, or is sailing before or with the wind, must get out of the way of the vessel that is close-hauled, or sailing by or against it. The vessel on the starboard tack has a right to keep her wind, and the vessel on the larboard tack is bound to give way to the other, and bear up or heave about, to avoid the injury, or be answerable for the consequences:" 3 Kent's Com. *230.

Accordingly, in either case, where the party damaged might easily have avoided the collision, but fails to do so, or in other words, where he has been guilty of contributory negligence, he acquires no right; for in such case the damage is as much the result of his own fault as that of the other party.

§ 82. [13.] General customs, also, frequently have the force of laws, and this perhaps is their most important aspect. The efficacy of custom in this respect is generally attributed to the fact that it necessarily constitutes an expression of the general will; and certainly custom is a more perfect expression of the will of the state than laws, which are often in conflict with the general will. Hence, so far forth as rights may be determined by the will of the state, custom, as being a more perfect expression of that will, should have a superior efficacy to law; and accordingly, this is practically the case; for with regard to private rights, laws in general become operative only when they conform to an existing custom, or generate a new one; otherwise, they may for a while, at the expense of infinite injustice and hardship, be imperfectly enforced; but ultimately they give way and become obsolete. And

as they become operative only by custom, so, too,
they cease to be operative, and are in effect repealed,
when the custom changes.[1] The assertion, therefore,

[1] " It is of the nature of the law to be realized in practice. A
principle of law never applied in practice, or which has lost its
force, no longer deserves the name; it is a worn-out spring in the
machinery of the law, which performs no service, and which may
be removed without changing its action in the least. This applies
without limitation to all parts of the law—to the law of nations as
well as to private and criminal law; and the Roman law has given
it its express sanction, inasmuch as it considers *desuetudo* as an
abrogation of a law:" Ihering's Struggle for Law, 65.

" Les lois conservent leur effet, tant qu'elles ne sont point abro-
gées par d'autres, ou qu'elle ne sont point tombées en desuetude.
Si nous n'avons pas formellement autorisé la mode d'abrogation
par la desuetude, ou le non usage, cést qu'il eut peut étré ete dan-
gereux de la faire. Mais peut on se dissimuler l'influence et
l'utilité de ce concert deliberé, de cette puissance invisible, par
laquelle sans secousse, et sans commotion, les peuples se font justice des mauvaises lois, et qui semblent proteger la societé contre
les surprises faites au legislateur, et le legislateur contre lui
même:" Discours Preliminaire, cited Sedgwick on Stat. & Const.
Law, 97.

" Inveterate custom is, not erroneously, observed as law (and
this is the law which is said to be *moribus constitutum*). For
since laws themselves bind us from no other cause than that they
are received by the judgment of the people, rightly also those
which, without any writing, the people have approved, shall bind
us. For what difference is there whether the people declare their
will by suffrage or by acts? Wherefore, most rightly, it is also
received that laws are abrogated, not only by the vote of the legislature, but also with the tacit consent of all by *desuetude:* "
Dig. 1, 3, 32; see also 1 Bla. Com. *74.

It may be interesting in this connection to refer also to the
Spanish law, which is subtantially to the same effect. " Legitimate custom has the force of law, not only where there is no law
to the contrary, but also to derogate from an anterior law opposed
to it; whence comes the saying, ' There is a custom *outside* of the
law, *against* the law, and *according* to the law ' (fuera de la ley,

made by Mr. Austin, that custom becomes operative
in the determination of rights only when adopted
by the political power,[1] or in other words, only
when it becomes law (in the strict sense), can not be
maintained; but it will be nearer the truth to say
that law becomes operative only when it becomes
custom, and for so long only as it continues to be
so.

It seems, indeed, part of the very nature and constitution of man that his actions shall in the main
be immediately determined by custom and habit;
and hence—using the term in its widest sense, as
including not only simple customs, but also those
which are accompanied by a conviction of their
moral rectitude (*mores consuetudinemque*)—morality
itself (and jurisprudence as a branch of morality)
depends mainly upon custom for its practical operation; though it is the function of morality as a
science to judge of the rectitude of customs, and as
an art to correct and reform them.[2]

contra la ley, y segun la ley). In order that a custom be legitimate,
it is required that it be introduced by the consent of the people, that
it be conformable to the general utility, and that it be observed for
the space of ten years:" Escriche's Dic. de Leg., tit. Costumbre.
This instance is the more striking from the fact that in theory the
Spanish law is supposed to be altogether *lex scripta*, Spain having
from the earliest period of its history been governed by written
codes.

[1] This view of Austin's, as to the nature of customary law, is
peculiar to himself and followers, and is manifestly absurd.

[2] "Customs are made by time and usage, and do obtain the
force of laws in particular places and nations; but not otherwise
than upon the supposition that they were reasonable at the
beginning:" 3 Mod. Rep., preface. The author, as an example
of an unreasonable custom, refers to the tenure of borough

§ 83. [14.] Custom, however, is not conclusive in the determination of rights, but its efficacy is confined to matters jurally indifferent. Thus the custom, spoken of by Blackstone, by which the landlord claimed the right of concubinage with the tenant's wife on the wedding night,[1] if in fact it ever existed, gave rise to no right in the landlord, but was a mere instance of successful oppression; and the same remark is true of many of the feudal customs which are better authenticated. Hence, customs enter into the determination of rights only as an element in the problem, and their effect, like that of laws, is determined by independent principles of right.

§ 84. Neither laws nor customs, therefore, any more than other events, of themselves originate rights, but they do so only by virtue of principles

English, the origin of which he explains, as stated by Blackstone in the note to the following section. " Custom to Puchta is nothing but a mere mode of discovering what conviction as to the legally (*i. e.*, *jurally*) right is:" 1 Ihering's Struggle for Right, 14.

[1] "The principal and most remarkable of which [customs] is that called ' borough English;' . . . . viz., that the youngest son, and not the eldest, succeeds to the burgage tenement on the death of the father. For which Littleton gives this reason: because the younger son, by reason of his tender age, is not so capable as his brethren to help himself. Other writers have, indeed, given a much stranger reason for this custom—as if the lord of the fee had anciently a right of concubinage with his tenant's wife on her wedding-night, and that, therefore, the tenement descended not to the eldest but the youngest son, who was more certainly the offspring of the tenant. But I can not learn that ever this custom prevailed in England, though it certainly did in Scotland (under the name of mercheta, or marcheta) till abolished by Malcolm III:" 2 Bla Com. *83.

of natural right, and therefore enter into the determination of rights merely as elements in the
problem. In this way, and in this way only, can
we reconcile the co-existence, in the law, of eternal
and immutable justice with laws which are purely
arbitrary, and customs which are, to a certain extent, accidental; and which are both, therefore,
often unreasonable and absurd.

§ 85. [15.] Nearly all questions as to rights (as
will be shown more fully hereafter) may be determined by the above principles. Where doubtful
questions arise which can not be so determined, the
principle of utility must be resorted to; for all
theories of right unite in the proposition that conformity to right must conduce to the welfare of
mankind; and utility, or tendency to promote that
welfare, may therefore be assumed to be, if not of
the essence, at least as a property of right, and
therefore universally to be affirmed of it. It therefore follows that nothing which is pernicious, or
contrary to utility, can be right.

§ 86. [16.] The wisdom of men is not always, or
even generally, adequate to judge truly as to the
utility of any given principle; and the question of
right is therefore generally more simple than that of
utility. Wherever a principle of right is otherwise
established, the question of utility can not be considered. In such cases we know it is useful because it
is right.

§ 87. The principle of utility, in the negative
form in which we have stated it, is embodied under
the name of the *argumentum ab inconvenienti*, in one

of the fundamental maxims of our law; and there are few principles more frequently referred to and relied upon by jurists than this. The maxim as given by Coke is, *Argumentum ab inconvenienti plurimum valet in lege;* and he adds, "The law, that is, the perfection of reason, can not suffer anything that is inconvenient;" and therefore he says, " *Nihil quod est inconveniens est licitum,*" and that "judges are to judge of inconveniences as of things unlawful."

CHAPTER VI.

OF THE RIGHTS OF THE STATE, OR PUBLIC RIGHTS.

§ 88. Right is divided into public right (*jus publicum*) and private right (*jus privatum*); the former relating to public rights, or rights of the state; and the latter to private rights, or the rights of individuals. We will treat of these in the order stated, so far as may be necessary to explain their general nature, and the nature of the proofs by which they are established.

§ 89. The state is, in effect, a corporation or body politic; that is to say, an aggregate of men, considered, with reference to their common rights, as a fictitious or ideal person, capable like natural persons of having rights and being subject to obligations. It may be briefly defined as a permanent autonomous aggregate of people occupying a common territory.

§ 90. The state is therefore to be distinguished from the government; the latter being the mere agent, or trustee of the state, and holding its rights only in a fiduciary capacity, and bearing to the state precisely the same relation as that borne to a corporation by its directory and officers.[1]

[1] "Every one who inquires into the nature of governments and what and of what kind are its several forms, should make this almost his first question: What is a state? For upon this point

§ 91. Public rights may be divided into two classes; namely, those which pertain to the individuals composing the state, and which differ from private rights only in being common to all, and those which do not pertain at all to private persons in their individual capacities, but to the state in its corporate capacity only. The former may be called the *social* and the latter the *political* rights of the state.

§ 92. The former class of rights includes the right to the maintenance of the public peace and security; the right to the preservation of the public morality, and the right to the lands of the state, and to other material things naturally existing, or which are not the product of labor. The existence of the social rights are essential to the existence of the rights, or rightful liberty, of each individual, and they therefore exist in the state because they exist in each of the individuals composing it.

§ 93. Thus with reference to the maintenance of the public peace and security, it is obvious that this is essential to the well-being and rights of every in-

there is a dispute; for some persons say the state did this or that, while others say it was not the state, but the oligarchy, or the tyrant. We see, too, that the state is the only object which both the politician and the legislator have in view in all they do; but government is a certain ordering of those who live as members of a state. Now, since a state is a collective body, and like other wholes composed of many parts, it is evident that our first point must be to inquire what a citizen is; for a state or a city is a certain number of citizens." Aristotle Pol. (Bohn's edition), b. 3, c.1.

"L'état c'est moi," is a natural expression of the egotism of political rulers; but is as an absurd as well as a pernicious proposition.

dividual; for the constant sense of insecurity which would result from the failure to maintain it would be as incompatible with the exercise of the just liberty of the individual as the actual invasion of such liberty.

§ 94. It is equally clear that the decent observance of morality is also demanded by the rights of individuals, and that its open violation is inconsistent with those rights. For such violation of the principles of morality generally observed by the community would constitute what is technically called a nuisance: N. Y. C. C., sec. 1949, and authorities cited; and is as incompatible with the comfortable enjoyment of existence, and the free exercise of the faculties in the pursuit of happiness, as a noxious smell, or poisonous exhalation.[1]

§ 95. The right of the state to the lands constituting its territory also rests, as will hereafter be fully explained, upon the right of personal liberty; which includes the right to use all unappropriated things.

§ 96. It is obvious, therefore, that the social rights of the state are but consequences of the prin-

---

[1] It is also obvious that the right to the maintenance of the public security implies the right to the preservation of the state; and the latter again implies the right to a certain extent to maintain and preserve the morality of the community; for no fact is more certain, historically, than that the decay of morality and the general corruption of society is incompatible with the well-being, and generally with the permanent existence, of the state. This right, however, so far as it rests upon this ground, does not pertain to any individual or individuals, but to the state only in its corporate capacity, and is therefore to be classed with political rights.

ciple that every man of normal *status*, within the limitations imposed by the rights of others, has the rightful liberty to use his natural faculties in such manner as he may deem most conducive to his own welfare; or in other words, that they rest upon and have their cause, or *raison d'etre*, in the right of personal liberty or self-ownership.

§ 97. The social rights of the state, like private rights, are fully effectuated by their mere exercise or enjoyment; and, so long as respected, do not call for or admit of the intervention of .the political force. Hence were it not for the liability of these rights to violation, or in other words, were mankind uniformly just, and voluntarily disposed to submit to the restraints demanded by the rights of others, private and social rights would include all rights whatever.

§ 98. Political rights spring from the necessity of an organized force to protect private and social rights, and they may therefore be all summed up in the one general right to govern or coerce; which includes not only the right to use force for the protection of private and social rights, but also the right to use it for the maintenance and protection of the government; the existence of which is essential to the principal end.

§ 99. With the exception of the right of organizing a government—which is extraordinary in its nature and only of occasional occurrence—political rights, from the nature of the case, can only be exercised by the government; and therefore, to distinguish such ordinary rights from the extraordi-

nary right of organizing government, they may conveniently and without impropriety be termed the
rights of the government.

§ 100. These rights are usually summed up
under three heads; viz., 1. The judicial right,
which consists in the right of determining by its
judgment questions of right between men, and between men and the state, and which would seem
properly to include the right of judicial legislation,
as well as that of jurisdiction, as ordinarily understood; 2. The legislative right, or the right of determining by its will how the government shall be
administered, and its force applied; and 3. The
executive right, or the right of enforcing the judgment, or the will of the state, as the case may be.

§ 101. Accordingly, in all the American governments, state and federal, the powers or rights of
the government are vested in three separate classes
of officers, or departments, termed respectively the
"Legislative," the "Executive," and the "Judicial;"
each of which is independent of the others, and
sovereign within its appropriate sphere.[1]

[1] Thus in the constitution of the United States, the legislative
powers are provided for in article 1, the executive in article 2, and
the judicial in article 3. The corresponding provisions of the
constitution of California are contained in articles 3 to 6 inclusive;
the first of which is as follows: "The powers of the government
of the state of California shall be divided into three separate departments—the legislative, the executive, and judicial; and no
person charged with the exercise of powers properly belonging to
one of these departments shall exercise any functions appertaining
to either of the others, except as in this constitution expressly
directed or admitted." Substantially identical provisions are contained in all the state constitutions.

§ 102. The executive power has for its object merely the execution of the judgment or the will of the other departments, as the case may be; and it is therefore subordinate to, and not co-ordinate with, them. Hence it would seem that the rights or powers of the government should be distributed in the first place into two classes only, viz., judicial and executive, and the executive powers assigned to the one or the other class, accordingly as they are designed to carry into effect the one or the other species of rights, and designated respectively as *judicial* and *non-judicial*, or administrative, *executive* powers.

§ 103. All political rights spring from the necessity of protecting private and social rights, and exist because essential to their existence: *Supra*, § 12, and note. Obviously, therefore, like private and social rights, they have their cause in the right of personal liberty or self-ownership.

§ 104. Whether the right of government extends any further than to the protection of the rights, or just liberty, of the individual,[1] is a point much controverted, and with reference to which opinions vary, from the extreme view of Spencer, that the rightful power of the state extends no further than to maintain the liberty of the individual to the fullest extent compatible with the equal liberty of others, to that of Hobbes, Austin, and others, that it is altogether unlimited.

[1] "It [the state] is first founded that men may live, but continued that they may live happily:" Aristotle, Pol. (Bohn's edition,) b. 1, c. 2.

§ 105. It may be said upon this point that the principle of personal liberty is not an ultimate principle, but must be resolved into another; namely, that the true end (or *summum bonum*) of man is the complete development and exercise of the faculties, and that justice or right, therefore, requires that every man should receive the highest physical, mental, and moral development which it is possible for him to receive consistently with a like development in others.

§ 106. If, however, we assume this to be the ultimate principle, it must also be assumed that in general the most efficient means of securing this development is to accord to every individual the most complete liberty compatible with that end, and with the just liberty of others; and that consequently the presumption, at least, is always in favor of liberty.

§ 107. It therefore devolves upon those who assert the existence of a more extensive right in the government to adduce some principle to justify it; and obviously no other principle can be adduced than that of utility—a principle utterly uncertain in its application except in its negative form; and which, at least in the present case, would seem to lead us to the opposite conclusion; for no historical fact is more certain than that the interference of government with the liberty of the individual, has been one of the most, and perhaps the most, fruitful of all sources of human misery and corruption;[1] and

---

[1] It would be difficult to find more error compressed in a few

6

it is perhaps doubtful whether a single instance of such interference, beyond what is necessary to protect the rights of individuals, can be adduced which has not, in all its consequences taken together, been productive of evil rather than good. In the present state of our knowledge, it would therefore seem safest to conclude that the right of the state is limited to the protection of the rights of its subjects; and that the end of scientific jurisprudence is to determine, and the end of government and law is to maintain, the equal jural liberty of individuals.

§ 108. At all events, it is only with reference to the general legislative power of the state that any serious question can arise; for with regard to the judicial right, or power of the state, including the right of judicial legislation, a clear and well-defined limit exists. For as it is the function of the state to protect and enforce the rights of individuals, this implies that it shall not violate them.

§ 109. There are, however, some claims which men have upon each other, which may, and indeed ought to, be enforced; and which may, therefore, be said to constitute rights, but which, until defined by law or custom, are so indefinite in their nature as not to admit of convenient enforcement. Such rights might with propriety be called *imperfect,* but on account of the loose sense in which that term is used, and to which we have referred, *supra,* § 11, it

words, than in the lines furnished by Johnson to Goldsmith for The Traveller:
    " How small of all that human hearts endure,
      The part that kings or laws can cause or cure."

will be better to denominate them *indeterminate* rights.

§ 110. Of this class the right of the parent to govern and control his child up to a certain age is an example. This right, as it is fiduciary in its nature, and exists only for the benefit of the child, may indeed be said to continue only until the child arrives at an age where control is no longer necessary for his own good; but the period at which he arrives at such an age varies in different cases, and even in each case is more or less indeterminate.

Rights of succession to intestate estates furnish another example of indeterminate rights. It seems clear, indeed, that where there is no widow the children should inherit, and perhaps that they should inherit equally; but if the intestate leaves a wife and a child or children, or a wife and no children, or if he leave only distant kin, there seems to be no principle of natural right by which it can be determined in what proportion the parties entitled should inherit.

So, too, all rights to the performance of obligations, though in other respects peculiarly clear and well defined in their nature, are indeterminate with regard to the kind and degree of force that may be employed to enforce them. Thus a man has a clear and definite right to compensation for an injury, or to the payment of a debt, and he also has the right to enforce, or to call upon the state to enforce, the obligation; but what particular kind or amount of force may be rightfully employed is indeterminate, except so far that it is clear that no more force can be rightfully used than is necessary to effect the object in view.

§ 111. It is obviously essential to the peace of society, and to the administration of justice, that indeterminate rights should be defined; but nature itself has provided for this necessity, by endowing men with a disposition to conform to custom, and by the operation of this natural tendency the jural relations of men become defined, and indeterminate rights determinate. Thus at an early period in the English law the age of majority, and also the rules of descent were fixed by custom; and indeed, so universal is the operation of this principle that in no system of law can any question remain for a long time unsettled.

§ 112. In the progress of society, however, new questions as to the jural relations of men continually arise, many of which, until settled by custom, are more or less indeterminate in their nature; and thus it devolves upon the state, in the exercise of its judicial function, to determine them. Its function also extends to the revision of the customary law, where, by reason of its original imperfection or by the change of manners and customs, it has become defective.

§ 113. As it is the function of the state to protect and enforce rights, it is clear that where rights are already defined by natural principles, there are no grounds for its interference, and that its legitimate power is limited by the condition that it shall not trench upon such rights, or even upon indeterminate rights, in so far as they are determinate. Thus it would be an abuse of power upon the part of the state, in undertaking to determine as to the respective claims of widow and children to intestate estates, to provide that such estates should go to strangers; nor would it have the right, on the one hand, to deprive parents altogether of the control of their children, or, on the other, to subject the latter altogether to the power of the former.

§ 114. Nor with regard to customs, is there any ground for interference with them by the state, where they are not unjust or irrational; for not only will legislation which runs counter to custom be productive of great hardship and injustice, but custom itself constitutes the most perfect expression of the will of the people, or in other words, of the state, and is, therefore, in general, entitled to a higher respect than the will of the few in whom, for the time being, the legislative power is vested.

§ 115. Nearly all questions between men as to the ownership of property or (as in the case of husband and wife, parent and child, etc.) of persons, and as to obligations, are clearly and definitely determined by the principles of natural justice, or by the manners and customs of the people; and hence the function of judicial legislation, in so far as it relates to the determination of rights, is extremely limited both in its legitimate and in its actual operation.

CHAPTER VII.

OF PRIVATE RIGHTS; AND HEREIN FIRST OF RIGHTS OF OWNERSHIP, OR RIGHTS IN REM.

§ 116. Of rights *in rem*, the fundamental right is the right of personal liberty, or (as it may be more accurately termed) the right of self-ownership or of property in one's self. The essence of all rights consists, indeed, in the liberty to act; and therefore, in the widest sense of the term, the right of liberty includes all rights whatever. But this liberty to act has reference to different objects; viz., to one's self, to other persons, or to things; and it is necessary, therefore, to distinguish the right which one has in himself from those rights which he has in or over other persons, whether *in rem* or *in personam*, and those which he has in things, or the right of property. To distinguish the former right, the term "personal liberty" is generally used; but the idea is more precisely expressed by the term "self-ownership," or property in the person; and to avoid the ambiguity of the former term, the latter will be generally used.

§ 117. The right of self ownership implies the absence of interference of any kind with the free exercise of the faculties, within the limits of the right; and this includes not only immunity from bodily harm, and from imprisonment or other physical restraint, but also from injury to the health or to the reputation, or from any other interference with the comfortable enjoyment of life, or with the pursuit of happiness, or with such other end as one may set before himself.

§ 118. Thus the right is violated, not only by injuries to the body, or corporal injuries—such as assault, battery, mayhem, imprisonment or murder —but also by libel or slander, by which the reputation is injured, and by threats of harm, by fear of which free action is impeded. The right is also violated, not only by direct injuries, such as above specified, but also by injuries occurring indirectly by the fault of others, as where one is injured in his health, or even annoyed, by a nuisance on a neighbor's land, or where, by the fault of another, he is injured by adulterated food or drink, or by a ferocious animal, or by a spring-gun or man-trap, or by a dangerous road, or by falling into an unguarded well. For all of these injuries are manifest invasions of the right to the free enjoyment and exercise of one's natural faculties; or in other words, of the right of self-ownership.

§ 119. This right includes also the right to use, to some extent at least, the material things naturally existing around us; for without the use of a certain amount of air, water, land, fuel, food and shelter, man can not exist; and without the use of a much larger amount of such things than is required for mere existence, he can not exist healthfully and comfortably, and freely exercise and develop his faculties. Just in proportion, therefore, as he is deprived of such things as he desires to use, and

which but for human interference he could use, he
is deprived of his liberty; and if he is altogether deprived of them, he is deprived of existence itself.

§ 120. The question is, therefore, not as to the
existence, but as to the limit of the right; and upon
this point, it is important to remember that the presumption is in favor of the right, and that to assign
any limit to it, such limit must be affirmatively
established. Now, as we have seen, there can be no
limits to the rights of jural liberty of the individual
other than some right in another or in others, and
such right can, in this case, only be a right in some
particular thing or things—*i. e.*, a right of property
—or the right of personal liberty or self-ownership
in others. We therefore conclude that the latter
right is the only limit to the right of any one to use
unappropriated things, or things in which no one
else has a peculiar right. .

§ 121. With regard to this limit, it is evident
that the use of anything by one must necessarily, to
some extent, detract from the personal liberty of all
others within whose power it would otherwise be to
use it; for a use by one takes away from all such
others the liberty of using the thing in any way inconsistent with the first use; and this is true, not
only of such things as are susceptible of being reduced to ownership, but also of those things which
can not be permanently appropriated, such as air and
water, and the sea, and navigable lakes and rivers,
and other highways. Thus, for instance, a ship
sailing on the sea must occupy a certain space, and
requires also new space in which to move freely in

the direction in which the master desires to go.
The right of personal liberty in the owner of the
ship, therefore, necessarily diminishes the personal
liberty of others, so far as to exclude them from the
use of the portion of the sea occupied by the former;
that is to say, not only the space actually occupied
by the ship, but also the space required for its
further movement in the direction it is going; for
the word "occupy" does not necessarily imply
actual physical or bodily occupation or holding, but
may consist merely in the manifestation of a will,
coupled with the power, to use. In other words, it
is not by the hand, or physical act, only, that a
thing is occupied; but, where it is within the natural
power of any one to use it, the manifestation of his
will or intention to use it is a complete occupation,
which can not be interfered with by others without
interfering with the personal liberty of the occupant. Where the movements of the ship, therefore,
indicate an immediate intention upon the part of
the master to move in a particular direction, or this
intention is otherwise manifested, the space thus indicated is occupied or appropriated for the time
being, and others are excluded from occupying it,
or from otherwise interfering with the movements
of the ship; for to do so would be to prevent the
free exercise of the will, or in other words, to interfere with the personal liberty of the owner of the
ship; and such interference could be justified only
by some right in the party interfering, which by
the hypothesis he does not have.

§ 122. With regard to things which are susceptible of permanent appropriation, it is obvious that the use of them by one must, in general, detract in a much greater degree from the liberty of others than in the case of the sea, and other things of that class. For many of the former class can only be used by consuming them, and the use of them therefore forever deprives others of the liberty to use them; and even with regard to those things which may be used without consuming them, the use is generally of a more permanent nature, and therefore must deprive others of the liberty of using them for a longer period.

§ 123. It is obvious, therefore, that the right to use unappropriated things is not limited by the condition that such use shall not interfere in any degree with the personal liberty of others; for in general, things can not be used without such interference. The problem therefore is, to determine the degree in which one may, by using unappropriated things, rightfully interfere with the personal liberty of others.

§ 124. In determining this question, it is necessary to distinguish between a direct and immediate interference with personal liberty, and such interference as is only indirect or consequential.

§ 125. With regard to the former, it is obvious that (unless by virtue of some clearly defined right) a direct interference with the personal liberty of any one is unjustifiable, and therefore, in general, no one has a right to interfere with any one in the use of any unappropriated thing which he has commenced to use.

§ 126. But with regard to the indirect interference with the liberty of others resulting from the use of a thing by any one, and its consequent withdrawal from the use of others, the question is not so clear. As we have seen, this kind of interference is to a certain extent inevitable and therefore justifiable; and hence, unless some clearly defined limit can be assigned, we must conclude (in view of the presumption in favor of the right) that it is unlimited.

§ 127. This limit, if it exists at all, must be found in the principle that the jural liberty of all men *in the same case* is equal; or in other words, that no restraint can be rightly imposed upon one that may not be equally imposed upon all others in the same case: Prop. 3, *supra*, § 62. Hence it would seem that of any class of things within the natural power of a certain number of persons to use (assuming that all desire to use them), the use by one is limited by the condition that the liberty shall be left to each* of the others to use an equal amount of such things, or so much as they may desire to use within this limit. And this, with regard to the moral limit, is doubtless true; for it is clearly not right, where the supply of natural things susceptible of use is limited, for any one to take more than his share. But though it may not be right for one to do so, it still may be true that he has a right to do it. For the problems as to the extent of *moral* and of *jural* liberty (as we have seen) are distinct; the former being to determine what a man may rightly do, and the latter in what case his liberty may be rightly re-

strained by others: *Supra,* § 47. The question,
therefore, as to the limit of the right to use unappropriated things reduces itself , to the question
whether any one else has the right to interfere.

§ 128. With regard to this, where the supply is
unlimited—that is, where there is enough to satisfy
the desires of all—it is manifest that there is no
limit to the right; for in such case the use by one
of what he needs leaves sufficient to satisfy others,
and therefore leaves them an equal personal liberty.

§ 129. But where the supply is limited, the use
by one of more than his share infringes upon the
equality of personal liberty. This, however, is an
injury common to all, who might otherwise use the
things appropriated; and it is, in general, manifestly impossible to determine the extent of the
injury to any one in particular, and therefore impracticable to determine the extent necessary for
any one to interfere in order to protect his right.
No individual, therefore, can have the right to interfere with the use of an unappropriated thing by another; but the right of all to equal personal liberty
in this particular must, as in other cases of undefined jural relations, be left to the state to define and
enforce. We therefore conclude that in general the
state only has the right to regulate the use of unappropriated things where the supply is limited;
and that, in the absence of restraint by the state, the
right to use such things is in general unlimited.

§ 130. This right, however, like all other rights,
is subject to the qualification that circumstances may
occur in which a right in another to interfere with

it may exist. Such cases—where they do not come
under the head of rights arising from contracts, injuries, or some other well-defined class—may be
summed up under the general denomination of
cases of superior necessity. For the conclusion we
have reached as to the right of any one to use exclusively unappropriated things rests upon the
proposition that in general the hurt or damage resulting from an unequal appropriation is common
to all who might otherwise use them, and that generally it is impossible to define with accuracy the
hurt or damage resulting to particular individuals;
it is manifest, therefore, that where a peculiar hurt
or damage would result to a particular individual
the argument fails. Thus a man in danger of
drowning would clearly have a right to land upon
ground appropriated by another, or to force an en-
trance upon a boat or raft occupied by another; or,
if one of two castaways upon a desert island should
appropriate all the fruit or other means of subsistence, the other would clearly have a right—within
the limit of equality—to as much as would be
necessary to his subsistence. In such a case, indeed,
each would have a right to an equal share, and
neither (except in case of unlimited supply) could
appropriate more without violating the right of the
other; though in the case of larger communities—
from the difficulty of defining the claims of individuals—the principle of absolute equality would
not apply. For the same reason, it is clear that
mere superior need does not give rise to a right in
any one to interfere with the appropriation of

things by another; for unless such need rises to actual necessity, it is impossible to define the degree of it that would give rise to the right of interference.

§ 131. Nor is mere necessity sufficient to give rise to such a right, unless it is also superior to the necessity of the person interfered with. Thus, in case of a shipwreck, where one has appropriated a spar which is sufficient to sustain him, but not to sustain another, no one has a right to interfere with him.

§ 132. The right of property in things is derived from and rests upon the right of personal liberty, or self-ownership. In the language of Cousin, "the first property is the person, and all other properties is derived from this:" The True, the Beautiful, and the Good, lect. 14, p. 289.[1]

§ 133. Where the supply of unappropriated things is unlimited, every man has the right, or jural liberty, to use them; and even where the supply is limited, in the absence of restraint by the state, he still has such a right. By the term "right to

[1] "It is a matter of indifference what the object of the right is. If mere chance were to put me in possession of an object, I might be deprived of it without any injury to my person, but it is not chance, but my will, which establishes a bond between myself and it, and even my will only at the price of the past labor of myself or of another; it is a part of my own strength and of my own past, or of the strength and past of another, which I possess and assert in it. In making it my own, I stamped it with the mark of my own person; whoever attacks it attacks me; the blow dealt it strikes me, for I am present in it. Property is but the periphery of my person extended to things:" Inhering's Struggle for Law, 55.

use" we mean not only the right to put to what in common language is called a useful purpose, but to put to any use whatever, useful or otherwise, or in other words, to act freely with regard to the thing as one's will may dictate. The right to use implies the right to take and to hold, or in other words, to occupy, any unappropriated thing, which one may desire to use; and while the occupation continues, the right to use is exclusive, and no one else has a right to interfere with the occupant in his use of the thing; for to do so would be a direct infringement upon his personal liberty. Any person, therefore, has a right to appropriate or make property of any unappropriated thing; or in other words, the mere occupation of an unappropriated thing creates in the occupant a right of property in it.[1]

§ 134. It has been said that occupation is indicated by a manifestation of the will, coupled with the actual power to take; and it continues so long as the will and the possibility to use continues: Bouv. Law Dict., tit. Occupancy. There is, however, a distinction between the facts necessary to initiate an occupation and those necessary to continue it. In the former case, an actual and immediate power is essential; but in the latter, it is sufficient if the occupant remains in such relation to the thing that it

---

[1] It seems to be universally agreed that property in land originated in occupation; and it is very generally agreed that this constitutes a sufficient title. There are, however, different opinions as to the grounds upon which this efficacy can be assigned to occupation. The history and nature of the question are well presented by Blackstone: 2 Bla. Com. 8; and by Mr. Christian, in his note on the passage cited.

is possible that he may resume the actual and immediate power; for while these conditions subsist, the taking by another of the thing occupied would be a direct interference with the liberty or free exercise of the will of the occupant. Thus, if a man cuts down a tree on unappropriated land to use in building a house, or for other purposes, and leaves it on the ground to season, his occupation in general continues during his absence; but if he altogether abandons his intention of using it, or places himself, or is placed, beyond the possibility of ever using it, *i. e.*, of either using it himself or conveying it to another, his occupation and his right ceases; for the appropriation of a thing by another would no longer interfere with his liberty of action.

§ 135. It has been said that the right acquired by mere appropriation continues only so long as the occupation continues, and that therefore it is to be distinguished from property in the true sense of the term; as, for instance, the right which a man has in the products of his labor. There does not, however, seem to be any ground for a distinction in this respect. For, in the one case as in the other, the right continues during occupation, and can continue no longer. For, even in the case of artificial products, if the owner should abandon them, or they should pass beyond the possibility of himself or his successor in interest using them, the right would cease.

§ 136. In another respect, however, there is a broad distinction between the two cases. The right of any one to appropriate and to hold things naturally existing is subject to the condition that the state may interfere to prevent the infringement of the equal personal liberty of others; but with regard to the products of ˙one's own labor, this is not the case. For such things would not exist but for the labor of the producer, and therefore their appropriation by him does not in any way tend to diminish the personal liberty of others with regard to them.[1] Therefore it would seem that they belong to the producer in a peculiar and higher sense than property acquired by mere appropriation.[2] For, if our faculties

[1] The distinction between the two classes of things is thus well explained by Mr. George: " The real and natural distinction is between things which are the produce of labor and things which are the gratuitous offerings of nature; or, to adopt the terms of political economy, between wealth and land. . . . . The essential character of the one class of things is that they embody labor, are brought into being by human exertion, their existence or non-existence, their increase or diminution, depending on man. The essential character of the other class of things is that they do not embody labor, and exist irrespective of human exertions; they are the field of environment in which man finds himself; the store-house from which his needs must be supplied; the raw material˙ upon which and the forces with which his labor can alone act:" Progress and Poverty, b. 7, c. 1, pp. 302, 303.

[2] The argument upon this point is thus stated by Mr. George: "What constitutes the rightful basis of property? What is it that enables a man to justly say of a thing, 'It is mine'? From what springs the sentiment which acknowledges his exclusive right against the world? Is it not, primarily, the right of a man to himself, to the use of his own powers, to the enjoyments of the fruits of his own exertions? Is it not this individual right which springs from and is testified to by the natural facts of individual organization, ... which alone justifies individual ownership? As a man belongs to himself, so his labor when put in concrete form belongs to him. And for this reason, that which a man makes or

7

are our own, the fruits of their exertion must be equally ours, except in the single case where one wrongfully exercises his labor upon the property of another; in which case he acquires no right.

§ 137. Upon this last principle Grotius bases an argument against the proposition that the right of property can be derived from labor. Assuming that originally all things belonged to all men in common, he infers that the common right of all to any particular thing can not be taken away by the act of any individual without the consent of all, any

produces is his own as against all the world—to enjoy or to destroy, to use, to exchange, or to give. No one else can rightfully claim it, and his exclusive right to it involves no wrong to any one else. Thus there is to everything produced by human exertions a clear and indisputable title to exclusive possession and enjoyment; which is perfectly consistent with justice as it descends from the original producer in whom it is vested by natural law. . . . . This is not only the original source of title from which all idea of exclusive ownership arise, ... but it is necessarily the only source. There can be to the ownership of anything no rightful title which is not derived from the title of the producer, and does not rest upon the natural right of man to himself. There can be no other rightful title, because : 1. There is no other natur..l right from which any other title can be derived; and 2. Because the recognition of any other title is inconsistent with and destructive of this:" Progress and Poverty, B. 7, c. 1, pp. 299–301. The propositions stated are in the main as correctly as they are forcibly expressed. The last sentence, however, asserts in fact two distinct propositions as though they were equivalent; namely, first, that there can be no rightful title " which is not derived from the title of the producer; " and secondly, that there can be none " which does not rest upon the natural right of man to himself." The latter is true; but the truth of the former is the very question in dispute, and, as is elsewhere shown, is inconsistent with the latter: *Vide* §§ 137 *et seq.*, and note.

more than that the property of an individual could be thus affected: 1 Rutherford's Inst., b. 1, c. 3, § 10.

§ 138. This conclusion, however, is based upon a misconception of the right which men have with reference to unappropriated things, and which they originally had to all things naturally existing. This right is not a mere abstraction, but consists in the liberty to use, and therefore to appropriate, unappropriated things. It can not be asserted, therefore, that all men have a right in all things, or indeed, that men have any right in unappropriated things at all, beyond that implied in the right of personal liberty; namely, the right to appropriate them.

§ 139. With unimportant exceptions, all movable property is produced by and receives its whole value from human labor; and therefore, in general, the title to personal property is absolute, and neither individuals nor the state have a right to interfere with it: *Supra*, § 136.

§ 140. With regard to lands, however, the case is very different; for, except in early or barbarous states of society, or in new settlements, the supply is limited; and therefore the appropriation of lands by some necessarily diminishes the personal liberty of others. No one, therefore, can acquire a right of property in land in the same sense or to the same extent as he may in personal property; for to assert that such rights exist is, in effect, to assert that a large portion of mankind have not even a right to live, and much less freely to exercise their faculties, except upon the sufferance of others.[1]

---

[1] The argument for this proposition is forcibly stated by Mr.

§ 141. It devolves upon the state, therefore, or upon the government as the representative of the state, to regulate the distribution and use of lands; and this is effected either by custom, which is the spontaneous expression of the will of the state, or by laws, which are the expressed will of its agent, the government.

§ 142. It does not follow, however, that the government, or even the state, can give a permanent right of property in lands; for the right of the state is simply the right of the individuals composing it to use the land as part of the right of personal liberty, and the right of the government is simply the right which it has to determine the jural relations of men in all cases where otherwise they are not sufficiently determinate; and this power is one that can not be alienated, but always remains in the existing government. It would therefore follow, if no other principle intervened, that the right of property in lands might be divested by the state at any time. For by the state is meant not only the

Spencer, Social Statics, c. 9, and also by Mr. George in the chapter of his work already cited. The argument of the latter, however, contains a very obvious fallacy. Starting from the principle of self-ownership, he legitimately infers that every man has a right to the product of his labor, and therefore, that the title to goods produced by the labor of man is clear and indisputable. It does not follow, however, that because a man has a right to the product of his labor he has no right to anything else; for this would exclude the very first principle from which we set out; namely, that every man is the owner of himself and his faculties, which certainly are not the product of his labor; and from this it follows, as we have seen, that a man may acquire a title to unappropriated things by mere occupancy: *Supra*, §§ 133 *et seq.*

existing people who for the time being compose it, but all future generations that may exist during its continuance, and therefore, if every individual in the state at a given time should consent to the permanent appropriation of the lands, it would only transfer their own right, and could not divest the rights of future generations. Still less can the government give a perfect title; for although the government, as the agent of the state, is from the necessity of the case vested with the power of regulating the common right, yet in point of fact, it often fails to act in accordance with the general will. So that to assert that the government can forever alienate the lands of the state, and permanently diminish the personal liberty of the individuals composing it, is to assert that individuals vested for the time being with political power may divest the right not only of all coming generations, but even of the existing generation without its consent.' The same fundamental principle, therefore, applies to this as to all other cases; namely, that no government can derogate from the powers of its successors; or in other words, that the latest law (or expression of the will of the government) must prevail, according to the maxim, *Lex posterior derogat priori*.' More-

---

¹ The logic of the Maoris, as given by Mr. George in the following argument, is therefore unanswerable: " This natural and inalienable right to the equal use and enjoyment of land is so apparent that it has been recognized by men wherever force or habit has not blunted first perceptions. To give but one instance: The white settlers of New Zealand found themselves unable to get from the Maoris what the latter considered a complete title to land; because, although a whole tribe might have consented to a sale,

over, it may be asserted as a historical fact, that
nearly all land titles originated in force or fraud;
and this, upon the theory that their validity rests
upon the consent of the state to their original acquisition, would be sufficient to invalidate them.

§ 143.   There is, however, another element which
enters into the problem, and which materially
varies its aspect.   For existing titles in general rest
upon *bona fide* investments in the purchase and im-
provement of the land; and these investments have
been innocently made upon the faith of the existing
laws and customs, and moral convictions of the
people.   Therefore the present owners of land are
what is technically called innocent purchasers, and
it is not difficult to prove that their rights, to the
extent of their investment, should be protected.[1]

they would still claim, with every new child born among them, an
additional payment, on the ground that they had only parted with
their own rights, and could not sell those of the unborn:" Progress and Poverty, b. 7, c. 1, p. 305, note.

[1] Mr. George altogether denies the right of the land-owner to
compensation, and this, in fact, is the only original part of his
doctrine upon the subject of property in land.   His argument
upon this point is based upon the same false assumptions as that
of Grotius, *supra*, §§ 137, 138, viz., that the land is the property
of all men.   Hence, he concludes that private ownership in it is
robbery.   "It is not," he says, "merely a robbery in the past; it
is a robbery in the present—a robbery that deprives of their birth-
right the infants that are now coming into the world.   Why
should we hesitate to make short work of such a system?   Because
I was robbed yesterday, and the day before that, is it any reason
that I should suffer myself to be robbed to-day and to-morrow?—
any reason to conclude that the robber has acquired a vested right
to rob me?   If the land belongs to the people, why permit the
owners to take the rent, or compensate them in any manner for
the loss of the rent?"   Progress and Poverty, b. 7, c. 3, p. 328.

For to do otherwise would be to deprive them of the fruits of their labor, or that of others acquired by them, without any fault of theirs; and this would be a direct attack upon the right of personal liberty; for this is equally attacked by depriving a man of that which is produced by the exercise of his faculties, as by depriving him of the use of his faculties themselves. Hence the owners of land have a clear right to compensation if deprived of the land; and, as against the state, the right of property in land can not be demonstrated to extend any further.

§ 144. In determining the just amount of compensation, regard must be had not only to the amount originally invested, but to the value of the investment; or in other words, the value of the land. For on the one hand, if the investment has been a losing one, the loss results from the land-

What has already been said is a sufficient reply to this argument: Vide supra, §§ 120 et seq., and especially §§ 137. 138; and we will only add a few words with regard to the practical method proposed by Mr. George for the application of his principles, viz., "that the state should confiscate the rental value of land by taxation." "What I propose," he says, "as the simple yet sovereign remedy which will raise wages, increase the earnings of capital, extirpate pauperism, abolish poverty, give remunerative employment to whoever wishes it, afford free scope to human powers, lessen crime, elevate morals and taste and intelligence, purify government, and carry civilization to nobler heights, is to appropriate rent by taxation; in this way, the state may become the universal landlord without calling itself so, and without assuming a single new function:" Id. 364. If this proposition (as has been supposed) went no further than simply to raise the revenue necessary for the state by a land tax, it might, though based on fallacious reasoning, possibly be accepted: for it has been maintained by some, who do not participate in his views, that this is

owner's own act, and is therefore his own; and on the other, if the investment has been advantageous, he is entitled to the gain.

§ 145. The family relations give rise at once to rights *in rem* and to rights *in personam*, and to understand the nature of either, these must be carefully distinguished. The former, as we have already observed, are of the same essential nature as the right of property, and are in effect mere rights of property of the owner or subject in the object of the right: *Supra*, § 16, note.

§ 146. In all cases of rights *in rem*, the essential idea denoted by the right is the relation existing between the subject of the right and third persons; namely, that the latter are excluded from interference with the free action of the former with reference to the object of the right.

the most economical as well as the most equal and just form of taxation. The proposition, however, goes further than this, and includes the confiscation by means of taxation (without reference to the needs of the government) of the whole rent, less a percentage equivalent to what it would cost the state to rent the lands itself: Id. A practical problem of great interest would thus be presented; viz., what to do with the surplus over what is necessary for the expenses of the government. And in view of the past experience of the world, it would not do to anticipate from the government its fair administration; for Lev`athan (to use the metaphor of Hobbes) has been a thief and a robber from the beginning of the world to this day, and until the world changes for the better, it must always be the most important of practical maxims to trust him no further than we can help. Nor, even if this difficulty could be surmounted, is it easy to devise a scheme by which the revenue of the government could be distributed in such a manner as to do more good than harm. It is indeed impossible not to perceive, with Mr. George, the unhappiness and

§ 147. From this it follows, in the case of the right of property, that the thing owned is subject to the will of the owner; but in the case of family rights, a new element is introduced; namely, the right of personal liberty in the object of the right, by which the power of the other party is necessarily limited.

§ 148. In general, where such power exists over the object of the right, it is a power corresponding to some specific obligation in him, and therefore belongs to the class of rights *in personam*, which are distinct from, and not to be confounded with, the class of rights we are now discussing. In addition to this, however, the right is sometimes accompanied by a power over the object of the right, similar in kind, though not in degree, to that of an

misery of mankind, or to doubt that this is in a large measure due, not solely to the particular cause assigned by him, but to that, in conjunction with other artificial and ill-contrived political arrangements. Nor is it difficult to participate with him in the faith that these evils are to a large extent remediable. He is, however, evidently mistaken, both in his diagnosis of the case and in the remedy proposed: in the former, because it is not difficult to show that there are other even more efficacious causes of the disease than the one assigned; and in the latter, to use his own expressive language, because "that alone is wise which is just, that alone is enduring which is right:" Id. 299. To us it seems that the true and only remedy is the more perfect establishment of justice by the reformation and development of the law upon true principles; and in view of the numerous patent nostrums put forward in lieu of this remedy by social reformers, we may well say, with the hero of Erchmann—Chatrian's Story (Histoire d'un Paysan)—" Mon Dieu, quand donc les hommes seront-ils justes?"

Another objection to Mr. George's scheme is that confiscation would be in any case unnecessary; for, if it could be shown that

owner over the thing owned; as, for instance, the right of a parent in the child, and possibly that of the husband in the wife; but the presumption in this, as in all other cases, is always in favor of liberty against the power; and perhaps such power can be only affirmed to exist in cases where the protection of the object of the right imperatively requires it.

§ 149. Where such power exists, it is an accidental and not an essential element of the right; for it does not in any way affect the relation between the subject of the right and third persons, in which, as we have seen, the essence of the right consists. Thus the right of the child in the parent, or the wife in the husband, is not less perfect than that of the parent in the child, or that of the husband in the wife, though unaccompanied by any

---

the acquisition of property by the government, beyond what is needed for its ordinary expenses, would be an advantage, nothing would be easier than to devise means for its acquiring it without robbery or confiscation. For, leaving out of view such obvious expedients as taxation, abolition of collateral inheritances beyond a certain degree of consanguinity, as for instance, that of first cousins, the acquisition and administration of railroads and canals, the issue of paper money redeemable in coin, and others that might be suggested, it seems extremely probable that by a proper use of available means government could, in a comparatively brief period, obtain by voluntary contribution all the means needed.

To this end, probably, all that would be needed would be the efficient organization of a department of the government to receive and administer bequests and gifts; for at present the desire so common with large classes of men, and with all men under certain circumstances, to contribute of their means to the welfare of their country, and of mankind, is checked by the lack of effi-

power or control over the object of the right; indeed, in all cases the right is most perfect, or at least most valuable, where the relations of the parties are governed by love freely rendered. The rights *in rem* growing out of the family relations consist, therefore, merely in the exclusive liberty of enjoying the society, affection and services of the object of the right; and whether these are freely rendered or denied, and whether in the latter case they can be compelled by force or not, affects merely the value, and not the nature, of the right. Hence the question of power over the object of the right belongs rather to the subject of *status*, and is immaterial to the present discussion, which is concerned only with establishing the relations of the subject of the right toward third persons.

cient means upon which they can rely to carry into effect their benevolent intentions; and it is probable that were a sufficient machinery provided there would· arise among men a constantly increasing disposition to avail themselves of it, and that ultimately, as in the case of the church, it would be found necessary to restrain rather than to stimulate such disposition. This proposition will probably at first view appear paradoxical to many; but we have only to call to mind the immense wealth now and in the past so freely devoted to objects of benevolence, and to consider that in the life of a nation a few generations constitutes but a short period, to perceive the immense capabilities of the principles of benevolence or love, or charity, (whichever we may call it,) and to conclude that the difficulty lies, not in the feasibility of the scheme, but in the doubt whether, in the present state of political organization, such wealth could be wisely administered, or could be made productive of more good than evil. To illustrate we need refer only to the immense wealth of the church in the times when it in effect performed the function which we would now assign to the proposed department of government; and especially

§ 150. The rights of husband and wife originate in contract, and in the right of each to dispose of himself or herself. To this extent, therefore, these rights are derived from and rest upon the right of personal liberty. This principle, however, is not sufficient to account altogether for these rights; but in order to do so we must have recourse to certain other principles established in the positive morality of the European race; such as the principle of monogamy, that of permanency in the marital relation, and that which forbids marriage within certain degrees of kindred. In the present state of ethical science, it is perhaps impossible to demonstrate the justice of these principles otherwise than by a resort to the principle of utility, and especially to that form of it to which we have referred as the *argumentum ab inconvenienti.* In this way, the necessity of these principles may be readily demonstrated, and the argument becomes stronger with the advance of science in its different departments.[1] At the same time, the

to its immense capacity for absorbing lands, which it was found necessary to check in all countries by the mortmain acts. We may refer also to the universities and public schools and other charitable foundations of England, to the old guilds or companies of London, (still possessed of immense wealth, though the purposes of their existence have long since ceased,) and to the modern charitable institutions so common in that and other countries. Indeed, without these illustrations it is sufficiently obvious that there is no limit to the wealth that may be acquired by any efficient corporate organization, endued with a permanent desire to accumulate; and that such an organization would be realized in its highest perfection in a political organization such as the one suggested.

[1] As is illustrated, for instance, by the physiological principle that marriage between near relations is apt to produce diseased offspring.

necessity of resorting to the argument from utility, conclusive as it is, seems to weaken the strength of the moral convictions already existing; for the mass of men who have advanced so far as to seek for a reason for thier moral convictions are prone to conclude, from their inability to perceive a more profound principle, that none such exists. It is perhaps better, therefore, until the progress of philosophy shall unfold to us the ultimate principle of right, to rest the argument upon the profound moral convictions of our race—the only one that has ever proved itself susceptible of a progressive civilization.

§ 151. The right of the parent in the child is directly derived from the right of self-ownership of the parents; for the child is the offspring of their bodies, which are theirs, and therefore *quoad* the rest of the world he is theirs also, as much as the offspring of their cow or other animal: Grotius, b. 2, c. 5, § 1; Puffendorf, b. 6, c. 2, § 1. It is true that their right in him is limited by his right in himself; but this, as we have seen, does not detract from the parent's right in the child, which consists exclusively in a relation between the parent and third persons. Indeed, the right of the child adds an additional sanctity to that of the parents; for his existence and education depend on their fostering care, which it is his right to receive, and with parents the most sacred and valued of their rights to afford.

§ 152. With regard to the right of the child in his parent, it is no less apparently derived from his right of self-ownership; for, leaving out of view all question of duty or obligation from the parent to the child, nature has so constituted men that in general they freely render to their children a protection and support which is essential to their welfare, and in part to their existence. To this extent, therefore, the parent is appropriated to and becomes the property of the child; and any interference with this appropriation by third persons is a manifest violation of his rightful liberty to enjoy the love and services of his parent.

CHAPTER VIII.

OF RIGHTS OF OBLIGATION, OR RIGHTS IN PERSONAM.

§ 153. Obligations and the corresponding rights *in personam* arise either from delicts, or torts (*ex delicto*), from contracts (*ex contractu*), or from mere right (*ex mero jure*), without the intervention of delicts or contracts.

§ 154. By a delict, or tort, is meant a violation of a right *in rem;* and such violation must necessarily consist in some interference with the object of the right. In the case of the right of self-ownership, the subject and the object of the right are one; and therefore any interference with the one is necessarily an interference with the other; but in the case of other rights *in rem,* the right can only be violated by an interference with the object of the right; for any other interference with the subject of the right would amount to a violation of the right of self-ownership. Thus, in the case of the right of property, a man may be prevented from exercising the right either by direct restraint imposed upon himself, or by the thing owned being taken from him; but in the former case, the wrong is a violation, not of the right of property, but of the right of personal liberty.

§ 155. Such interference with the object of the right may consist in a permanent removal of it from the possession or power of the subject of the right;

as, where one imprisons another, or takes away his property, or his wife or child; or it may be a mere temporary interference. Where the object of a right *in rem* is taken away from the owner's power or possession, it is an obvious consequence, from the definition of the right, that the object of the right should, if practicable, be restored.

§ 156. It seems equally obvious that if from the destruction of the object, or otherwise, it should become impracticable to restore it, compensation should be made; and also that, even should the object of the right be restored, the party injured should be compensated for the temporary deprivation of its use, and for any other loss or damage resulting from the injury.

§ 157. In reality, however, the principle of compensation, though apparently self-evident, requires a somewhat abstruse argument to establish it, in making which, we will in the first place confine our attention to the right of property, and afterwards consider the modifications the argument must receive in its application to other rights *in rem*.

§ 158. All rights, as we have observed, are merely particular parts or instances of the general liberty or power which every man rightly has to pursue his own welfare or happiness. The violation of a right consists in depriving the owner of this liberty or power, and restitution in restoring it to him.

§ 159. Applying these principles to the right of property, such right consists in the power to use the thing owned for the advancement of the welfare of the owner. The capacity of the thing owned to subserve this end constitutes its *utility*, or value to the owner; and such utility, or capacity for use, is in fact the object of the right—the thing owned being altogether immaterial to the right, except as being the means or vehicle of this utility. Hence, where one takes the property of another, the injury, in its ultimate analysis, consists in depriving the owner of the utility of the thing owned, and restitution in restoring to him the utility of which he has been deprived.

§ 160. Different utilities, or the utilities of different things, are susceptible of being measured the one by the other; and the equivalent of every utility may be stated with more or less accuracy in terms of the others; for the right itself being in its essence merely the power of using the faculties in a certain way, different things which serve equally well as the means to this end may be said to be in this regard equivalent or identical; for by restoring to the owner a thing of equal utility to him as the thing lost, we restore to him the power of action, the loss of which constitutes the gist of the injury.

§ 161. There are, however, important differences in things with respect to their capacity of being measured in utility by other things; and accordingly, with respect to this quality, things are divided into *fungible* and *non-fungible;* the former, according to Thibaut, being "things of such a nature that it is, generally speaking, wholly immaterial whether a person has any one in particular, or some other like it; things in which this is material [being] non-fun-

8

gible:" Lindley's Introd. to Jur., sec. 153; *vide* also Austin's Jur. 807.

§ 162. With regard to the former, the utility of one thing is precisely equivalent or equal to that of others of the same class; and in such case, the identity of the thing is altogether immaterial to the value of the right, and therefore its utility is the only material element to be considered; for evidently the power to use one thing and the power to use another of precisely the same kind and quality, and for all purposes of use precisely equivalent, is of equal value, and may be said in all material circumstances to be identical. Thus, where the thing taken is wheat, or corn, or money, it is evidently immaterial whether the identical thing taken is restored, or an equal quantity of another thing of the same kind and quality; for the owner in either case receives, and the wrong-doer restores, a precisely equivalent utility or value, and it is therefore immaterial to either which course is pursued. Still more clearly is this the case where the thing taken is money, for in such case it is not even necessary that coins of the same denominations should be returned, but it is sufficient if the aggregate value is returned; for by receiving this, the injured party receives a utility or value precisely equivalent to what he would have received by the return of the identical coins taken from him.

§ 163. On the other hand, in the case of non-fungible things, each thing has a utility peculiar to itself and not common to the class, and the substitution of the one for the other would, in general, be to substitute a utility different both in kind and value. It is true, indeed, that things generally have an exchange value, and that their relative exchange values may be compared and measured, and one exchanged for the other; but the utility or value we are now discussing is the utility or value of the thing to the owner, which, in general, differs from the exchange value. Thus, where one's horse is taken from him, to give him another horse, or to give him a cow, or a piece of land, of the same exchange value, would not, in general, be to restore him an equivalent utility; for, not only might the thing given to him be less useful to him than the thing lost, but if he had no need of it, he would have to incur trouble and perhaps loss in selling it.

§ 164. These objections, however, do not to any considerable extent apply to money, the use of which is to serve as a standard of value and medium of exchange,[1] and which is a commodity by which the utility of the thing to the owner can in general be accurately measured, and which can be readily disposed of without trouble or loss. Hence it is generally practicable by means of money to restore to the owner a utility of value equivalent to that of which he has been deprived.

§ 165. Even in this case, however, the restitution of utility is not always complete; for often the thing

---

[1] "Therefore it is necessary that all things, of which there is interchange, should be in some manner commensurable. And for this purpose money came into use; and it is in some sense a medium, for it measures everything:" Aristotle, Eth., b. 5, c. 5, fols. 4, 5.

taken has a utility or value to the owner based on sentiment, or taste, or some other peculiarity of his circumstances, which is not susceptible of precise measurement.[1] This, however, constitutes no reason why the injured party should not receive in restitution the utility which it is practicable to return to him; for the right to recover the whole utility of which he has been deprived obviously includes the right to recover part of it; precisely as the right to recover a number of things includes the right to recover any of them, or the right to recover a whole thing the right to recover a part of it.

§ 166. The same reasoning that leads us to the conclusion that where a thing is taken from the owner, and can not be restored, he is entitled to compensation for its loss, also establishes the proposition that, even where it is restored, he is entitled to compensation for the temporary deprivation of its use; for the owner has thus been deprived of a utility or value which can not be otherwise restored to him.

§ 167. It may sometimes happen that the taking of a thing may cause to the owner a loss or damage other than the mere loss or value of the thing. Thus the taking of a man's horse might prevent him from keeping an engagement on which his fortune depended; or the taking of his seed grain might prevent him from planting his crop. In such cases, it is obvious that by the wrong he

---

[1] It is upon this principle that the specific performance of contracts is decreed in equity; and hence this relief is limited to cases where damages at law do not afford a complete remedy: 2 Story's Eq. Jur., §§ 717 et seq.

has been deprived, not only of the utility or value of the thing taken, but in addition, of other utility which he otherwise would have had; and it is clear that, to the extent the loss can be traced to the wrong, he should be compensated.

§ 168. The conclusion we have reached with reference to the right of property, and the reasoning upon which it is based, apply equally to the violations of other rights *in rem;* the only difference being that with reference to the latter the utility of which one is deprived is not in general susceptible of being so accurately measured as in the case of the right of property, or in other words, that the measure of damages is not so certain; and hence this measure must to a large extent be left to some rule established by the State, or to the conscience or discretion of the jury or judge (*arbitrio boni viri*). Thus, where a woman sues for the killing of her husband, while his mere pecuniary value to her can be calculated with considerable accuracy, his utility in other respects is not susceptible of accurate measurement; and the only practicable measure of damages is therefore the judgment of impartial men. So in other cases, outside of the mere loss of utility, the wrong may occasion physical or mental pain which can be measured only in the same way.

§ 169. We conclude, therefore, that in all cases of violations of right *in rem* the party injured is entitled to restitution of the object of the right, if it can be returned to him, together with compensation for its temporary loss or its deterioration; and that where it can not be returned to him, he is entitled to compensation for its loss; or, as it may be otherwise expressed, that he has a right to restitution in kind as far as practicable, and otherwise in value or utility.

§ 170. We come now to consider obligations *ex contractu*, or arising from contracts; and with reference to these, to inquire what it is that gives to them their binding force; or in other words, what is the cause or reason of such obligations.

§ 171. A contract is defined by Blackstone as "an agreement upon sufficient consideration to do or not to do a particular thing:" 2 Bla. Com. *442; and this definition has since been generally received by the profession in this country and England.

§ 172. The definition is, however, objected to by Mr. Parsons, on the ground that it assumes that the consideration is an essential part of a contract—which he denies is the case; and accordingly he defines a contract merely as "an agreement between two or more parties for the doing or not doing some particular thing:" 1 Parsons on Contracts, *6.

§ 173. With regard to this point, it will be seen hereafter that Blackstone is clearly right; but his definition is perhaps objectionable, as assuming a controverted proposition; and it would be better, therefore, to define a contract as an agreement to act or forbear—in other words, an executory agreement—which gives rise to an obligation, and a corresponding right *in personam;* or (as an executory agreement is nothing more nor less than a promise) a contract may be defined simply as *an obligatory promise.*

§ 174. A different view as to the nature of contracts has, however, been taken by Mr. Wharton in his late work on contracts, who, following the German jurists, defines a contract as "an interchange by agreement of legal rights:" 1 Wharton's Law of Contracts, 1, and note; according to which a contract includes not only obligatory promises or executory contracts, but also grants or transfers of rights of ownership, which are called executed contracts.

§ 175. An obvious objection to this definition is, that it excludes all contracts, whether executed or executory, which have no consideration; which is clearly a mistake. For whatever may be the case with reference to executory contracts, it is clear that a consideration is not necessary to the validity of a grant; for the right of property necessarily includes the right to dispose of it according to the will of the owner, who may therefore give it away as well as sell it.

§ 176. This objection may, however, be obviated by defining a contract as *a jurally binding agreement*, or as an agreement resulting in the transfer of a right; and thus defined, the term will include both executed and executory contracts; and this agrees substantially with the definition of Kant, as cited by Mr. Wharton (Id., note), except that the latter seems to regard a contract rather as an agreement for the transfer of a right than as one by which a right is in fact transferred.

§ 177. Thus amended, the definition is correct, and is perhaps preferable to the definition commonly received in our law, both as embracing a wider generalization of related facts, and also, as will be presently shown, as being more in accord with the ultimate analysis of rights and obligations.[1]

§ 178. According to this view, an executory contract is regarded as a transfer of a portion of the power or dominion which the obligor has over his own person; or in other words, as a transfer of a right in the person of the obligor, precisely as an ordinary grant is a transfer of a right in an external object; and this in its ultimate analysis it really is. For, in spite of our natural aversion to this view, all rights of obligation consist in a limited dominion over the obligor, which differs in degree only, and not in kind, from the dominion which a master has over a slave; for looking to the bottom of the matter, the obligor is, to the extent of the obligation, the property of the obligee—precisely as land subject to an easement is to the extent of the easement the property of him in whom the easement is vested; and hence, according to a common and not improper usage, obligations are classed as a species of property; as, for instance, by Blackstone, 2 Com. *388, *400, et seq., and by the California Civil Code, § 14, subd. 1, 3; though this is euphemistically expressed by saying that the object of ownership is the obligation instead of the obligor: Id., § 655; N. Y. C. C., § 160.

§ 179. In opposition to this view, it may be

---

[1] Mr. Austin is, however, of the opinion that "the confusion of contract and conveyance . . . . is one of the greatest obstacles in the way of the student:" Austin's Jur. 1006, 1001, 56.

urged that there is an essential difference between the power of a master over a slave and that of the obligee in a contract over the obligor, consisting in the fact that the latter power rests upon or is created by the consent or agreement of the obligor. If, however, *mere* agreement is a sufficient cause for an obligation, and for the corresponding power or right of the obligee over the obligor, it must also be sufficient to justify the relation of master and slave, where it is founded upon the contract or agreement of the latter; for if a man may by his own agreement transfer to another a limited power over himself, no reason can be assigned why he should not also be able to transfer an absolute dominion; which, however, it is universally admitted he can not do.[1]

§ 180. In this respect, therefore, the right of self-ownership differs essentially from the right of property in things; the latter of which, from its very nature, includes the absolute and unrestricted power

[1] "It is said that slavery may begin *jure civili*, when one man sells himself to another. This, if only meant of contract to serve or work for another, is very just; but when applied to strict slavery in the sense of the laws of old Rome or modern Barbary, is also impossible. Every sale implies a price, a *quid pro quo*, an equivalent given to the seller in lieu of what he transfers to the buyer; but what equivalent can be given for life and liberty?— both of which in absolute slavery are held to be in the master's disposal. His property, also, the very price he seems to receive, devolves *ipso facto* to his master the instant he becomes his slave. In this case, therefore, the buyer gives nothing, and the seller receives nothing; of what validity, then, can a sale be which destroys the very principle upon which all sales are founded?" 1 Bla. Com. *424.

of alienation; while the former is in its nature inconsistent with such a power.

§ 181. With reference to the former, as the power of alienating one's personal liberty admittedly exists to some and yet not to an unlimited extent, it becomes necessary to inquire as to the limit of this power; and this question again resolves itself into an inquiry as to the nature of the cause of the right in the obligee, and of the obligation in the obligor; or in other words, as to what is the reason upon which they rest for their justification; for in jurisprudence, as in physics, the effect must always be precisely commensurate with the cause; as is expressed or implied in the maxims, *Cessante causa, cessat effectus,* and *Ubi eadem ratio, ibi idem jus.*

§ 182. According to an opinion which seems universally to prevail, the mere agreement or promise of the obligor creates in him an obligation to perform it;[1] and this if we use the term "obligation" in its loose sense, as synonymous with duty, may as a general proposition be taken as true. But it is not true that it is of itself a sufficient cause to create an obligation in the proper sense, or a right *in personam.* For in many cases it is obvious that it would be iniquitous and unjust for the obligee to exact or to have the power of enforcing the promise; and therefore, in such case, *ex vi termini,* he has no such right. Thus in the case of a gratuitous promise, while there may be, and probably is in

---

[1] This opinion is embodied in the maxims of the Roman law, *Pacta legem faciunt inter partes,* and *Pacta quælibet servanda sunt: Infra,* § 263, note.

every case, a duty upon the part of the promisor to perform his promise, there is no right in the promisee to exact it, or obligation in the promisor to perform it. And accordingly, neither in our own nor in the civil law are such agreements enforced. It follows therefore, that the agreement by itself does not constitute the cause of the obligation.

§ 183. It is, however, obvious that where the obligee gives or does something in consideration of the promise, an obligation arises in the obligor either to render the agreed equivalent or otherwise to make restitution; and the obligee acquires a corresponding right to exact the performance of this obligation. For here the obligee is induced to suffer detriment by the act of the obligor; and though he suffers this detriment with his own consent—and, as a general rule, one who consents is not injured (*volenti non fit injuria*)—yet this consent is upon the condition that the promise shall be performed, and if it is not performed, the case is precisely the same as where the obligee is made to suffer detriment by force or by fraud. It will also generally happen that, in addition to the detriment thus suffered voluntarily by the obligee, further detriment will also be suffered by him, either in consequence of the agreed detriment, or in consequence of his reliance upon the promise of the obligor; and for this involuntary or collateral detriment, which is equally caused by the obligor, he is equally obliged to make restitution. The case is, therefore, thus far precisely identical with that of delict, the detriment caused to the obligee by the obligor being in either case a sufficient cause for the obligation to make restitution.

§ 184. The detriment suffered by the obligee, which is contemplated or agreed to by the parties, is called in our law the consideration, and in the civil law the cause, of the contract or obligation.[1] It would, however, be more correct to distinguish between the consideration or the cause of the contract and the cause of the obligation; and to say that the former consists of the agreed detriment only, and the latter of all the detriment suffered, whether agreed or collateral.

§ 185. The cause of the obligation being therefore the detriment caused to the obligee by the acts of the obligor, it follows that this constitutes also the limit to the extent of the obligation; and that the obligee has no right to exact more than to be restored

---

[1] "Nothing is more remarkable than the modification, in recent English and American cases, of the doctrine of consideration. For nearly a century it was held that a consideration must be either a benefit to the promisor or a detriment to the promisee. The conclusion, it was true, was not very lucidly expressed; the consideration, it was said, must 'flow' from the promisee, but no matter how the rule was stated, it is now settled. There must be a detriment of some kind to the promisee; it may or may not be that the promisor is benefited by the bargain, but detriment to the promisee there must be. Now, it is an interesting fact that this is the conclusion to which Schlossman comes after a copious and subtile discussion, not only of the Roman standards, but of the philosophy of modern jurisprudence. . . . . Other illustrations of the way in which German authorities have recently been invoked to sustain the conclusions of English judges will hereafter be given in detail. It is enough now to say that even if our sole object be to reproduce English jurisprudence, no book on contracts can meet the present need, unless it at least gives us what is said by great German commentators, now recognized in England as authoritative in the jurisprudence common to Germany and England:" Wharton on Contracts, pref. pp. 5, 6.

to the position he would have been in but for the acts of the obligor; namely, his promise and his failure to perform. This conclusion is apparently paradoxical, but the presumption is in favor of liberty, and the burden of proof upon those who assert the existence of a more extensive right; and we know of no principle that can be adduced in favor of such a claim.[1] Indeed, the affirmative of the proposition follows from the principle stated in §§ 61–65, viz., that, subject to the exceptions there stated—of which this is not one—every man is entitled to the highest degree of liberty compatible

[1] Except, indeed, that of general utility, which may always be urged in favor of any opinion of which one happens to be convinced, and to which all that is said by Bentham and Austin about conscience, or the moral sense, may with more propriety be applied; as, for instance: "One tells you that he has in himself something which has been given him to teach what is good and what is evil, and this he calls either his conscience or moral sense. When looking at his case, he decides such a thing to be good, such another to be bad. Why? Because my moral sense tells me so; because my conscience approves or disapproves it:" Bentham's Theory of Leg. 3, 1. "As for the moral sense, ... conscience, they are merely convenient cloaks for ignorance or sinister interest; they mean either that I hate the law to which I object, and can not tell why, or that I hate the law, and that the cause of my hatred I find it incommodious to avow. If I say openly, I hate the law, *ergo* it is not binding and ought to be disobeyed, no one will listen to me; but by calling my hate my conscience, or my moral sense, I urge the same argument in another and more plausible form—I seem to assign a reason for my dislike, when in truth I have only given it a sounding and specious name:" Austin's Jur. 221. Substituting for "conscience" and "moral sense" the terms "perception of utility" and "sense of utility," the sentiment expressed will become as just as it is forcibly expressed. For a full discussion of the theory of utility, see book 3, Chap. 8, §§ 575 *et seq.*

with an equal degree of liberty in others; from which it follows that no one can have the right to control the liberty of another, except so far forth as may be necessary to secure his own, and to this end it is not necessary that the obligee in a contract should have the power to interfere with the liberty of the obligor any further than to be restored to his original condition.[1]

§ 186. It also follows that, in the absence of fraud or imposition, the extent of the obligation is limited also by the agreement; or in other words, that the performance of the agreement extinguishes the obligation, without regard to the comparative value of the consideration; for where one disposes of his property or his services freely, and for an understood consideration, the loss sustained by the inadequacy of the consideration to compensate him for the detriment which he agrees to suffer, is the consequence of his own free act, for which the obligor is in no wise responsible.

§ 187. It follows, from the principles stated in § 185, that where the consideration for a promise is inadequate, and there is no collateral detriment, the promisee has no right to exact the specific performance of the promise, or to exact anything more from the obligee for a breach than the restitution of the consideration, or its value. For inadequacy of

---

[1] Nothing is said expressly by Mr. Spencer in his Social Statics, upon this point; but it is to be inferred, from what is said in his thirteenth chapter, that he participated in the commonly received notion as to the obligation of contracts. It is, however, obvious, as shown in the text, that this notion can not be deduced from his first principle, and indeed, that it is inconsistent with it.

consideration is, in fact, to the extent of the inadequacy, no consideration; and upon the same principle that we affirm that a promise without a consideration is not jurally binding, we must also affirm that no obligation rests upon the promisor to
perform a promise for which the consideration is
inadequate, or to do more than to compensate the
promisee for the detriment which he has suffered.
Thus if one agrees to pay another a hundred dollars, either in money or in labor, or in goods not
specifically determined, for a horse which is worth
but five, there is obviously no consideration for the
promise as to ninety-five out of the hundred dollars
agreed to be paid; and the obligee therefore has no
right to exact anything more than a return of the
consideration, together with compensation for such
collateral detriment as he may have suffered.

§ 188. In applying this principle, however,
there is always involved a question of fact with
reference to the value of the consideration, or
agreed detriment; and this question is always one
of great difficulty. For it is not the exchange value
of the consideration, but its value or utility to the
obligee, that is to be ascertained—a question often
altogether indeterminate, and with reference to
which, as a general rule, the obligee is himself
obviously the most competent judge. Hence, as a
practical rule, it is reasonable to assume, unless the
contrary clearly appears, that the value of the consideration to the obligee is as agreed upon by him.

§ 189. We therefore conclude that the detriment
caused to the obligee by the acts of the obligor, viz.,

the promise and the breach, is at once the cause and the measure of the obligation of the obligor, and of the corresponding right of the obligee; but that, in determining this detriment, the agreement itself must, unless the contrary appears, be taken as its measure.

§ 190. The rules of the law as to the measure of damages in cases of contract, though not altogether consistent with the principles of right here laid down, yet obviously rest upon them. For, though it is held as a general rule "that the contract itself furnishes the measure of damages" (Sedgwick's Meas. of Dam. *200), yet the proposition is not to be taken as universally true; but is subject to numerous exceptions, which qualify the rule in such a way that the general result is substantially as stated in the preceding section, with the exception that, owing to the erroneous notions which prevail as to the cause of the obligation, the presumption in favor of the fairness of the contract is perhaps too strongly insisted upon. A brief examination of the rule, in connection with the exceptions referred to, will make this apparent.

§ 191. 1. To assert that the agreement is absolutely the measure of compensation for the breach of a contract is in effect to assert that it is the cause, and of itself a sufficient cause, for the obligation. Hence it would follow that all agreements, whether with or without consideration, would create obligations in the obligors to perform them, and corresponding rights in the obligees to exact their performance. But it is admitted, as we have already observed, that where there is no consideration, there is no obligation or right; and accordingly, neither in our own nor in any other system of law are such agreements enforced.

2. It would also follow, if the agreement is to be taken absolutely as the measure of damages, that the obligee would in all cases have the right to exact, not only the value of the agreed equivalent for the detriment suffered by him, but the agreed equivalent itself; or in other words, he would have a right, not merely to compensation for the failure of the obligor to perform his promise, but to the specific performance of the promise itself; for if the agreement is to control, the obligee is entitled to what was agreed upon, and can not justly be put off by the substitution of another thing to which he has not agreed. But neither in our own nor in any system of law is such a right recognized; but, with certain well-defined exceptions, compensation only is given: Sedgwick's Meas. of Dam. 10.

3. Even in the exceptional cases, where specific performance is as a general rule allowed, it is refused if the consideration is inadequate: N. Y. C. C., § 1894, and cases cited.

4. Upon the same principle, in the case of promises to pay money or goods, the obligee would in all cases be entitled to recover the full amount agreed to be paid; and this is no doubt the general rule. There are, however, numerous exceptions, to some of which we will refer. Thus it has always been a rule of equity, and is now equally the rule at law, that an agreement to pay a penalty for non-per-

9

formance of a promise can not be enforced; and the rule applies to all cases of alternative promises to pay money in case of non-performance, where it does not appear that the amount agreed to be paid is a *bona fide* estimate of the actual damage sustained: Sedgwick's Meas. of Dam. 497 *et seq.* In other cases, also, the courts refuse to enforce agreements which are manifestly unequal; as, for instance, in such cases as Thornborow *v.* Whitacre, 2 Ld. Raym. 1164, where one for valuable consideration agreed to deliver two grains of rye-corn on Monday next, and four grains on the next Monday, and doubling on each Monday for a year; or as in James *v.* Morgan, 1 Lev. 111, approved by Lord Chancellor Hardwicke in Earl of Chesterfield *v.* Jansen, 1 Wils. 286–295, where one agreed to pay for a horse a barley-corn for the first nail in the shoes of the horse, two for the second, four for the third, and so on for twenty-four nails; or as in the case of usurious contracts, and numerous other similar cases in which the courts refuse to enforce the agreement in its entirety, and give compensation only.

From all of which, it clearly appears that the rule of law which makes the agreement the measure of damages in cases of contracts rests merely upon the presumption—which is indeed perhaps carried too far—that the parties themselves are the most competent and safest judges of value; and not, as is commonly assumed, upon the principle that the agreement itself is the cause, and consequently the measure of the obligation.

§ 192. The remaining class of obligations to be

considered are those arising from mere right (*ex mero jure*), amongst which may be instanced the following:

1. The parent is under obligation to support his minor child, and the child has a corresponding right to exact such support.

2. Where property comes into the hands of any one without the consent of the owner—as, for instance, where lost property is found, or property delivered by mistake—the person receiving the property is under obligation to restore it. In such case, if on demand he refuses to restore it, an obligation *ex delicto* arises, but antecedently to such demand and refusal, an obligation *ex mero jure* exists.

3. Upon the same principle, where one receives money which justly belongs to or should have been paid to another, as, for instance, where money is paid by mistake to one which ought to have been paid to another, an obligation arises in favor of the latter; which in the absence of an express agreement to pay, is an obligation *ex mero jure*.[1]

4. Where one without the knowledge or consent

---

[1] " When a defendant receives money which belongs to plaintiff, or which in equity and justice he should not retain, and which ought to be paid to plaintiff, *assumpsit* or debt lies against him for the amount of it, as for so much money had and received to plaintiff's use: " 2 Saunders' Pl. & Ev. *670. " This kind of equitable ac. tion to recover back money which ought not in justice to be kept is very beneficial, and therefore much encouraged. It lies only for money which, *ex æquo et bono*, the defendant ought to refund. . . . In one word, the gist of this kind of action is, that the defendant, under the circumstances of the case, is obliged, by the ties of natural justice and equity, to refund the money:" Mansfield in Moses v. McFerlan, 2 Burr. 1012.

of the owner takes charge of his property, he is
under obligation to use due diligence in its care
and preservation, and to render a just account of
profits received.

5. In the same case, where labor is performed or
expense incurred, which is necessary to preserve
the property—as, for instance, in the case of lost
property on land (2 Kent's Com. *356), or derelict
or captured ships at sea (3 Id. *245)—an obligation
arises in the owner to make compensation to those
performing the labor or incurring the expense.

§ 193. In the above, and in all cases of obligations of the class under consideration, the cause of
the obligation is a detriment suffered by the obligee
or impending over him, for which the obligor is
responsible; and they may all be brought under the
one general formula which is equally applicable to
cases of delict and contract; viz., that every man is
under obligation to make restitution for detriment
suffered by another for which he is the responsible
cause; and is equally under obligation to prevent
the happening of such detriment. Two elements
must therefore concur in this, as in the case of delict and that of contract; namely, detriment, actual
or impending, to the obligee, and responsibility for
such detriment in the obligor.

§ 194. Thus, in the case of a parent and child,
it is evident that the child must suffer a detriment
by the failure of the parent to provide it with the
necessary means of life; and that such detriment,
if it happens, will be the effect of the parent's voluntary act in bringing him into the world, conjoined

with his failure to supply him with the necessaries of life. The case is therefore the same in principle as where one man imprisons or wounds another, or otherwise puts him in a situation that he must suffer unless assisted. So where one has the money or other property of another, it is obvious that the latter suffers a detriment so long as he is deprived of it, which is caused by the former; and it is equally clear that where one takes charge of the property of another without his consent, he is responsible for any damage that may happen to the property, or for any loss of profits caused by his negligence or fault.

§ 195. The case of the obligation of the owner of property to compensate another— as, for instance, the finder of lost property, or the salvors of a derelict or captured ship—for labor performed or expenses incurred in the preservation of property, though apparently clear, is somewhat more difficult to explain.[1] Here the detriment suffered by the obligee is sufficiently obvious, but the responsibility of the obligor is not so clear, for there is neither fault nor consent upon his part. The obligation, indeed, obviously rests upon the implied or presumed consent of the owner; for if the obligee had interfered not only without his consent but against his will, no liability would have arisen. But implied consent is not consent at all; nor is actual consent possible in such a case. Some other principle must therefore be sought, in order to explain the cause

---

[1] Obligations of this class are designated in the Roman law by the term *de bonorum gestione:* Inst., b. 3, c. 28, § 1; Austin's Jur. 944.

of the obligation; and such a principle may perhaps be found in the maxim of the Roman jurists, that it is just that no one should profit by the detriment of another, justifiably or innocently incurred. *Nam hoc natura æquum est, neminem cum alterius detrimento fieri locupletioem:* Dig. 12, 6, 14. In this case the interference is not only innocent and justifiable, but seems to be imperatively demanded by the principles of morality; nor could there be any possible motive in the owner to refuse an assent which, had it been possible, it is certain he would have given, except the desire to avail himself of the detriment of an innocent person without compensation.

NOTE.—In this book we are concerned only with the principles of justice, and with showing that their observance is an essential condition of civilization. (*Supra* § 12, n., *ad fin.*) It is important however, to observe (in order to show the relation of jurisprudence to social science in general), that justice is not of itself a sufficient principle of social organization, but that it must be supplemented by benevolence, or love in its various forms; love of family, of friends, of neighbors and of mankind.

The broad and essential distinction between justice and benevolence is that the one is free, the other compulsory. (*Supra*, § 11 and note.) Hence all socialistic schemes are to be condemned as violating justice, not only because they generally agree in proposing the confiscation of property, but, chiefly because the destruction of personal liberty is one of their essential characteristics. Such schemes derive their whole plausibility from the admitted evils of the existing state of society; which are assumed to be the offspring of free competition, or, as it is called, individualism, and hence, the principle of liberty, which implies free competition, is condemned. But this assumption is not admissible. The principle of liberty has never yet been consistently applied, and hence, existing evils can not be charged to it, but most probably are in the main the result of its violation; or, in other words, are due to the failure of society to realize perfect justice, which is but another name for the protection of liberty. (*Supra*,

§§ 21 *et seq.*) Among the most potent causes of the inequality of human conditions, may probably be enumerated the original unequal distinction of land, or its appropriation by the few at the expense of the many; the misconceptions hitherto universally prevailing as to the obligations of contract (*supra*, §§ 170 *et seq.*), and the system of enforced credit and usury based upon it, the protective system and other abuses, whether ignorant or intentional, of the taxing power, monopolies, including (what are generally considered unobjectionable) patent and copy rights, and the indiscriminate creation of corporations; to which is to be added the inefficient organization and administration of government. That these (with the exception of the last) have been potent factors in the production of wealth, is not to be denied; but that they have been equally potent causes of its unequal distribution is perhaps also true; and it is at least doubtful whether on the whole, the masses have profited by the result.

At all events, it can not be assumed that the principle of liberty and the resulting principle of free competition, are to be held responsible for existing evils, until they have had a free operation; which can only be when the principle that no man's liberty can be rightfully restrained except so far as necessary to maintain the equal, or at least the just, liberty of others is recognized and consistently applied. (*Supra*, §§ 21 *et seq.*) Then perhaps it will be found that nothing more will be needed for the highest perfection of society than the free and spontaneous operation of the principle of benevolence—a principle as real, if not as strong in human natures as self-interest. This principle did not fail to manifest itself in the conflict of mere force which preceded the settled state of modern Europe, and still manifests itself in the scarcely less fierce struggle of mingled intelligence, cunning and fraud, in the pursuit of wealth, that characterizes our modern era. Nor are we to judge of the force of this principle from its present or its past manifestation. Benevolence withers amid conflicts, whether of force or fraud, and hence flourishes only in proportion as justice reigns. For the end of justice is to suppress, and its perfect realization would altogether suppress conflict and war among men, for that realization would consist in no man's interfering with the just freedom of others, and in this way only is conflict to be avoided. Hence we may hope that, with a settled political organization, and a more perfect administration of justice, benevolence, or love will play a larger, and more beneficient part in human affairs than has hitherto been anticipated. Much also may be anticipated from what may be called the organization of benevolence to which we have referred (*Supra* § 14, 3 n.), and still more perhaps from an increased capacity for voluntary co-operation, which may reasonably be hoped for.

Hence it follows that jurisprudence is the most inviting of all fields for the labors of those who seek the good of mankind; and that it stands before all other branches of political science in importance and dignity. How great, therefore, the misfortune that at least in this country and England, it has been so entirely left either to professional lawyers, who in general regard their profession as a trade, or to theorists, who have entirely misunderstood its nature, and who have devoted their labors to the establishment of a slavish and immoral theory, which is entirely destructive of its most fundamental principles. (See Preface and *infra*, §§ 427 *et seq.*)

BOOK II.

OF THE ELEMENTS OF THE LAW.

CHAPTER I.

ANALYTICAL OUTLINE OF THE LAW.

§ 196. We propose in this book to treat of the nature and general principles of the law. This term, properly speaking, denotes the law of the particular state or country of which the speaker happens to be a citizen; but in America, although the several states are, with reference to each other, and, with certain well-defined exceptions, also with reference to the federal government, sovereign or independent political communities, each with its own law, yet substantially the same system of law is administered in the tribunals, with one exception, of all the states and of the United States; and it is this system that in America we generally have in view when we speak of *the law*. Accordingly, it will be understood that the law of which we propose to treat is the common law of England as administered by the courts of this country.

§ 197. With reference to this, the first step of our investigation will be to inquire as to its nature, or rather, as all systems of positive law are in essential nature the same, to inquire as to the nature of positive, or, as Blackstone calls it, municipal, law in general.[1]

§ 198. The definitions of the law given in our books, though varying widely in terms, may all in effect be reduced to three.

The first in substance defines the law as being a mere expression of the will of the state, or in other words, as consisting altogether of laws (*leges*) or statutes.[2] To this effect is the definition of Blackstone, as emended by Christian, viz., that the "law is a rule of civil conduct prescribed by the supreme

[1] "Municipal or civil law, that is,.the rule by which particular districts, communities, or nations are governed, being thus defined by Justinian, ' *Jus cirile est .quod quisque sibi populus constituit:* ' " 1 Bla. Com. *44. It is to be observed that, in confounding municipal law with the *jus civile* of the Roman lawyers, Blackstone falls into a very egregious error; for, according to their views—as will be more fully explained in the sequel—the municipal law, or law of the state, was made up of the *jus civile* and the *jus gentium;* and the former constituted but a comparatively inconsiderable part of it: See *infra*, §§ 263 *et seq.* That a blunder so obvious should have escaped the attention of his numerous annotators does not speak well for the proficiency of English and American lawyers in the civil law. For an interesting discussion of this definition, see dialogue between Alcibiades and Pericles, Xenophon's Memorabilia, b. 1, c. 2, §§ 40-46.

[2] According to Horne Tooke and later writers, this is the original and proper sense of the term: See Diversions of Purley, and 1 Bla. Com. *39, note 1. There seems, however, no ground for this opinion; for the original meaning of the term seems to be merely something fixed or established: See Skeat's Etym. Dict. Accordingly the term is applied with equal propriety to physical and customary laws as to laws established by a human superior. Indeed, laws of the latter class are probably of a later date than the term itself. Hooker, therefore, was not wrong in regarding this as the true sense of the term "law;" "whose seat," he says, " is the bosom of God, whose voice is the harmony of the universe;"

power in a state:" 1 Bla. Com. *44; and also the definition of Austin, that a law is a command of the sovereign, and that the law is an aggregate of such commands: 1 Austin's Jur. 91; and that of the code of the New York code commissioners, which defines the law as "a rule of property and of conduct prescribed by the sovereign power of the state:" N. Y. C. C., § 2. These definitions are all in effect the same, and though embodying a conception of the law now almost universally prevailing in this country and England, are obviously incorrect; for not only are there many laws or statutes which form no part of the law, but those which do constitute in fact but a small and comparatively inconsiderable part of it.[1]

§ 199. The second definition defines the law as consisting of the general customs of the realm or state: 1 Bla. Com. 63. This definition is of earlier date than the former, and rests upon higher authority; but, though more nearly correct, can not be accepted as satisfactory. For it is obvious on the one hand that the law is not made up altogether of customs, and on the other that there are innumerable customs with which the law has no concern.

§ 200. The third definition regards the law (or rather that part of it which is sometimes called sub-

and which he thus defines: "That which doth assign to each thing the kind, that which doth moderate the force and power, that which doth appoint the force and manner of working, the same we term a law:" Ecl. Pol. This agrees with the definition of Chrysippus: *Lex est omnium divinarum & humanarum rerum regina:* Pandects, Pothier's ed., 1, 3, 2.

[1] "Private law does not spring wholly, or chiefly from the will of the ruler:" Bliss on Sovereignty, 12.

stantive law) as identical with justice. This is implied in our common speech; as, for example, when we speak of "courts of justice," or of "the administration of justice;" and is expressly asserted by the highest authorities. Thus Bracton, following the Roman lawyers, defines jurisprudence, or the knowledge of the law, as "the science of the just and the unjust," and the law as "the art of the good and equitable" (*ars boni et æqui*): *Vide infra*, § 419, 1; and Coke says (which is in effect the same thing) that "the common law itself is nothing else but reason:" *Vide infra*, § 419, 4; and indeed the books are full of expressions by eminent jurists which in effect assert the same proposition. This definition, however, to say the least, is obviously inaccurate; for the law is undoubtedly made up in part of laws and customs; the former of which are purely arbitrary, and the latter to a large extent accidental, and both of them often unreasonable and absurd.

§ 201. The common fault of all these definitions is, that they each regard only a part of the law and ignore the remainder. For the law is in fact made up of laws or statutes, customs and principles of natural reason, and no definition which ignores either of these elements, or which fails to express the manner in which they are related to the law and to each other can be accepted as satisfactory.

§ 201a: A definition or supposed definition has however been suggested, which is free from any of the objections stated. According to this "a law is a general rule of external conduct enforced by a sovereign power, and the law merely an aggregate of laws."

(Holland's Jur. 12, 34.) It is obvious, however, that this definition is based upon a merely accidental quality of the subject defined; for whatever may be the nature of the law, it can not be assumed that it will always be enforced; but on the contrary it is certain that its operation will often be defeated by the ignorance or corruption of judges or juries, and by the uncertainty of evidence.[1] Except in this respect, however, the definition is equally consistent with all the definitions given, and indeed with any definition that can be devised. Hence it furnishes a common ground upon which the advocates of all theories of jurisprudence may stand at least equally well and may be conveniently used as giving a rough and approximately correct description of the law.

Let it be assumed, therefore, for the purpose of defining the scope of our inquiries, that the law, whose nature we are seeking to ascertain, is the law

[1] Accordingly Mr. Pollock very properly amends the definition of Mr. Holland by substituting for the word " enforced " "purporting to be enforced;" for, as he properly observes, " not every sovereign can make sure of enforcing his own commands." Indeed he might have said, " not any." (Essays on Jur. and Morals, 9.)

According to Mr. Holland's definition, a right is defined as " a capacity residing in one man to control, with the assent or assistance of the state, the actions of others "; and he says, " that which gives validity to a right is in every case, the force which is lent to it by the state." (Jur. 62.) It is obvious, however, that the question of the existence of a right does not depend upon the fact that it can, or can not, be enforced in any particular case; but upon the general principles of the law, whether these be of natural origin, or of legislative imposition. His definition of right is therefore as defective as that of the law. (*Infra*, § 214.)

which the courts enforce, or which at least they are supposed to enforce.[1]

§ 201*b*. This description of the law, however, gives us no information as to the essential nature of the rules of conduct which are thus enforced, and which, according to it, constitute the law. It remains therefore to investigate the nature of these rules or principles—a problem purely historical and which can only be solved by an examination of the actually existing law.[2]

§ 201*c*. It is, however, first to be observed that the law is not a homogeneous whole, but consists of several different parts or branches, which differ essentially in their nature. To understand the nature of the law, we must therefore first understand the nature of its several parts. Our first step, therefore, will be to examine and analyze the law as it is actually administered by the courts.

§ 202. If we observe the course of business in the courts of justice, we will find that they are exclusively occupied either in determining controversies between individuals with reference to their reciprocal claims and demands upon each other, or in de-

---

[1] This is in effect the definition of Hale cited in note to § 213, and of Von Ihering, who defines the law as "embracing all the principles of law, (recht) enforced by the state" (Struggle for Law, 5); and also of Bliss, who defines it as "the aggregate of the rules recognized or prescribed by the supreme power of the state. . . . regulating the property and personal relations of men." (Sovereignty, 52.) In fact, however, these are not definitions at all, but merely statements of the subject to be defined.

[2] In making this investigation, we will, for obvious reasons, generally have in view our own law; but what we will have to say will be equally applicable to all systems.

termining accusations of crime, which in effect are controversies between individuals and the state.

§ 203. The power to hear and determine such controversies is called *jurisdiction: Vide supra*, § 3; and is either *civil* or *criminal;* the former consisting in jurisdiction over civil cases, or controversies between individuals, and the latter in jurisdiction over criminal cases, or accusations of crime.

§ 204. An obvious division of the law, therefore, is into the *civil* and the *criminal* law—the former being the branch of the law which governs the exercise of civil, and the latter that which governs the exercise of criminal jurisdiction.[1]

§ 205. The criminal law in this country consists almost wholly of statutory enactments, which are simple in their nature and readily understood; and a sufficient knowledge of it for purposes of the general practitioner can, therefore, readily be acquired by the perusal of the criminal code of his particular state, and perhaps also of some good text-book on the subject. It differs so essentially from the civil law in its nature, that it will only produce confusion to consider them together; and we will therefore, for the present, dismiss it from consideration, adding only that the civil law is the branch of the law with which lawyers in general are principally, and indeed almost exclusively, concerned.

---

[1] The criminal law differs so essentially in its nature from private right, that it would seem impossible to confound them. Yet this has been effected by Bentham and Austin, who seem indeed to have formed their conception of the whole law from this branch of it only; both of them defining obligation as consisting in the fear of punishment: *Infra*, §§ 550 *et seq.*, 566.

§ 206. The civil law is that branch of the law by which the determination of civil cases is provided for and governed; and it consists of the *law of civil procedure* and the *law of private right* (*jus privatum*).

§ 207. The former will first be briefly explained. To every civil controversy there are two parties, viz., the plaintiff and the defendant (*actor* and *reus*). The former is he who demands relief from the court against another; the latter, he against whom the relief is demanded. The proceeding by which the demand is made by the plaintiff and resisted by the defendant is called a *suit* (*litis*), and also an *action* (*actio*). The latter term, however, has a more appropriate signification, in which we will be compelled habitually to use it, and we will therefore, in the present connection, use the former exclusively.

§ 208. In general, the determination of a suit involves two classes of questions, which are distinguished as *questions of law* and *questions of fact.* The latter depend for their determination upon the evidence; the former, upon general rules and principles which in the aggregate constitute the law.

§ 209. Questions of law are again of two kinds, viz., those which relate to jurisdiction or other points of procedure; and those which relate to the merits of the controversy, or, as they are called, *questions of right.* The determination of questions of fact is part of the procedure in a case, and the subject of evidence therefore belongs to the law of civil procedure; the whole object of which is to elicit and present to a competent tribunal the question of right involved in the case.

§ 210. The law of civil procedure may therefore be described as that branch of the law which provides for the creation of a jurisdiction, and which regulates the mode of procedure to be followed by the parties and the court in the conduct of the case (including the determination of all questions of fact), in order to elicit the questions of right involved; and which also regulates the subsequent proceedings necessary to carry the judgment of the court into effect.

§ 211. The subjects embraced in it may be enumerated with sufficient accuracy as follows, viz.: jurisdiction, pleading (which consists of the statement of the demand and the defense by the plaintiff and defendant respectively), evidence, and practice—the last including all that is not embraced in the other subjects named.

§ 212. In England, and in many of the states, the law of civil procedure is reduced to statutory form, and a competent knowledge of it can be obtained only by the study of the code of civil procedure of the state in which the student proposes to practice. It presents no great difficulty in its acquisition, and will therefore, at this time, require no further remark.

§ 213. The law of private right may be described as consisting of the aggregate of the rules and principles, whether statutory, customary, or of natural reason, by which the courts are, or are supposed to be, governed in determining the questions of right involved in civil cases or controversies.[1] This de-

---

[1] This is in effect the definition of Hale; according to which, "the common law of England is the common rule for administer-

scription, however, though it serves to direct and define the object and scope of our investigations, gives us no information as to the essential nature of the rules and principles which constitute the law of private right. We must therefore seek further for a definition, and in doing this, we can not do better than to pursue still the method originally marked out, namely, to observe and analyze the actual course of business in the courts.

§ 214. In every civil suit the immediate question to be determined by the court is whether the force of the government shall be used in behalf of the plaintiff to compel some act or forbearance on the part of the defendant. This power of coercing another by means of the force of the state is called *an action;*[1] and the immediate question in such controversies is, therefore, to determine whether the plaintiff has an action against the defendant, or otherwise. An action, however, does not imply the

ing justice within this kingdom, and asserts the royal prerogatives, and likewise the rights and liberties of the subject; it is generally that law by which the determinations in the king's ordinary courts are guided : " Jacob's Law Dict., tit. Common Law.

[1] " An action is nothing more than the legal demand of one's right:" Co. Lit. 285 a. Bracton, following Justinian's Institutes, thus defines it: *Actio nihil aliud est quam jus persequendi in judicio quod alicui debitur;* which may be rendered, " An action is nothing else than the legal power of prosecuting in a judicial proceeding what is due to any one."

The Latin *jus* has a somewhat wider signification than the English term " right," and is used with propriety to denote actions as well as rights: *Infra,* § 231. On account of this ambiguity, the definition of Heineccius (cited Austin's Jur. 792) seems to be preferable: *Actio non est jus, sed medium jus persequendi.*

actual power of coercion; nor does such actual power necessarily constitute an action. Thus, should A have the property of B, which he refuses to return, or should he owe money to B, which he refuses to pay, in either case B would have an action against A, even though in attempting to enforce it he should be defeated by perjury or defect of evidence, or by the ignorance or corruption of the judge. And this is true, whatever theory we adopt as to the nature of the law; for even if we should assume that the law is composed altogether of laws or statutory enactments, enumerating all possible injuries, and prescribing the corresponding actions, yet the most absolute power could not always render the remedy effectual.

Whether an action exists, therefore, is to be determined in every case, not by the result of the particular suit, but by general principles applicable to all similar cases.

§ 215. Of these principles the fundamental one is, that wherever there is a right, there shall be an action; or, as it is expressed in a maxim common to our own and the Roman law, *Ubi jus ibi remedium* (where there is a right, there shall be a remedy). And the converse of this proposition is also true, for all actions are in theory mere means of enforcing rights.

§ 216. The law of private right, therefore, treats of two principal subjects; viz., *rights* and *actions*. Of the former we have already treated at length in our first book, and of the latter to some extent in this. Some further remarks will, however, be necessary, to explain more fully the nature of actions, and the nature of their relations to rights.

§ 217. It is only when a right is violated by a breach of the corresponding duty that force can be directly applied to effectuate it, and then only by the enforcement of the duty. We say directly, for it is obvious that rights may be indirectly enforced by the threat of punishment for their violation, or in other words, by the criminal law; but this constitutes a branch of the public law (*jus publicum*) which for the ˙present we are not engaged in discussing.

§ 218. In the case of rights *in personam*, the corresponding duty is an obligation exactly commensurate with the right, and therefore such rights may be directly enforced. In the case of rights *in rem*, the only corresponding duty is the general negative duty resting upon all men not to interfere with the right; and this can only be directly enforced when the right is violated or threatened, in which case there arises a specific duty in the particular person invading the right; or in other words, an obligation, and a corresponding right *in personam* in the person injured. Hence, rights *in rem* can not be enforced directly, but only indirectly, either by the fear of punishment or by enforcing the rights *in personam* arising from their violation.[1] In certain cases of violation of rights *in rem*, the party injured may himself enforce the corresponding obligation; as for instance, where this is necessary in defense of himself or property: 3 Bla. Com. *3; but in general the

---

[1] Hence the duties corresponding to rights *in rem* are not, in the proper sense, obligations.

natural liberty which every man, in the absence of
government, would have to enforce his right is, by
the institution of government, taken from him and ·
vested in the courts, and in lieu of it, there is given
him an action, or power of invoking the exercise of
the force of the state to compel the performance of
the obligation.[1]

§ 219. As we have observed, obligations are
divided, according to a classification commonly
received in our law, into obligations arising from
contracts, express or implied, and obligations arising
from torts; and a corresponding division is made of
actions; viz., into actions *ex contractu* and *ex delicto:*
Supra, § 18, note.

§ 220. It is convenient, however, to divide obligations, considered with reference to actions, into
those obligations which arise upon an actual or
threatened invasion of a right *in rem* to restore the
party injured to its free enjoyment, and obligations
to transfer to the obligee money or other property
belonging to the obligor. The obligation resting
upon any one who has possession of the property of
another to restore it is an instance of the former
class; and an obligation to pay a debt or compensation for an injury is of the latter. The former
may be called *vindicative,* the latter *commutative,* obligations; or, more properly, the corresponding

---

[1] "Self-defense, that original right of man which, as Cicero
says, is a law enacted by nature itself, and which the Roman
jurists were ingenuous enough to believe could not be ignored in
any body of laws in the world." *Vim ri repellere omnes leges
omniaque jura permittunt:* Ihering's Struggle for Law, 122.

rights *in personam* may be called respectively *vindicative* and *commutative*.

§ 221. Actions to enforce the former class of obligations are called actions *in rem*, or real actions; those to enforce the latter, actions *in personam*, or personal actions.[1] This division of actions was originally taken from the Roman lawyers, but is

---

[1] "*Omnium autem actionum . . . . summadivisio . . . . in duo genera deducitur; aut enim in rem sunt, aut in personam; namque agit unusquisque aut cum eo, qui ei obligatus est, vel ex contractu, vel maleficio; quo casu proditæ sunt actiones in personam, per quas intendit, adversarium ei dare aut facere oportere, et aliis quibusdam modis; aut cum eo agit, qui nullo jure ei obligatus est, movet tamen alicui dealiqua re controversiam; quo casu proditæ actiones in rem sunt; veluti si rem corporalem possideat quis, quam Titius suam esse affirmet, possessor autem dominum ejus se esse dicat; nam si Titius suum esse intendat in rem actio est.*" Justinian's Inst. 4, 6, 1.

"*Appellamus autem in rem quidem actiones vindicationes; in personam vero actiones, quibus dare aut facere oportere intenditur, condictiones.*" Id. 4, 6, 15. This division of actions was adopted into our law at an early day, and will be found explained by Bracton, precisely as by the Roman lawyers. The true nature of the distinction, however, was afterward lost sight of, and real actions came to be considered as including only actions affecting real estate, and personal actions as including all others: Stephen on Pleading, *3. Thus detinue, which was an action for the recovery of the possession of personal property, though in reality a real action, was classed by the English lawyers as a personal action.

The old real actions, with one or two important exceptions, finally became obsolete, and were replaced by the action of ejectment; which was in form a personal action for trespass, but was made to serve also for recovering possession of the land. The meaning of the distinction thus became altogether lost to the profession, and the distinction itself faded out of the law. As the old forms of action are now generally abolished, there is no reason why we should not return to the more rational classification.

now generally received in our own law as at once the most convenient and the most scientific.

§ 222. The terms used are, however, open to the objection that they seem to imply that actions *in rem* do not have for their object the enforcement of obligations, which is not the case. For such actions, as well as actions *in personam*, have for their immediate object the enforcement of rights *in personam*, or obligations; and the only difference is, that in the one case the enforcement of the obligation is the ultimate as well as the immediate object of the action, while in the other the obligation is merely subsidiary, and the ultimate object is the vindication of the right *in rem* which has been invaded or threatened.[1]

§ 223. It would be more appropriate, therefore, to term the two classes of actions *vindicative* and *commutative;* the former having for their ultimate object the vindication of rights *in rem* already existing in the obligee, and the latter the transfer to the obligee of a right *in rem* previously belonging to the obligor. The use of the terms "actions *in rem*" and "actions *in personam*" is, however, so familiar that it will be well to retain them.

---

[1] "All rights of action must, it is evident, be founded on rights *in personam*, that is, on rights which avail exclusively against the determinate person or persons against whom the action will lie, although these persons may have been brought under that designation by committing an offense against a right *in rem*. Actions *in rem* are rights of action founded on an offense against a right *in rem*, and seeking the restitution of the party to the enjoyment of that very right, and not merely satisfaction for being deprived of it:" Austin's Jur. 389. As to the use of the term "rights of action," *vide infra*, § 238.'

§ 224. Actions *in rem* may again be divided into *restitutive* and *preventive* actions; the former having for their object to restore the plaintiff to the enjoyment of a right *in rem* which has actually been invaded, and the latter to prevent a threatened invasion.

§ 225. Actions *in personam* may be subdivided into actions for the *specific performance* of contracts and *compensative* actions, or actions for damages; and the latter again into actions *ex contractu* and *ex delicto*.

§ 226. The following examples will illustrate the nature of the different classes of actions, viz.: an action to recover real or personal property is a *restitutive* action *in rem;* an action to enjoin interference with the plaintiff's property is a *preventive* action *in rem;* an action to compel the performance of a contract to convey land is an action *in personam* for *specific performance;* an action for damages for breach of contract is a *compensative* action *in personam ex contractu;* and an action for damages for trespass on property or person is a *compensative* action *in personam ex delicto.*

§ 227. In our law, actions are also divided, according to the forum in which they were originally established, into *legal* and *equitable;* the former being those which while the two jurisdictions were kept separate, were enforced in the common-law courts, and the latter those enforced in courts of equity. The division, however, is only historically important, and will be sufficiently familiar to professional readers without further explanation; for the benefit of others, it will be found fully explained in a subsequent chapter: *Infra*, chap. 6.[1]

[1] The following is a list of the ordinary common-law actions, viz.: debt, covenant, trespass, trespass on the case, including *assumpsit*, detinue, replevin and ejectment, all of which are classed as personal actions, though in reality the last three are real: See Stephen on Pleading, *passim*. Equitable actions may be classed, according to the nature of the jurisdiction exercised, into *concurrent*, *ancillary*, and *exclusive*. The most familiar are actions for relief against fraud, accident or mistake, contribution among sureties, marshaling securities, settlement of partnership affairs, specific performance of contracts, the enforcement of trusts, and for injunction and bills of interpleader, and *quia timet*: See Story's Eq., *passim*. This and other works on equity may be considered simply as treaties on equitable actions.

CHAPTER II.

DEFINITIONS OF THE LAW AND OF COGNATE TERMS.

§ 228. It is the function of government to protect and enforce rights; but from the inherent imperfection of all human instrumentality, this function must necessarily be more or less imperfectly performed. While in theory, therefore, actions are mere means of enforcing rights *in personam*, or obligations, they may, in fact, be either just or unjust, and hence they differ essentially in their nature from rights.

The science of rights and the science or doctrine of actions are, therefore, to be distinguished from each other; and for this purpose, it is essential that clear and well-defined terms should be used to denote them.

§ 229. The term "right" is the most appropriate term to denote the aggregate of the principles by which rights are determined, and we have therefore adopted it for that purpose. This term, indeed, in its most usual and proper sense, includes in its signification the whole domain of morality, and therefore presents the same ambiguity as presented by the terms "justice" and "a right," or "rights:" *Supra*, §§ 10, 11. But the two senses of the term are so clearly distinct, that the ambiguity needs only to be pointed out in order to be avoided.

§ 230. The term "*jus*," though somewhat ambiguous, is, on the whole, the most appropriate term to denote the body of rules and principles by which actions are determined, and when clearly defined, will answer for the purpose.[1]

[1] "Right," as Haffter remarks, "is either guaranteed under the protection of a competent power (as we see it in the state), or free, that is, the individual power or person must protect and preserve itself :" Woolsey's Intern. Law, § 6. The distinction between *jus* and *right* corresponds precisely to what is here denoted by the terms "guaranteed" and "free" right. "*Jus* denotes, in its objective meaning, those laws and rules which men, as rational beings, in their mutual relations are to respect as the standards of their free action (*jus est norma agendi; jus* is a rule of conduct). These laws and rules are juridical when they establish rules which the inhabitants of a state may, if necessary, be compelled through its public authorities to observe; or ethical when they consist merely of moral precepts, for the observance of which no coercion is practicable. The voluntary conduct of men in conformity with the precepts of law is called justice (*justitia*). . . . . *Jus* (law), in its objective meaning, is usually divided, according to its foundation, into natural and positive law. By natural law is understood the law discoverable by and derived from the abstract ideas of human reason, or the doctrine of the general and necessary conditions upon which the external liberty of each individual may comport with the liberty of the whole community. Positive law, on the contrary, is the law established by historical facts, or is the sum of those principles which are acknowledged in a state as principles of law, and consequently have authority as such. In every state general acknowledgment and observance form the foundation of all positive law; and upon it, in every nation, the character of the people, the manners, religion, form of government, and many incidental facts and events, exercise the greatest influence. This explains, on the one hand, the reason why positive laws are dissimilar among different nations, while the natural is everywhere one and the same; and on the other hand, why the latter, on account of its being derived from reason, forms, and ought to form, the basis of every positive law. . . . . No body of positive law depends merely upon the enactments of the legislative power. A great number of its maxims and principles originate and are formed, in all nations and at all times, by the opinions and manners of the people, by the decisions of the judges, and by

§ 231. This term, indeed, from its etymology, seems originally to have denoted merely the aggregate of the principles of justice generally received, and therefore regarded as binding, in the community, but, according to a notion generally, and until a late period universally, received, it has always been regarded as the function of the state to enforce such received principles;[1] and hence, at the earliest period of political organization, *jus* became the appropriate term to denote in the aggregate the principles actually enforced by the state in the administration of justice, and was naturally adopted for that purpose. While, therefore, according to its strict or original sense, it denoted the aggregate of received principles of justice, and was in effect identical with that term, in its later and more usual sense it denotes merely the body of rules and principles, whether statutory, customary, or of natural reason, by which the courts are governed in deciding questions of right, or by which, in other words, actions are determined.

§ 232. The signification of *jus* has also been naturally extended so as to include, not only the

---

scientific exertions for the elaboration and development of the law which already exists, as well as that which lives in the minds of the people. Those legal (*jural*) rules which are not founded in explicit precepts of the legislature, but are introduced by public opinion and manners, are termed the law of custom or usage—a legal maxim of this kind, introduced and established by public opinion, habit, and custom, by the practice of the courts, or by the jurists, has equal force with an explicit law:" Mackeldy's Modern Civil Law, introd., §§ 2, 3, 6.

[1] "The severance of law from morality, and of religion from law, [belong] very distinctly to the later stages of mental progress:" Maine's Ancient Law, c. 1, p. 15.

principles by which actions are determined, but also the practical means adopted in each state for their determination and enforcement. These means consist in the organization of a jurisdiction and in its actual exercise; and *jus*, therefore, in this sense, includes the laws and institutions by which a jurisdiction is organized, and also the rules and principles by which its mode of procedure is regulated; or in other words, the law of procedure. In this sense, the term "*jus*" is precisely equivalent in meaning to our word the "law;" and we will therefore make use of the latter term exclusively to denote this sense of the term.

§ 233. The term "jurisprudence" denotes the science or knowledge of *jus*, and therefore varies in meaning according to the sense we give to the latter term. We will generally use it according to the sense above adopted; viz., as the science or doctrine of actions—but in accordance with the common usage, we will also use it to denote right, or the science of right—always, however, in doing so prefixing the adjective *theoretical* or *scientific*, in order to distinguish it from practical or positive jurisprudence.[1]

---

[1] "*Jurisprudentia est, divinarum atque humanarum rerum notitia, justi atque injusti scientia:*" Inst. 1, 1, 1. "Jurisprudence is the science of actions so far as they may be termed just and unjust:" Leibnitz, cited Heron's Jur. 523. "Leibnitz defines jurisprudence to be the science of right, *scientia juris*, on some case or fact being proposed:" Id. 521. "*Juris civilis prudentia*, the science of civil rights, is nothing more than a certain application of moral philosophy to regulate and govern the political morals of the state:" Suarez de Legibus, cited Heron's Jur. 306.

§ 234. As we have already had occasion to observe, the term "a right, or rights," in its proper sense, and indeed in its almost universal acceptation, connotes or necessarily implies the quality of rightness. Thus to say that one has a right to property is but another mode of saying that it is right for him to have it; or to say that he has a right to the payment of a debt, or to the return of a deposit, or to the performance of any other obligation is, in effect, to say that it is right for him to exact it.[1] All rights, therefore, are moral rights, and it is a contradiction in terms to speak of a right that is not. It follows, therefore, that right, or theoretical jurisprudence, is identical with justice, and constitutes one of the departments of morality; and it may be added that of all other parts of that science it is the most clear and definite in its nature.

§ 235. The problems presented by *jus* and by right respectively, though intimately connected, are yet essentially different in their natures—being in the one purely scientific and in the other historical. For in the one, the problem presented is to determine,

---

[1] "Right . . . . signifies consistency with the will of God. . . . Right is a quality of persons or of actions; of persons, as when we say such a one has a 'right' to this estate, etc.; . . . . of actions, in such expressions as the following, 'it is right,' etc. . . . . In this latter set of expressions you may substitute the definition of right above given for the term itself, 'it is consistent with the will of God,' etc. . . . . In the former set, you must vary the construction a little, when you introduce the definition instead of the term. Such a one has a 'right to this estate,' that is, it is 'consistent with the will of God' that he should have it; parents have a 'right,' to reverence from their children, that is, it is consistent with the will of God 'that children should reverence their parents,'" etc.: Paley's Moral and Political Philosophy, b. 2. c. 9.

in view of all existing facts, including laws and customs, the cases in which rights exist; while in the other it is simply to ascertain in what cases actions, whether just or unjust, are given by the state. The former question must, *ex vi termini*, be determined solely by the consideration of what is right, and is not affected by the question of whether the right is or is not in fact recognized and enforced by the state; while on the other hand, the question of actions is determined simply by considering the cases in which it is the custom of the courts to accord to individuals a power or control over others.

§ 236. These problems, however, though essentially different in nature, are nevertheless intimately and indissolubly connected. It is indeed conceivable that governments might exist in which actions should have no relation to rights; and if we suppose such a state of society (and also assume that the government has in advance established rules by which all actions are to be determined), then we might adopt as correct the definition of *jus* as being a mere expression of the will of the state, and that of rights as being mere actions, or powers conferred by that will. But in point of fact, except in the dreams of some modern theorists, no such state of society has ever existed, or can exist. For so formidable is the power of government that nothing would induce men to submit their lives and fortunes to it except absolute necessity. While, therefore, it may be among the legitimate ends of government, after it is constituted, to promote the welfare of the people in other ways, yet its only necessary end is the protection of rights. This, therefore, constitutes its *raison d'etre*, the sole justification of its existence; and the substantial performance of this function constitutes also, at least with civilized nations, a necessary condition of its permanence. For, whether we reason *a priori* or from historical experience, it is certain that the same necessity which alone leads to the establishment of government must also in the end lead to its destruction, when it ceases to answer substantially the principal end for which it exists.[1]

§ 237. Hence it is assumed in all systems of law that it is the function of the state to protect rights in the ordinary and familiar sense of the term, or in other words, what are sometimes, but unnecessarily, called *moral* rights; and accordingly, as we have observed, it is a fundamental principle both of our own and the civil law, that wherever there is a right there is a remedy (*ubi jus, ibi remedium*); and from this maxim the converse also follows, to wit, that an action shall be given only where there is a right; for to give any one an action where he has no right must necessarily infringe upon the right of some one else, and deprive the latter of its corresponding action. In theory, therefore, *jus* includes *right;* and positive includes theoretic jurisprudence.

§ 238. In theory there is, and in fact there should be, a perfect correspondence between rights and actions, and in the present state of the law a very close correspondence does exist; and hence actions are sometimes, but not with strict propriety, called rights of action, regard being had to what ought to be

---

[1] As is illustrated by the case of the Roman and of the first French republic.

rather than to what is.[1] This correspondence, however, is not, and from the intrinsic imperfection of all human instrumentality can not be, altogether exact; and there must therefore always exist rights without corresponding actions, and actions without rights.

§ 239. Hence arises a capital distinction between *actionable* and *non-actionable*, or as they are more generally called, between *juridical* and *non-juridical* rights: Kaufman's Mackeldy, introduction, 1, 1, 12. This distinction is identical with that made in ordinary speech between what are called legal and moral rights; the former being those which are, and the latter those which are not, enforced by the state. This use of terms, however, is improper; for, as we elsewhere observe, the term "rights" necessarily implies the idea of rightness, and all rights are therefore moral rights, and there can not be a right of any other kind. Hence there can not be such a thing as a legal which is not a moral right.

§ 240. A distinction must also be made between just and unjust actions, or in other words, between actions to which there are corresponding rights, and actions to which there are none.[2]

---

[1] "*Prætor quoque jus reddere dicitur, etiam cum inique decernit; relatione scilicet facta, non ad id, quod ita Prætor fecit, sed ad illud, quod Prætorem facere conrenit:*" Dig. 1, 1, 11.

[2] For example, in California an action may be maintained to recover compound interest, where it is stipulated for in a written contract: C. C., § 1919. Under this law, a judgment for over $27,000 has been recovered on a note originally of about $1,000; and one for about $500,000 on a note of $28,000. To California lawyers there does not appear to be anything wrong about this;

11

§ 241. All actions are indeed supposed to be founded on rights; and hence, even to an unjust action, there always corresponds some supposed right, or in other words, some legal power assumed to be a right. These powers are in their nature in all respects similar to rights, except in not being right or just, and hence, and also because they are in effect asserted to be rights, they must, when we are treating of practical jurisprudence, be considered along with them. They are not, however, rights in the true sense, and must be carefully distinguished from them; and for this purpose they may be termed *quasi*, or still more appropriately, were the innovation not too violent, *pseudo* rights.

for to confess the truth, the sense of justice seems almost altogether to have abandoned us; but a different view was taken by the Pennsylvania courts, who, in action upon an ordinary California note to one Syme for interest at 1½ per cent. per month, compounding monthly, very properly held, on the authority of *Thornborow* v. *Whitacre* and *James* v. *Morgan*, cited *supra*, § 191, that the contract was unconscionable, and allowed the plaintiff reasonable interest only. On the other hand, an instance of a right without an action is presented by the case of *Ybarra* v. *Lorenzana*, 53 Cal. 197—if that decision can be sustained—which was the case of a conveyance of land made with *bona fide* intent to secure the payment of a debt to the grantee, but also with the motive of preventing other creditors from attaching it; and in which the court held, upon the principle *In pari delicto, melior est conditio defendentis*, that the plaintiff was not entitled to redeem. On the same principle, the New York courts hold that where A, with intent to defraud creditors, sells land to B, taking the note of the latter for the purchase-money, A can not recover either his land or the money. These and similar cases are, however, very justly criticised by the court in *Clemens* v. *Clemens*, 28 Wis. 637, 9 Am. Rep. 520, where it is shown that the principles upon which they are decided have no application to cases of the kind.

§ 242. We have defined *jus*, or rather jurisprudence, as the science or doctrine of actions. It includes also the subject of actionable rights and *quasi* rights, but this subject is material only as bearing upon the ultimate problem—which is the determination of actions—and is therefore logically included in the definition.

§ 243. The object of the law, as we have often had occasion to observe, is to enforce rights, and in the present state of the law this function is fairly well performed. Hence instances of non-actionable rights are of comparatively rare, and those of false or *pseudo* rights of still rarer, occurrence. The doctrine of actionable rights, true and false, therefore, in the main coincides with theoretic jurisprudence, or right,[1] and hence the most practical method of mastering the law is first to investigate and determine rights scientifically, regarding statutes, precedents, and customs like other acts or events, as mere elements of the problem, and noting at the same time the cases of non-actionable and *quasi* or false rights. For the results of the scientific investigation of rights so nearly coincides with their historical development, that positive right or jurisprudence can be understood in no other way than by mastering theoretic right, and noting the divergence be-

---

[1] Hence *jus* has been well defined as " that which neither altogether recedes from the natural law, or *jus gentium*, nor altogether follows it." *Jus civile est, quod neque in toto a naturali vel gentium recedet, nec per omnia ei servet:* Pandects, Pothier's ed., 1, 1, 8. *Jus civile* is used here as denoting the whole law, and not in its proper sense as denoting part of the law only.

tween the two.[1] This is the true method of jurisprudence, and to distinguish it we will call it the
scientific method.

§ 244. The difference between right and *jus*, or
between theoretical and positive jurisprudence, is
that between the science of rights and the body of
rules which govern its practical application; and
accordingly *jus* has been defined as the art of right:
Infra, §§ 403, 420 (1). Hence the courts are called
by lawyers and legislators, as well as by the people
generally, courts of justice, and the exercise of jurisdiction, the administration of justice; which is in
effect to say that *jus*, or the body of principles by
which the exercise of jurisdiction is governed, is the
art of justice or right. The definition implies, not
that in fact justice is always administered by the
courts, or that, in the present state of political organization, the courts are in all cases so organized
as to be at liberty to do justice, but that it is the
function of the courts to administer it, and that in
an ideally organized government no impediment to
the performance of this function would exist; and it
may be added, that the existing judicial organizations in the United States approximate very nearly
to this ideal. Hence we may say that the definition
is in theory true, and as a description of the existing

---

[1] "The only preparation and grounding which a university is
either able or, I suppose, would be desirous to give, is in law considered as a science; or at least, if that is not yet possible, in law
considered as a collection of principles capable of being systematically arranged, and resting not on bare authority, but on sound
logical deduction, all departures from which, in the existing
system, must be marked and explained:" Markby's Elements of
Law, introduction, p. x.

system very nearly true. We must not be understood, however, as implying that the actual administration of justice in this country is in a satisfactory condition. On the contrary, its condition is deplorable. It is the law only we praise, not the lawyers who administer it.

CHAPTER III.

OF THE JUS GENTIUM AND THE JUS CIVILE.

§ 245. The prevailing theory of the law altogether ignores, and indeed expressly denies, this connection between actions and rights; and distinguishes actionable rights and *quasi* rights from rights in the ordinary sense, by calling the former *legal*, and the latter *moral*. The former are defined as legal powers, or mere creations of the legislative will; and it is asserted that it is with these alone that the law is concerned, and that with moral rights it has nothing to do.

§ 246. According to this view, it belongs to the legislative function of the state to determine in advance the principles by which justice is to be administered, and for this purpose to establish rules by which the courts are to be governed. These rules, ought, indeed, to be just, and in an ideal state would be so; and in such case, the exercise of jurisdiction would be in fact the administration of justice; but it is the function of the state to determine the question of their justice or injustice; and the decision of the state is therefore conclusive upon the courts. The administration of justice, or what is so called, consists, therefore, merely in interpreting the will of the state, and is, therefore, merely the exercise of the art of hermeneutics, or interpretation.

§ 247. Hence the exercise of jurisdiction is not in fact the administration of justice, but something quite different, and is only improperly so called from a regard rather to what ought to be than to what actually is. This is the view which, perhaps, embodies the notion of the law now most generally prevailing in this country and England.

§ 248. In fact, however, the assumption upon which this view rests is far from being true; for in no system of law do laws in the ordinary sense, or statutes, constitute the whole or any considerable part of the law.

§ 249. Hence those who hold this view have found it necessary to assert that judicial decisions are a species of laws or statutes, differing from others only in being enacted by judges instead of by ordinary legislators; and accordingly it is asserted that the function of the courts consists merely in interpreting and applying statutes and precedents. This view rests upon the fact that there are many rules established by judicial precedent, or the custom of the courts, which though not enacted by the legislature, are identical with laws in their effect and operation; and upon the assumption that the law is in fact made up altogether of such rules and of laws.

§ 250. This assumption, however, is also unfounded; for such rules, though far more numerous than those which rest upon statute, constitute but a comparatively small part of *jus;* and the contrary assumption rests upon a misapprehension of the nature of the elements of which the law is composed, and a failure to observe the essential and clearly marked distinction between the principles and the rules of the law.

§ 251. For rules established by statute or by precedent or custom are from their nature confined in their operation to classes of cases specifically determined by the express will of the legislator, or by the custom, and hence can not be extended to other cases not coming within the intention of the legislator, or the operation of the custóm as the case may be, and are therefore not susceptible of logical development. While, on the other hand, the principles of the law are principles in the true sense, or in other words, propositions either true or assumed to be true, not only in their explicit statement, but in all their implied logical consequences, and hence are susceptible of scientific definition and logical development, precisely as are the principles of geometry, or any other science.

§ 252. Of the one, the principles of personal liberty, or self-ownership, and those of property, of contract, and of restitution, and compensation in case of injury, are instances; of the other, such rules as that no action shall be maintained on certain contracts unless in writing; or to enforce parol trusts, and the rule that where a grant or executory contract has been made with intent to defraud creditors the court will not interfere either to enforce the one or to rescind the other, but will leave the parties without remedy.

§ 253. Hence a broad distinction is made in the law between reasoning from principle and reasoning from authority; of which the one consists merely in applying the established rules of the law to cases coming within their explicit terms, and the other in logical deduction from principles. To the former applies the maxim, *Quod vero contra rationem juris receptum est, non est producendum ad consequentias:* Dig. 1, 3, 14, cited also in Broom's Leg. Max.; to the other the maxim, *Ubi eadem ratio, ibi idem jus.* Or as the distinction is expressed by Bacon: "Let reason be prolific, but custom sterile, that it may breed no cases. Therefore what is received against the reason of the law, or even where its reason is obscure, is not to be drawn into consequence:" De Augmentis, b. 8, c. 3, aph. 11. And hence it is said that the law consists "not in particular instances and precedents, but in the reason of the law:" Holt, C. J., in Ashby *v.* White, 2 Ld. Raym. 957.

§ 254. The rules of the law, therefore, are either mere applications of its principles or exceptions to their application; and hence they do not enter into the development of *jus*, except merely to limit or restrain it.

§ 255. That development itself, except so far as thus restricted, consists merely in the logical definition and development of principles of natural right universally recognized in all systems of law. And though this development has been obstructed, especially in our own law, by a lack of philosophical knowledge, and of logical consistency and scientific method, yet, on the whole, it has gone on with reasonable and ever-increasing consistency; and even where it has erred, its errors have been quickly made apparent, and generally corrected, by the necessity of testing the deductions arrived at, by applying them to actual practice, or have quietly been eradicated by the establishment of some inconsistent principle.[1]

§ 256. Hence *jus* at all times more or less perfectly represents the notions of justice prevailing among the people, and is, as it were, a mirror reflecting the general conscience. Hence the justification of the maxim that every one is presumed to know the law; for it is in the main written in his conscience, and otherwise the maxim would be unreasonable and absurd. Hence, also, *jus*, in the main without legislation, and often in spite of it, has in all civilized countries advanced hand in hand with civilization; and thus all systems of *jus*,

[1] A striking illustration of this is furnished by the case of *Hunt* v. *Rousmanier*, 8 Wheat. 175; 1 Pet. 1. In that case the plaintiff had borrowed of Lewis Rousmanier, the defendant's intestate, · certain sums of money, and to secure the repayment of the same executed to him two irrevocable powers of attorney; the one authorizing him to sell the brig Nereus, and the other the schooner • Industry. Each power contained a proviso "reciting that the power was given for collateral security for the payment of the notes mentioned, and was to be void on their payment; on the failure to make which, the plaintiff was to pay the amount thereof and all the expenses out of the proceeds of said property, and to return the residue to the said Rousmanier." Rousmanier having died before the sale, it resulted from a well-settled rule of the law that the powers of attorney as powers were revoked, and the court, in an action against the administrator, so held; and held further, that the parties having, with a full knowledge of the facts, by a mistake of law, selected the particular form of security that was given, the plaintiff could not be relieved. This decision was followed by the supreme court of Virginia in a case subtan-

though differing widely in rude ages with the progress of civilization, gradually assimilate; and *jus* becomes, though like the water we drink, as it were, tinctured by locality, essentially the same throughout the civilized world.

§ 257. There is therefore nothing extravagant in the opinion of Coke, that the law "is nothing else but reason;" or in that of Burke, that it "is the pride of the human intellect, which, with all its defects, redundancies, and errors, is the collected reason of ages, combining the principles of original justice with the infinite variety of human concerns:" *Infra*, § 420, subd. 4, 10.

§ 258. Hence the absurdity of the opinion so commonly entertained, that the law is developed from the arbitrary or accidental rules prevailing in

tially identical (the name of which I have forgotten), reversing a previous decision in the same case, in which they held that the transaction constituted an equitable mortgage; and it has been approved and quoted as authority by Judge Story, 1 Eq. Jur., §§ 114, 115, and by other text-writers. It has, so far as we are informed, never been expressly disapproved, or even adversely criticised, but has always been treated as a leading case. There can. however, be no doubt that the original decision in the Virginia case was correct, and that at the present time such a transaction would be held in any court to be an equitable mortgage, as the document itself showed that it was the intention of the parties to create a security upon the particular property: 1 Jones on Mortgages, § 102. Indeed, it is doubtful whether any court would now hold the principle to be correct upon which the case was professedly but erroneously decided, viz., that equity will not relieve against a mistake of law—a principle strongly insisted upon by Judge Story in the work cited, and which, upon his authority, has been persistently taught to law students as a settled principle, and has also been asserted by many courts; but which, somehow or other, seems to have become, as it ought to be, obsolete.

the early periods of society; as, for instance, from the laws of the twelve tables,[1] or from the more or less barbarous laws and customs of our own ancestors. On the contrary, its development consists in the eradication of such anomalous elements, and the substitution of principles of reason and justice.

§ 259. *Jus*, therefore, as it now stands, is not a body of arbitrary enactments or accidental rules, but, in the main, a systematized body of principles logically deduced the one from the other, and ultimately, by a more or less rigid and consistent logic, from principles of natural right; and its principles, in the main, differ from the notions of justice commonly received—like the conclusions of scientific geometry from the notions of geometric truth held by uneducated people—merely in being a more scientific, and therefore a more perfect, expression of natural right: See opinion of Leibnitz, cited *infra*, § 408.[2]

[1] "It is not claimed that this famous code embodied anything new, or covered the mass of rules that regulated personal and property relations; it contained but little more than what we should call the Law of Civil Procedure:" Bliss on Sovereignty, 28.

[2] This is well illustrated by the story of Lord Mansfield, who, being consulted by a military friend upon his appointment as governor of Jamaica, with regard to the duties of chancellor—which, it seems, would devolve upon him—advised him to hear patiently the cases presented to him, and to decide them as it should appear to him right and just, but to refrain from giving his reasons for the decision. "Your decisions," he said, "will probably be right, but your arguments infallibly wrong:" Campbell's Life of Mansfield; Stewart's Philosophy of the Mind, 2, 2, 1. The general belief in the truth of this principle is also illustrated by the system of popular courts so common in America; as, for instance, in Virginia, where from the earliest times the county court, consisting of unlearned justices of the peace, exercised a general jurisdiction, substantially co-extensive with the circuit courts.

§ 260. Nor are the principles of the law any the less principles of natural right from the fact that they are universally recognized and acknowledged; for this is the common characteristic of all scientific truth when once discovered and expressed; and the objection may therefore be urged against every science, and with increasing force as it approximates toward perfection.

§ 261. Nor does the fact that principles of natural right are confirmed by statute or consecrated by judicial usage and observance in any way alter their essential nature; for it is the function of the state to provide for the administration of justice, and all law, however formulated, is therefore in theory an attempted expression or application of natural right;[1]

[1] " Universal and absolute law is natural justice, which can not be written, but speaks to the reason and heart of all. Written laws are the formulas wherein it is sought to express, with the least possible imperfection, what natural justice requires in such and such circumstances. . . . . Positive right rests wholly on natural right, which at once serves as its foundation, measure and limit. The supreme law of every positive law is that it be not opposed to natural law; no law can impose on us a false duty, nor deprive us of a true light:" Cousin's The True, the Beautiful, and the Good, lect. 15. "Nevertheless, although laws have no other virtue than that of declaring what exists before them, we often found on them right and justice, to the great detriment of justice itself, and the sentiment of right. Time and habit despoil reason of its natural rights, in order to transfer them to the law. What then happens? We either obey it, even when unjust, which is not a very great evil, but we do not think of reforming it little by little, having no superior principle that enables us to judge it; or we continually change it, in an invincible impotence of founding anything, by not knowing the immutable basis on which written law must rest. In either case, all progress is impossible, because the laws are not related to their true principles, which is reason,

and hence just so far as it answers the end of its existence—which in all civilized countries it very fairly does—it is, except so far as it provides for matters jurally indifferent, in fact natural right.

§ 262. Thus the principles that one has a right to the return of his property which he has intrusted to another, or of which he has been unjustly deprived by another, is a principle of natural justice logically deducible from the principle of property, which is also a principle of the same kind; and neither is the less a principle of natural right because it has been generally recognized and enforced in all political communities. Nor does a principle of natural right cease to be such ·even though its observance be enjoined by a statute. Thus the principles of personal liberty and security, and of property, still continue to be principles of natural right, although the provisions of Magna Charta, and also of all the. American constitutions, expressly enjoin their observance, and forbid their violation. ·So, also, the principle of the obligation of contracts

conscience, sovereign and absolute justice:" Id. This agrees substantially with the description of the law given by Demosthenes, which Mr. Christian thinks is perhaps the most perfect and satisfactory that can either be found or conceived: 1 Bla. Com. *44, note. "The design and object of the law is to ascertain what is just, honorable, and expedient; and when that is discovered, it is proclaimed as a general ordinance, equal and impartial to all. This is the origin of law, which for various reasons, all are under an obligation to obey; but especially because all law is the invention and gift of heaven, the sentiment of wise men, the correction of every offense, and the general compact of the state, to live in conformity with which is the duty of every individual in society." Assuming these to be his views, it is difficult to understand the grounds of the objection made by him to Blackstone's definition.

is not less a principle of natural right in America than elsewhere, although the federal constitution expressly forbids the enactment of any law impairing their obligation.

§ 263. Accordingly, it has been generally recognized by jurists, from the time of Aristotle down to the advent of Bentham and his followers, that the law is made up of two elements; namely, principles of natural right common to all people, and an arbitrary or accidental element peculiar to the particular system at any given time; the former of which is, in its nature, permanent and immutable, except as to degree of development, and the latter transitory, and everchanging with the changing views of legislators and the manners and customs of the people. The former constitutes what is called by Aristotle the *nomos koinos*, or common law, and by the Romans *jus gentium*, or *jus naturale;* and the latter by Aristotle the *nomos idios*, or peculiar law, and by the Romans *jus civile*, and also *jus singulare:*[1] *Infra*, §§ 389 *et seq.*,

---

[1] "*Jus singulare est, quod contra tenorem rationis propter aliquam utilitatem auctoritate constituentium introductum est:* " Dig. 1, 3, 10; see also Lindley's Introd. to Jur., p. 30, and app. 23.

"The positive laws either contain and confirm the common and natural rule of right (*regula juris s. ratio juris*), or establish for special reasons something that differs from this rule. In the first case they contain a *jus commune;* in the second, a *jus singulare s. exhorbitans:* " Kaufman's Mackeldy, Gen. Part, 4, 2; to which the translator adds the following note: "The meaning of a *jus singulare* might have been more accurately defined in the text. *Jus singulare* is every irregularity, exception, or peculiarity which runs counter to the *jus commune*, or common natural rule of right. Such a *jus singulare* may relate to individuals, to an entire class of persons, or even to the whole community, since its distinguish'ng characteristic is simply that it establishes

403.   The arbitrary or accidental rules constituting the *jus civile*, or *nomos idios*, are not principles in any sense, but operate only to limit or restrict the application of the principles of the *jus gentium*, or *nomos koinos*, and are therefore, except where they are legitimate applications of those principles, in the nature of anomalies or exceptions.   On the other hand, the *jus gentium*, or common right, rests for its authority upon the principles of natural justice, and is purely rational in its nature.   It is, therefore, another name for right, as we have defined that term. The one is therefore the normal, as the other is the abnormal, part of the law.   The *jus civile* is the principal source of the confusion that prevails with regard to the nature of the law, and it will therefore be necessary to investigate more fully its nature. It is, as we have seen, founded either upon statute or custom; and the problem presented is, therefore, to inquire how and to what extent statutes and judicial precedents enter into the determination of actions, and constitute elements of *jus.*

something abnormal; thus a *jus singulare* is, for instance, the allowing of an individual, contrary to the common and natural rule, to make a will for another; or the excepting of certain classes of persons from the common rule, *Ignorantia juris nocet;* or the imposing restrictions with regard to the general rate of interest. Even this last case, although referring to the whole community, belongs to the *jura singularia,* insomuch that it is opposed to the common and natural rules, *Pacta legem faciunt inter partes,* and *Pacta quælibet servanda sunt.*   It is in consequence of their anomalous nature that *jura singularia* are not permitted to be extended by way of analogy; since, on the one hand, everything that disagrees with the rule must be treated *stricte;* and on the other hand, the extension of peculiarities would only tend to deform the law."

CHAPTER IV. *

OF LAWS AND JUDICIAL PRECEDENTS AS ELEMENTS
OF JUS.

§ 264. In general, the chief difficulty in the way
of a just decision of cases arises from the intrinsic
uncertainty of human testimony: Paley's Moral and
Political Philosophy, 6, 8; and so great is this uncertainty, that in the attempt to administer justice
there is always great danger of violating the rights
of the defendant; which the state is bound to enforce, ·
and which, especially, it is bound not to invade.

Hence the perfect enforcement of all rights is impossible; and all that can be done is to secure as perfect an approximation to that result as practicable,
by establishing rules for determining in certain cases
the nature and amount of evidence necessary in order
to maintain an action.

§ 265. Accordingly, it has been found, or at
least deemed, advisable to prescribe the nature and
amount of evidence requisite to maintain actions in
certain cases. Of this species of legislation a familiar instance is furnished by the act of 29 Car. II, c.
3, commonly known as the statute of frauds and
perjuries, the most important provisions of which
have been re-enacted in all the American states,[1]

[1] This statute has always been, and still is, one of the most
fruitful causes of litigation; and it has been said that the construction of each one of its clauses has cost a subsidy. It may be
added that it still annually costs a subsidy to administer it.

12

and also by the statutes of limitations of the several
states, and by the statutes requiring certain formal-
ities to be observed by married women in conveying real estate; and by numerous other enactments
which will readily suggest themselves.

§ 266. Nearly all judicial legislation relating to
actions is of this kind, and is designed merely to
prevent men from being deprived of their rights by
false testimony; and their effect, therefore, is simply
to establish rules of evidence. Such laws, therefore,
are to be regarded as mere rules of art to guide the
courts in the application of the principles of justice;
and though many and perhaps most of them—as
well as of similar rules established by precedent or
custom—do not in fact answer the end for which
they were designed, but probably in the majority of
cases serve to protect rather than to prevent fraud,
yet the principle upon which they rest is entirely
justifiable; for where in any class of cases it is clear
that the attempt to enforce rights resting upon parol
evidence is as likely as not to result in violating the
more fundamental rights of personal liberty and
property, it is within the legitimate power of the
government to decline to undertake their enforcement, and to restrict the jurisdiction of the courts
accordingly.

§ 267. There are indeed instances of the interference of the legislature with the determination of
actions upon other grounds than the one above stated;
but in general the evil consequences resulting from
such enactments have been such as to lead to their
speedy repeal. A striking instance of this class of

laws is presented by the Connecticut law referred to in Goshen *v.* Stonington, 4 Conn. 209, which in effect ▪ declared void all marriages not solemnized by a minister "ordained and settled in the work of the ministry;" the effect of which was to make, or to attempt to make, adulterers of people honestly married and bastards of their children, with the further consequences of diverting the property of the parents upon their decease from their children to more distant kin. Other instances are also presented by statutes of various states, now happily repealed, which declared void all contracts made in contravention of the usury or the banking laws, the effect of which was merely to authorize the robbery of one of the parties by the other, though equally guilty.

§ 268. In discussing the subject of right, we have seen that it is immaterial to our definition what theory may be adopted as to the extent of the right, or function of judicial legislation; for it is admitted by the jurist that where the state acts within the limits of its right, whether that be unlimited or otherwise, the expression of its will is conclusive, and that rights in the true sense exist or otherwise as it may determine. With reference to *jus*, however, the question is material; for here the immediate problem to be determined is in what cases actions exist, or in other words, in what cases the power of the state is in fact habitually exercised at the suit of private individuals to coerce others.

§ 269. The immediate problem, therefore, is purely historical, and though there are certain natural tendencies, or as they may be called, laws of human

nature, which govern the historical development of
. human society in this as in other respects, yet the
solution of the problem must be different for different systems of law, and different periods in the same
system, according to the greater or less approximation of *jus* to perfection. It is therefore necessary
for us to consider not only what *jus* in theory ought
to be, but also what in the particular system under
consideration it actually is; and in considering this
problem, it is important to determine at the outset
the actual limits which, in the given system, are in
fact imposed upon the legislative power; for, having
once determined this limit, we can affirm, at least,
that no actions can exist outside of it.

§ 270. In American jurisprudence there prevails
a theory and practice with regard to the legislative
power and the validity of legislative acts or laws
very different from that which prevails in Europe.
For with us it is the universal practice to restrict
and limit the powers of government by written constitutions; and these universally contain declara-
tions or bills of rights by which the existence of the
fundamental rights are declared, their violation prohibited, and their observance enforced. Under the
rights thus enumerated in all the constitutions, state
and federal, are included the rights of life, liberty,
and property, and in addition, it is expressly provided by the federal constitution that no state shall
pass any law impairing the obligation of contracts;
so that in effect these provisions, though rudely and
inartificially framed, include all or nearly all conceivable rights. Besides, it has uniformly been held

by the courts of highest authority that independently of express constitutional provisions there is, in
the nature of things, a limit to the legislative power
beyond which its acts are void;[1] and though this
principle has not been accurately defined or consistently applied, the prevailing and growing opinion
seems to be that the legislature has not the power to
interfere with vested rights, except in the case of
clearly defined rights vested in the state. So that
the opinion of Coke that if a statute "is against common right and reason, the common law will control
it and adjudge it void," is in America not only good
but familiar law.[2] Nor is this with us a mere theory;
for both in the state and federal constitutions the
powers of government are divided between three independent and co-ordinate departments called respectively the legislative, the executive, and the

[1] "It may well be doubted whether the nature of society and
government does not prescribe some limit to the legislative power;
and if any be prescribed, where are they to be found if the property of an individual, fairly and honestly acquired, may be seized
without compensation?" Marshall, C. J., in *Fletcher* v. *Peck*, 6
Cranch, 135. "The fundamental maxims of free government
seem to require that the rights of personal liberty and private
property should be held sacred. . . . . We know of no case in
which a legislative act to transfer the property of A to B, without his consent, has ever been held a constitutional exercise of legislative power in any state in the Union. On the contrary, it has
been constantly resisted, as inconsistent with just principles, by
every judicial tribunal in which it has been attempted to be enforced:" Story, J., in *Wilkinson* v. *Leland*, 2 Pet. 657, 658.

[2] Mr. Campbell in his lif of Coke speaks of this as a foolish remark. It has, however, been consistently asserted by the great
jurists of England and this country, and is so obviously just that
Mr. Campbell may be more justly charged with folly in disputing
it: See authorities, *supra*, and also § 420, *infra*.

judicial; each of which is independent of the other, and, within its own sphere, vested with sovereign or supreme power.

§ 271. The above remarks apply equally to the state and federal governments; but with regard to the latter there is a still further restriction. For the state governments in their different departments are vested with all the legitimate powers of government, except such as are expressly denied to them by the state or federal constitution; but the federal government is vested with only certain specific powers, granted to it either expressly or by necessary implication by the constitution; and it is expressly provided by that instrument that "the powers not delegated to the United States by the constitution, nor prohibited to the states, are reserved to the states respectively or to the people:" Const. U. S., amend., art. 10.

§ 272. Under these provisions, it is an established principle of American law that if any law violates any constitutional provision, or trenches upon the powers of the other departments, or in the case of an act of congress, is in excess of the powers delegated to it by the federal constitution, it is absolutely void; and it is the familiar practice of the courts, both state and federal, when in the course of judicial proceedings it comes before them so to adjudge it.[1]

---

[1] A curious instance of how the nature and operation of this principle is misconceived by foreign lawyers is furnished by Mr. Austin, in his statement of what was told him by Colonel Murat; which, however, he *must* have misunderstood: Jur. 678.

§ 273. Hence, so far as the exercise of the judicial function and the protection of rights is concerned, the ultimate power of the state is vested in the courts of justice; and upon them is imposed the duty and the authority and actual power to protect and defend the rights of individuals as well against the state as against private wrong-doers.

§ 274. Nor has this practice of submitting the validity of legislative acts or laws to the judgment of the courts—incomprehensible as it seems to be to foreign jurists—been productive of any serious inconvenience; but on the contrary, it has, after nearly a hundred years' experience, proved so satisfactory in its practical operation, and has become so familiar to the American mind—in which there is a great and constantly growing distrust of legislative power —that with every amendment of the state constitutions new restrictions have been imposed; and it is perhaps not too much to expect that with further experience their power may be reduced to an extent not now conceived practicable.

§ 275. The theory of the American law with reference to the power of the legislature and the validity of its acts is therefore substantially the same as that of theoretical right; which is that rights avail against the state as well as against individuals, and are to be protected against political as well as against private invaders; and one of the greatest advances that has ever been made in political organization is the principle of American constitutional law, that it is essential, in order that right may be protected against legislative interference, that the judicial department of the government shall, within its appropriate sphere, be vested with supreme or sovereign power.

§ 276. This theory, indeed, has not as yet been consistently carried into practice; nor, in view of the inveterate superstition in favor of legislative power, which at the time of the American colonization had so long prevailed, and which in Europe seems still universally to prevail, is it strange that this should be the case; but nevertheless, the principle has been established, and under its influence there has been a constantly increasing tendency upon the part of the courts to extend its application.

§ 277. It is, however, the right, as it is the principal end, of government, to determine controversies between individuals as to their rights and obligations; and within certain limits (not necessary here precisely to determine) this right implies the power —either in exercising the function of judicial legislation or that of jurisdiction—to decide erroneously; and from the necessity of the case its decision, in many cases, whether erroneous or not, must be conclusive upon the question of the interference, or non-interference, of the state in the particular case or class of cases, as the case may be; and hence, within the limits referred to, the decision of the state, in the exercise of its function of judicial legislation, is conclusive in the determination of actions. The action of the state is also, in certain cases, conclusive upon this question upon other grounds; for it is within the power or right of the state, and—except so far as the matter is disposed of by constitutional provisions—within that of the ordinary legislature, to determine the jurisdiction of the courts; and it has therefore the power or right to restrict jurisdiction in certain cases so as to leave some rights unprovided for.

§ 278. Such legislation, or failure to legislate, does not, however, affect rights, but actions only; and this is not only a principle of right necessarily following from the very nature of a right, but also a recognized principle of American law.

§ 279. Thus, it is a well-settled principle of our law that a right barred by the statute of limitations continues to exist, though the remedy be forever gone: Sichel v. Carrillo, 42 Cal. 493. So also it has been repeatedly held with reference to contracts declared void by the usury and banking acts, and with reference to conveyances of married women declared void by statute on account of defective acknowledgments, and with reference to marriages technically void for want of compliance with statutory provisions as to the mode of solemnization, that rights existed under and by virtue of such contracts, conveyances, and marriages, though expressly declared to be void by statute; and accordingly, subsequent statutes declaring them valid have been upheld on the ground that the validating acts did not create new rights, but simply provided remedies for rights already existing: Syracuse Bank v. Davis, 16 Barb. 108; Dentzel v. Waldie, 30 Cal. 144; Goshen v. Stonington, 4 Conn. 309. Otherwise, such laws would be clearly unconstitutional; for, on the theory that there were no pre-existing rights, such laws would operate to transfer the property of one set of persons to another; which is forbidden by all the American constitutions, state and federal.

§ 280. With regard to the effect of judicial precedents, it is often asserted, and indeed it is accepted as a fundamental principle by certain theorists to whom we have referred, that the courts in deciding particular cases also establish a rule or principle in the nature of a law which is binding upon other courts in deciding similar cases; and that consequently judges exercise the function of legislation.

§ 281. This assertion involves two propositions, one of right and one of *jus;* namely, that judicial decision in theory ought to be, and that according to the established principles of *jus* they in fact are, conclusive and binding upon the courts.[1]

§ 282. With regard to the first proposition, it is impossible to conceive of any principle of right or reason, or even of expediency, to justify it; for the proposition asserts, not merely that the decisions of a court (whose judges are assumed to be men skilled in their art) ought (upon the principle *cuilibet in sua arte perito est credendum*) to carry with them a certain weight and authority, but that, whether right or wrong, such decision ought to be held conclusive, not because it is or is presumed to be correct, but because the courts are vested with legislative power, and therefore that the will of the judge, in accordance with a maxim applicable to all legislators, stands as a sufficient reason for the decision—*voluntas stat pro ratione.*

§ 283. With regard to the second proposition, although confidently asserted, it also is absolutely

---

[1] " There is such a thing as idolatry of precedents, and an idolatry it is which at times has slaughtered Justice at her own altar: " Lieber cited Bliss on Sovereignty, 43.

untrue with reference to the English or Anglo-
American law, if not also with reference to all other
systems. For, while in England at one period, the
doctrine of *stare decisis* was carried, with disastrous
consequences to the law, to extreme and absurd
lengths; and while in that country, and also here,
the courts are still disposed to pay a due, and perhaps more than due, respect to former opinions—
yet such opinions are viewed merely as authority of
more or less weight, according to the character of
the judges pronouncing them; and the courts assume and freely exercise the power of overruling
them when they deem them erroneous.[1] A concur-

[1] "Nevertheless, the rule [*stare decisis*] must not be so rigidly
pressed as to shield error needlessly, or shut out advanced knowledge. . . . . Although prior decisions are not lightly to be de-.
parted from, yet any error may be corrected when any substantial
injury is to be expected from the change, or when the evils of adherence are manifestly greater than those of departure. It must,
of course, be clear that there is an error; . . . . but when this
is clear, and a plain rule of law is manifestly violated, and especially if the rule established is mischievous rather than beneficial
to the community at large in its practical operations, or to a particular class of the community, as, for example, the holders of
commercial paper, it should be abrogated without delay. Indeed,
it may, under certain circumstances, become as imperative a duty
to arrest the damage resulting from the active power of a false
principle as in other circumstances to abide by the standards of
doctrine established by deliberate consideration and practical utility. Where a case arose in which a prior decision was attacked,
on the ground that it had no support in the cases from whence it
purported to be derived, the court yielded and said: ' Do we violate the doctrine of *stare decisis* by now correcting the mistake,
and going back to the well-established doctrine which that case
has disturbed? If we do, we commit a greater error than the one
we have felt bound to correct; for that doctrine, though incapable
of being expressed by any sharp and rigid definition, and there-

rence of decisions may indeed in certain cases establish a rule which courts will not feel at liberty to disregard; which is simply to say that a rule may become established by custom; and such rules may become more or less inveterate from the continuance of the custom; but no matter what may be the concurrence of decisions, if the rule established is erroneous, or in other words, contrary to the principles of

fore incapable of becoming an institute of positive law, is among the most important principles of good government. But, like all such principles, in its ideal it presents its medial and its extreme aspects, and is approximately defined by the negation of its extremes. The conservatism that would make the instance of to-day the rule of to-morrow, and thus cast society in the rigid molds of positive law, in order to get rid of the embarrassing but wholesome diversities of thought and practice that belong to free, rational, and imperfect beings; and the radicalism that, in ignorance of the laws of human progress, and disregard of the rights of others, would lightly esteem all official precedents and general customs that are not measured by its own idiosyncrasies;—each of these extremes always tends to be converted into the other, and both stand rebuked in every volume of our jurisprudence. And the medial aspect of the doctrine stands everywhere revealed as the only practical one, not as an arbitrary rule of positive law, attributing to the memory of cases higher honors and greater value than belong to the science and natural instinct and common feeling of right; not as withholding allowance for official fallibility, and for the changing views, pursuits, and customs that are caused by and that indicate an advancing civilization; not as indurating, and thus deadening the forms that give expression to the living spirit; not as enforcing "the traditions of the elders," when they "make void the law" in its true sense, nor as fixing all opinions that have ever been pronounced by official functionaries —but as yielding to them the respect which their official character demands, and which all good education enjoins. When the varied surface of this earth is changed into a dead level, and the ocean's waves are still, then man will need another habitation. And when the variety of human action and development is subjected to judi-

the law, the courts feel themselves at liberty to disregard it, except in certain well-defined cases; as for
instance, where it has entered into the course of
business and habitual mode of action of the people;
or in other words, become, not merely a custom of
the courts, but of the people generally; and even
where a rule has become so firmly established that
they hesitate at first to attack it, yet by the progres-

cial and legislative prescriptions, and the rule of man's free and
educated reason is proscribed, with all its improving diversities, and
all reasoning becomes illegal, if the subject has already been reasoned upon by judges, or decided upon by them without reasoning,
then men will need another jurisprudence and another legislation,
without, perhaps, being capable of enjoying them. The doctrine
of *stare decisis* is indeed one of the most important in the law; for
in its simplicity it expresses man's reverence for civil authority,
and the demand of his nature that it shall be obeyed; and this
feeling is the surest foundation of social order. It is the expression of the people's expectation that all government should be
administered with great care, and with a reasonable degree of consistency, and of their confidence that it is so; and it involves the
injunction that official functionaries shall not, for light reasons,
abandon the expressed judgments of themselves or of their prede-
cessors, especially if any serious embarrassment of public order
may be the consequence. It regards all governmental, and especially judicial, decisions as the official representation of the public will in relation to civil rights and duties, and as being entitled
to respect and reverence for this simple reason. To these feelings
and principles we owe official reverence, and we desire to cherish
it as a necessary element of social order and of political character.
We do not violate it when we declare that a decision made four
years ago, in opposition to all previous legislation and jurisprudence, is open to correction. We should violate it by declaring
that decision conclusive evidence of the law, and should at the
same time announce a judicial heresy involving the assertion that
judicial decisions are equivalent to positive law, and that courts
not only apply the law, but make it. . . . . If it should be said
that the principle of the decision in *Ewing* v. *Furness* has entered

sive development of the principles of the law and
the establishment of more rational rules inconsistent with it, sooner or later, if the law retains its
vitality, it is eradicated: *Vide supra*, § 255, note.
Moreover, precedents are manifestly, as we have assumed them to be, a species of custom; and all customs, however permanent they may seem to be,
with the continually occurring changes in society,

into the customs and practice of the country, then the claim that
it should stand as law would be founded upon a different principle expressed in the maxim, *Communis error facit jus:'*" *Callen-
der's Adm'r* v. *Insurance Co.*, 23 Pa. St. 474. "Apart from all
express authority, reason must convince us that no such inexorable rule could exist. The rule itself implies that the doctrine protected by *stare decisis* can not stand by itself. . . . . It is a sole-
cism to say that causes should be tried upon wrong principles—be
decided against the law—whether it be for the purpose of justice
or not so to decide them. The law is not so false to itself as to require its own permanent overthrow. For as the rule of *stare
decisis* is avowedly put upon the ground of policy, we can not
conceive that the application of this rule could be rightly so made
as to overthrow the paramount public policy of deciding causes by
the rules of law:" *Linn* v. *Minor*, 4 Nev. 407. "Even this back-
wardness to interfere with previous adjudications does not require
us to shut our eyes upon all improvements in the science of the
law, or require us to be stationary while all around is in progress.
. . . . Perhaps no general rule can be laid down upon the subject.
The circumstances of each particular case, the extent of influence
upon contracts and interests which the decisions may have had,
whether it may be only doubtful or clearly against principle,
whether restrained by some authority or opposed to all—these are
all matters to be judged of whenever the court is called upon to
depart from a prior determination:" Id., cited Wells on Res Ad-
judicata and Stare Decisis, c. 45.

"Although the case of *Smith* v. *Acker* plainly departs from the
law as it had been previously settled, it has been strongly urged
that as the decision of a court of last resort, it is a conclusive precedent which must be followed until the legislature shall change

fall into desuetude and pass away; and accordingly
it would be easy to fill a book with rules of the law
once firmly established, which have never been abrogated by legislation or directly overruled, but which
have ceased to be a part of the law, and would if in- ·
voked in a court of justice receive no respect.

§ 284. It is nevertheless true that erroneous rules
become established in the law by the force of prece-

it. It is undoubtedly true that the other courts of Westminster
Hall have generally considered themselves bound by the decision
of the House of Lords, when sitting as a court of review, though
more than one instance might be mentioned where the doctrine
· did not prevail. . . . . The reversal by the House of Lords of
Lord Somer's decree in *Kettle* v. *Townsend*, 1 Salk. 187, is one
instance. Sir John Trevor, M. R., denied the authority of that
decision, affirming, moreover, that if the same case were to come
again into the House of Lords, they would decide differently:
Watts v. *Bullis*, 1 P. Wms. 60, 61. Lord Harcourt seems also to
have refused to follow it as a precedent: Id. 61, note. Of the same
case, Lord Loughborough spoke as follows: ' I have no difficulty in
saying I think of that determination of the House of Lords as Lord
Harcourt and other judges have done,' adding: ' Upon the jour-
nals of the House of Lords, it appears no one was present upon the
reversal who could know much of the matter; it was not determined by lawyers; and Lord Harcourt speaks of it certainly as not
such a decision as he would follow; and one or two other judges
have not treated it with much respect: ' *Hills* v. *Downton*, 5 Ves.
565. . . . . It is going too far to say that a single decision of any
court is absolutely conclusive as a precedent. It is an elementary
principle that an erroneous decision is not bad law—it is no law
at all. It may be final upon the parties then before the court,
but it does not conclude other parties having rights depending
on the same question. I will refer to a few cases for the purpose
of showing that our court of errors does not abide by its decisions.
. . . . These examples are sufficient to show that our court of
dernier ressort does not regard its own decisions as conclusive by
way of precedent; and if not so regarded by that court, it would
be strange indeed if other courts were bound to follow them at all

dent; and although where the law is in a healthy
condition these will almost certainly sooner or later
be abrogated by legislation, or, more frequently,
overruled by the court, or silently fall into disuse,
yet in the meanwhile they enter into the determination of actions, and therefore for the time being constitute a part of *jus*.

§ 285. Such rules, however, like unjust laws,

events, and without looking into the reason on which they stand:"
Bronson, J., in *Butler* v. *Van Wyck*, 1 Hill (N. Y.), 461–463.

" The judicial rule, *stare decisis* does, however, admit of exceptions where the former determination is most evidently contrary
to reason—much more if it be clearly contrary to the divine law.
But even in such cases, subsequent judges do not pretend to make
a new law, but to vindicate the old law from misrepresentation.
For if it be found that the former decision is manifestly absurd or
unjust, it is declared, not that such a sentence was bad law, but
that it was not law; that is, that it is not the established custom
of the realm, as has been erroneously determined: " 1 Bla. Com.
*69, *70.

"Even a series of decisions," says Chancellor Kent, "are not
always conclusive evidence of the law, and the revision of a decision very often resolves itself into a mere question of expediency,
depending upon the consideration of the importance of certainty
in the rule and the extent of property to be affected by a change
in it. Lord Mansfield frequently observed that the certainty of a
rule was often of much more importance in mercantile cases than
the reason of it, and that a settled rule ought to be observed for
the sake of property; and yet perhaps no English judge ever made
greater innovations or improvements in the law, or felt himself
less embarrassed with the disposition of the elder cases when they
came in his way to impede the operation of his enlightened and
cultivated judgment." " The law of England," he observed,
"would be an absurd science were it founded upon precedents
only:" 1 Kent's Com. 47.

As is said by Chancellor Wentworth, speaking of this maxim:
" While another maxim—*Humanum est errare*—remains true,
there must occasionally be a reconsideration and overruling of

affect only the determination of actions, and not that of rights; and it may be remarked here, with equal propriety as of laws, that this is a principle not only of right, but of *jus* also; and that it is to this principle alone that we owe the development of equity jurisprudence in our law; which development has consisted mainly in the giving of actions for rights not recognized by law, and therefore non-actionable

former judgments. If on a re-examination the former error is clear, our duty is plain; we must be, as Lord Coke said Sir John Fortescue was, ' not amongst the number of those *qui suos amassent errores*, but one of those who yielded to the truth when he found it: ' Preface to 10 Coke. To overrule a decision clearly erroneous on principle is always a duty, un'ess there has been a uniform course of corrobating decisions for a series of years; and even then the doctrine of *stare decisis* has been most strongly applied in real-estate cases. I believe that a single decision has never in any case been allowed to stand if found opposed to principle.''

The effect of an irrational rule established by a series of judicial decisions is limited to the case or class of cases in which it was originally established; and generally, it follows that the rule itself (by what has been well called the *vis medicatrix* of the law) is gradually undermined and finally eradicated. '' It has been the constant labor of judges,'' says Sir James McIntosh, cited *infra*, § 367, ''through all changes of society, to keep the common law consistent with reason and with itself; '' and thus in the language of Lord Mansfield, Id., ''the law works itself pure by the fresh streams which it draws from its original fountains of equity and reason.''

It is to be observed, also, that in America the maxim is less strictly observed than in England. In the latter country the law has been administered from time immemorial by a few courts sitting in the same locality and in constant communication with each other, and all subject to a common appellate jurisdiction; and it has therefore been practicable, by means of the rule, to attain a degree of certainty in the law unattainable elsewhere. But in the United States, the decisions of the courts of all the states, as well

13

until the action was supplied by the chancellor. Thus, under the old English law, the right of the *cestui que trust* in land was not recognized by the courts of law, which regarded the holder of the legal title as the absolute owner, although the right of the *cestui que trust* was precisely the same in its nature as that of the owner of personal property intrusted to another—a right which was in fact recognized by

as those of the federal and English judiciaries, are habitually cited as authority, and consequently, among the conflicts necessarily arising in the decisions, the American courts are generally left free to decide cases upon principle, unembarrassed by authority. In each state, indeed, the courts generally pay more regard to their own decisions than to those of other states; but even in this case, where a rule is at once against principle and the concurrent decisions of other states, it is more easily overruled.

The strictness of the rule is also greatly relaxed by the fact (elsewhere referred to) that American writers on jurisprudence, with few exceptions, do not treat of the law of any particular state, but of American law generally, and therefore are not bound by the precedents, except when they concur. which in general only occurs where they are all supported by reason. The American jurist is therefore generally at liberty to confine himself to the strictly scientific aspect of the subject, and American jurisprudence is therefore, beyond all other systems, susceptible of a scientific development: See also Ram's Leg. Judg., c. 14, § 1.

It is therefore evident, as asserted in the text, that judicial decisions are not in any sense laws, or analogous to laws; and that they are binding on other courts only in so far as they are right, or if erroneous, only when they become established by custom.

In view of these authorities, and innumerable others that might be cited to the same effect, the hallucination of Mr. Austin and his followers, with reference to the nature and force of judicial precedents, must strike the professional reader with surprise.

It may be added, that so far as the rule of *stare decisis* enjoins upon the judge a respect for his own former decisions, it is apt rather to be unduly observed than otherwise, and that judges,

the courts. The right of the *cestui que trust* was therefore a true right; and the fact that it was without an appropriate action, so far from destroying the right, simply induced the chancellor to supply the defect.

§ 286. Clearly, therefore, our proposition is true, that precedents, like other customs and laws, are mere elements in the determination of rights, whose effect, like that of other facts, is to be determined by the principles of right; and it is also true that this principle, though not always consistently applied, is also a recognized principle of *jus;* and that, in the determination of actions, precedents and other customs and laws are mere elements of the problem— the only difference being that the principles by which their effect is in fact determined are, owing to the inherent and . necessary imperfection of all human instrumentality, somewhat different in *jus* from those of right; the latter of which are purely scientific in their character.

§ 287. Hence we conclude that jurisdiction is not, as is commonly supposed, a mere power to carry out the will of the state, or to apply the accidental results of custom, but is in its nature a general power to administer justice between men; and that this power is in no way altered in its character

therefore. in this respect, need the bridle rather than the spur. In this regard, we may therefore say with Cujacius: " *Utinam qui hoc tempore jus nostrum interpretantur, Papinianum imitati, quævel falso vel inepte aliquando et senserint et scripserint, ingenue retractent; nec eis, contra quam postea resciverint, tam obstinato tamque obfirmato animo (uti faciunt) perseverunt:* " Kaufman's Mackeldy, preface, 18.

by the fact that it is a part of the administration of justice to determine the jural effect of laws and customs, as is that of contracts, injuries and other human acts.

CHAPTER V.

OF THE PRACTICAL IMPORTANCE OF THE DISTINCTION
BETWEEN ACTIONS AND RIGHTS, AND BETWEEN JUS
AND RIGHT.

§ 288. The problem we have been discussing relates to the nature of the law as it is, and is purely
historical in its character. The consideration of
what the law ought to be is therefore irrelevant to
the point under discussion.

§ 289. In view, however, of the almost universal
tendency to confound rights with actions or remedies, and of the confusion resulting from the failure
to distinguish between things so essentially different, it will be well to point out some of the practical
bearings of the distinction, and to show that it is
not only essentially necessary, but also of vital
practical importance.

§ 290. In the first place, to assume that the essence of a right consists in the fact that it will be
enforced by the state is in the highest degree subversive of morality. For the term "a right"—as
can not be too often observed—connotes the idea of
rightness; and hence the notion that a man has the
right to exact from another whatever the law will
enable him to exact inevitably carries with it the
idea that it is not wrong for him to do so. Hence
there is added to the power of doing injustice, itself
demoralizing, a specious theory that clothes the

wrong with the name of right, which must necessarily have a powerful tendency to corrupt the
average conscience. Nor is it less clear that the
effect upon the person wronged must also be demoralizing.[1]

[1] The effect on the lawyers and judges is also necessarily demoralizing. In order to participate in injustice, or in any other
iniquity, with any degree of mental quietude, men must in self-
defense stifle the natural instincts of their conscience. Hence the
false theory is asserted that it is not the function of the courts to
administer justice, but the law; which is held to consist of the
mere arbitrary will of political rulers, or of the often absurd
opinions of judges; and thus the responsibility is shifted to the
law, where it does not belong. For in the hands of competent
judges the law is seldom wanting in resources to make its rules
subservient to the ends of justice; and it is the glory of its great
jurists that they have known how to arrive at justice through all
technicalities. "I commend the judge," says one of them, "that
seems fine and ingenious, so it tend to right and equity;" and in
this he but expresses a sentiment common to all of them: Hob.
125; Broom's Legal Maxims, 81; see also opinion of Mansfield in
Rex v. *Phillips*, 1 Burr. 301, 304. It is natural, also, that in
justification, the theory in which they find their excuse should be
frequently and emphatically asserted; and hence we often hear
these "priests of justice" (*vide infra*, § 350) expressing a
thorough contempt for the principles of justice which they are
supposed to administer. What, for instance, can be thought by
plain men of expressions such as these, cited from Ram's Leg.
Judg. 25—all of them from the lips of reverend judges:
."Perhaps it is less important how the law is determined than
that it should be determined and certain, and that such determination should be adhered to:" *Goodtitle* v. *Otway*, 7 T. R. 419;
or, "Where things are settled and rendered certain, it will not be
so material how, as long as they are so, and that all people know
how to act:" *Butler* v. *Duncomb*, 1 P. Wms. 452; or, "No matter what the law is, so it be certain:" 2 Ch. Cas. 221; or the expression we often hear, that "hard cases make bad law"—a
proposition exactly opposite to the truth, which is, that the re-

§ 291. Accordingly, it can not be doubted that the prevalence of this theory has in fact been the source of a wide-spread and profound corruption of the public morality. It is essential, therefore, to the conservation of morality, that the distinction

lief of hard cases is the very principle to which the law owes its rational development. Nor does the conduct of the bar or the bench in this respect belie their professions. For there is no fraud, oppression or villainy so great that respectable lawyers—who would themselves scorn to perpetrate it—will not undertake to prosecute it for a client, and which respectable judges will not help to carry out, provided that judges before them, either through inadvertence, mistake, or crookedness of mind, have been guilty of similar wrongs.

An instance of this is presented by the doctrine already referred to, that where, for the purpose of protecting it from his creditors, one conveys property to another in trust, equity will not enforce the trust—a doctrine founded upon a misapplication of a rule of law thought by Lord Thurlow to be itself irrational: *Nevill* v. *Wilkinson*, 18 Ves. 382; 1 Bro. Ch. 547, 548; and which yet has been generally affirmed by American courts, and is now regarded by the mass of the profession as settled law. This doctrine, which has for its professed object the prevention of fraud, not only violates the rights of the *cestui que trust*, and inflicts upon him a punishment out of all proportion to his offense, but directly incites to a far more outrageous fraud, by offering to the trustee, who might naturally be inclined to be honest, a bribe often enormous for the betrayal of his trust and the violation of one of the most sacred of human obligations. And thus judges, in the name of virtue and the law, but in violation of both, become willing accomplices in a crime abhorrent to the ordinary conscience, and which is in fact more villainous than any for which men are sent to the penitentiary, except perhaps murder.

Another instance is presented by the California law of defaults, by the operation of which a trifling neglect on the part of the defendant in answering in a suit results in a judgment for the plaintiff; and the hardship of this law, itself unjust and cruel, is aggravated by the rule judicially established, that the client is responsible for the negligence of his attorney. Thus if a man un-

between rights and actions should be observed; and
even should we adopt the extremest views as to the
power of the state and the necessity of absolute submission to its will, there can be no reason why we
should corrupt our language and debauch our con-

justly sued, even for his whole fortune, employs in due time—to
put in his answer—a lawyer, who holds the commission of the
state as the guaranty of his competency, and the lawyer fails to
do so, the mischief is irreparable. The plaintiff's claim may be
admittedly villainous; the defendant's whole fortune may be involved; himself and innocent family may be plunged into destitu-
tion; he himself may have exercised the utmost diligence to prevent these disastrous results; but the rule is inexorable, and one
remedy only remains to him, namely, the right to sue his lawyer—
a right like the right to shear the wolf, undoubted, but of ques-
tionable value. For the lawyer is in general secure in his skill in
his profession, in the sympathy of his brethren, and in the
liberal rules adopted by the judges for the measurement of his responsibility.

Still another instance is presented by a rule adopted by the
California supreme court with relation to appeals, and which was
enforced with the most rigid consistency until lately abolished by
statute—the statute itself illustrating how tardy is legislative
relief even in the plainest cases. The original statute provided
that an appeal should be made "by filing with the clerk . . . . a
notice stating the appeal, ... and serving a copy of the notice
upon the adverse party or his attorney:" Prac. Act, § 337; and it
was further provided that to render the appeal effective, the undertaking for costs, etc., on the appeal "shall be filed with the
clerk within five days after the notice of appeal is filed:" Id.,
§ 348. Upon a fair construction of these provisions, it would seem
to be a matter of indifference in what order the several steps
should be taken, and accordingly it is so expressly provided by the
present law. It was, however, held at an early date, by the
supreme court, that if the order as stated in the law was departed
from—that is to say, if the notice was served before it was filed,
or the undertaking filed before the filing of the notice—the appeal
was void; and this rule was rigidly enforced down to the amendment referred to, which was not passed until July 1, 1880, though

science by calling the unjust just and the wrong right.

§ 292. Secondly, the observance of the distinction is also essential to the practical administration of justice. It is, indeed, as we have observed, a common supposition with people not familiar with

in the mean time a new code had been adopted. When it is added that every step after judgment, in the proceeding for new trial and on appeal, is beset by technicalities rigidly enforced by the courts, and that in California, as in other states, not even a decent competency of professional knowledge is required from the lawyers, it will be readily understood that in a vast number of instances the litigant has but little chance of having his case decided on its merits.

Other instances might be given—instances enough to make a book which would be at once one of the most melancholy and one of the most useful that ever was written—but these are sufficient to illustrate our proposition.

We may say, therefore, with Burke, that while the law "is one of the first and noblest of human sciences—a science which does more to quicken and invigorate the understanding than all other kinds of learning put together— . . . . it is not apt, except in persons happily born, to open and liberalize the mind exactly in the same proportion." It may be added, also, that while to the higher minds—the Cokes, the Hales, the Mansfields, and the Marshalls of the profession, who have always regarded the law as the mere means of administering justice, or, in the words of Bracton (infra, § 420 p. 247), "justice as the end, jurisprudence as the means"— the pursuit is also one of the most ennobling, it is not so with the ordinary mass—the ignoble vulgus; for upon the average lawyer such sentiments and such rulings as those we have cited necessarily have a most demoralizing effect, and absolutely destroy in him the capacity of discerning the just from the unjust. Hence, we can readily understand the cause of the unsavory reputation which the profession has always had in the opinions of plain people, nor is it altogether clear that Dick the butcher was not without show of reason in proposing "to hang all the lawyers" as a preliminary measure of reform.

the law that it consists mainly or altogether of rules
established by statute or precedent, which at least
have the merit of being permanent in their nature
and certain in their expression and application; and
that the chief source of uncertainty in the administration of the law consists in the tendency to be
swayed by what are supposed to be the loose and
ill-defined, and consequently varying, notions of
justice as commonly received; and hence, that certainty in the administration of justice can only be
secured by its formulation into rules of rigid and
unbending character, and by a strict and unvarying
application of such rules without regard to the question of their justice or injustice. 'But in point of
fact, these notions are altogether unfounded. For
the most certain as well as the only permanent
and immutable element of *jus* is that portion of it
which consists of principles of natural right, logically defined and scientifically expressed. And the
element which approaches most nearly to this in
certainty is the sense of justice held by jurists in
common with the people generally. And the least
certain as well as the least permanent of all is the
part composed of arbitrary or accidental rules resting upon statute or precedent: *Infra*, § 364. For
these rules are not only generally uncertain in expression and frequently contradictory in effect, but
are also often in conflict with the principles of the
law, or, to speak more definitely, with the principles
of natural right recognized and firmly established
in the law; and in such cases it is at least necessary
that, in accordance with the maxim we have quoted

above, they should be restricted in their application. Hence it results that unless the judge is guided in the application of such rules by the principles of the law—which are in fact principles of natural right—or, in default of knowing such principles applicable to the case, by his sense of justice, such rules are generally extremely uncertain in their application, and apt to give rise to the widest divergence of opinion as to their meaning and as to their legitimate scope and operation. Hence in all periods in the history of the law it has been the practice of the courts to refer constantly to "justice," "good conscience," "equity," "reason," or "common sense"[1] as it is variously expressed, as the grounds of their decision; and in this way only has the practical administration of justice been kept steady.[2] And there is no doubt

---

[1] This gives Austin occasion to complain that "justice is commonly erected into an entity, and spoken of as a legislator, in which character it is supposed to prescribe the law, conformity to which it should denote." "The veriest dolt," he continues, "who is placed in a jury-box, the merest old woman who happens to be raised to the bench, will talk finely of equity or justice—the justice of the case, the equity of the case, the imperious demands of justice, the plain dictates of equity. He forgets that he is there to enforce the law of the land; else he does not administer that justice or that equity with which alone he is immediately concerned. This is well known to have been a strong tendency of Lord Mansfield—a strange obliquity in so great a man:" Jur. 223. All the great English judges, along with Lord Mansfield, must be included among the old women referred to: *Vide infra*, § 367.

[2] " The attempt to divorce law from conscience, from the natural perception of right and justice, ... while seeming to simplify, really confuses our notions: Bliss on Sovereignty, 23.

but that since this tendency has of late years been weakened by the prevalence of the legal theory, the uncertainty of the administration of justice has greatly increased; nor can there be any doubt that if that theory were to be finally realized in practice and the law reduced to statute, and natural right or justice entirely removed from the consideration of the judges, it would result, not only in an unjust

The following passage from the Central Law J.urnal, of June 18, 1886, may be cited as indicating a view almost universal with the best class of lawyers. It occurs in a review of an address by George H. Christy, Esq., upon "The Evils of Case Law:"

"The author proceeds to state what he deems the proper course for the practitioner, thus: 'To keep in mind the principles of right and wrong which, theoretically at least, underlie all law, and to apply those principles to the facts under consideration, and thereby seek a righteous verdict or adjudication. In this work, previous decisions in so far as they apply, are an obvious, important and desirable aid; for the reason that they indicate the conclusions which previous judges have reached on the consideration of like questions under conditions at least favorable to a just decision.'

"The practice which he deprecates he states in these words: 'The other course is to leave out of consideration entirely, or give but little weight to, the underlying principles of right and wrong, and to look through prior decisions to see if one can not be found which, either in the plain meaning of the language used, or by a distortion, or perversion, or stretching of such language, will secure a favorable result.'

"Three classes of practitioners are charged with thus abusing instead of properly using, case law: 'The beginner, the lazy practitioner and the *shyster*.' "

The non-professional reader can readily verify the correctness of these views by consulting almost any old lawyer of good reputation for professional ability, and asking him to explain the process by which he arrives at his opinion upon any case submitted to him. The answer, if the author's own observation can be trusted, will almost always be in substance the same as given above by Mr. Christy.

and oppressive tyranny, but in a state of unparalleled uncertainty in the actual administration of the law.

§ 293. Thirdly, as a question of method, whether we aim at the further development of *jus*, or simply to understand it as it is, it is absolutely essential to distinguish between rights and actions, or in other words, between right and *jus*, and to treat the former independently. This follows from the relation of the two, as science and art, for though in all subjects of knowledge art is in point of time first cultivated, it is essential to the perfection even of the art itself that the science should be treated independently.

§ 294. Accordingly, as we have seen, the development of *jus*, in so far as it has been rational and satisfactory, has been the result of this method: *Supra*, § 255.[1] For it is the recognition of the existence of non-actionable rights, and of the necessity of providing remedies for them, which in the past has produced and governed the development of our law; and this is true not only of equity jurisprudence—to which we have already referred—but of the whole law. For it is inevitable where a right is once recognized that the remedy shall sooner or

---

[1] "It must be admitted that the law, like language, has an unintended, unconscious development, or, to call it by the traditional expression, an organic development from within outward. To this development we owe all those principles of law which are gradually accumulated from the autonomous balancing of the accounts of the legal (juridical) rights of men in their dealings with one another, as well as all those abstractions, consequences and rules deduced by science from existing laws, and presented by it to the consciousness:" Ihering's Struggle for Right, 8.

later follow; and that this has been a necessary, and not an accidental, mode of development is proved by the precisely similar development of the Roman law and other systems.

§ 295. This, indeed, is the principle embodied in the maxim we have cited, that wherever there is a right there shall be a remedy (*ubi jus, ibi remedium*); and although from the intrinsic imperfection of which *jus* in common with all art partakes, the maxim is not, and can not be in fact, altogether observed; yet it expresses a fundamental principle of the law which in all progressive countries governs its development, and to the actual realization of which, as we have seen, it constantly approximates.

§ 296. That at a certain stage in the history of the law the principle became less marked in its application results from its having in the main accomplished its function in the perfection of the remedial part of the law; and hence it is a common tendency of the professional mind to regard the function as completely performed, and the law itself as finished and complete. Hence the maxim is inverted, and it comes to be asserted that where there is no action there is no right. It is, however, clear that had the maxim originally been so interpreted, there would have been an absolute arrest of development in the law, and consequently of civilization; for no fact is more certain than that, at least in the past, legislation has been the least considerable and least efficient of the agencies by which the law has been developed; and that without that capacity of spontaneous development which it has always exhibited,

and which has been well called the *vis medicatrix* of
the law, it would still be in a state of barbarism.
Nor is it less clear that the recognition of the existence of natural right and non-actionable rights is
as essential to the future as it has been to the past
development of the law—whether that development
is to take place in the main spontaneously, as here-
tofore, or by legislation; for the end of government
and of law is the establishment of justice; and
whether the art of doing this pertains to the legislator or to the judge, it is necessary that the principles of the science should be recognized and asserted: See observations of Cousin, cited *supra*, § 261,
note.

§ 297. In fact, however, the principle embodied
in the maxim, *Ubi jus, ibi remedium*, is still a principle of the law, and the capacity for spontaneous
development which results from it still continues;
and in view of the recent legislation in England
and in many of the United States, abolishing the
old forms of action, it is perhaps not too much
to expect—unless the genius of the profession
has failed—that, under its beneficent influence, the
maxim may come to have a practically universal
application.

§ 298. But though the present development of
the law, so far as it is rational, is due altogether to
the recognition of the existence of natural rights,
and of the necessity of providing them with appropriate remedies, and though the method of the jurists has therefore in the main been rational and
scientific, yet the operation of this method has been

embarrassed by their failure to keep consistently in view the essential difference between the principles of natural right, which in the main compose the law, and its arbitrary and accidental part, the *jus civile;* the latter of which, as we have observed, is anomalous and exceptional in its nature, and therefore can not legitimately enter into the development of *jus* otherwise than by merely limiting or restraining the application of its principles.

§ 299. Thus not only has the development of the law been retarded, but the law itself has been corrupted; so that, as it now stands, it is not only backward in its development, but contains also numerous arbitrary and irrational rules, which judges in their ignorance mistake for principles, and which are consequently pushed to unjust and absurd consequences. Of late years, also, the evil has been aggravated both in this country and in England, by the increasing prevalence of a false theory as to the nature of law; and in the former especially,[1] by other causes, among which may be noted the lack of general and even of professional education in the lawyers, and more particularly in the judges, and the enormous multiplicity of precedents,[2] from

[1] In England, also, according to Mr. Markby: Elements of Law, § 194.

[2] The decisions of the supreme court of all the different states, those of the federal courts, supreme, circuit, and district, and those of the English courts—in all from sixty to a hundred—are habitually cited by judges and text-writers in the United States. That all these precedents should agree is of course impossible, and as Gibbon remarks, the most rigid rule as to the observance of precedents can require the precedents to be followed only where

which has resulted a state of confusion and conflict in the law, inconceivable to any one who has not been so unfortunate as to participate as a practicing lawyer in what is called the administration of justice.

§ 300. With regard to form especially, so chaotic is the condition of the law, and so innumerable the books in which it is supposed to be contained, that it is. not within the bounds of human capacity to master the authorities; and even in particular cases it is as a general rule impracticable for the lawyer to examine and digest the authorities bearing upon the question involved; and still less practicable to secure from the courts anything like an exhaustive examination even of those which are cited.[1]

§ 301. Hence along with the increasing tendency to regard authority to the exclusion of reason, and largely as the result of that tendency, there has resulted such uncertainty in the administration of justice, that in the large majority of cases no lawyer

they agree. Accordingly, this has given occasion to Mr. Pollock to remark that "authorities are criticised [in the United States] with a freedom which seems to an English lawyer to imply a growing sense that after all it is a matter of opinion, and nothing more." Essays on Jur. and Eth., 245.

[1] The decision of cases, therefore, depends in large measure upon the number and character of the precedents with which the judge happens to become acquainted; and as the number of these is far beyond any human capacity of acquisition, it results that the principle of decision with different judges—which is sometimes called the *judicial conscience*—varies in quantity and quality far more than the natural consciences of different men; so that Selden's witty remark about the latter would in these times be far more applicable to the former: 1 Pomeroy's Eq. Jur., § 57, and note.

14

can make even a reasonable guess as to the result
of litigation; and men's fortunes, in the language of
Bacon, "are tossed at this day as upon a sea, in such
sort that it is hard to say which bark will sink, and
which will get to the haven:" Reading on the Stat.
of Uses.

§ 302. With regard to the remedy for these evils,
an opinion prevails that it is to be found in the re-
duction of the law, by means either of legislation or
of a stricter adherence to authority, to a body of
rigid and precisely defined rules; but this, as we
have already shown, would be but to aggregate the
evil, and, fortunately for the welfare of the human
race, is as impracticable as it would be disastrous.

§ 303. The history of the law itself, however,
suggests the true and only practical remedy; for the
law owes whatever is good in its present development to the use of a scientific method, and its defects
to a failure to apply that method consistently. It is
not unreasonable, therefore, to anticipate that a
more consistent employment of the same method
will be productive of results in perfecting the law
and ameliorating the condition of the human race
hitherto unanticipated. The true method of treating the subject, therefore, is to treat it scientifically
—dealing with received opinions, customs, · and
laws, as elements of the problem, without suffering
ourselves to be misled, or in any way influenced by
authority, either legislative or judicial; but at the
same time, noting wherein the principles of *jus*
actually established in and enforced by the state
differ from those theoretically established; and in

this way the principles of the philosophical and the historical methods are reconciled.

§ 304. In adopting this method, we are not, however, to be understood as asserting that it is the duty of the judge in the practical administration of justice to decide always according to the principles of abstract justice, or always to disregard statutes and precedents which are opposed to those principles. Whatever view may be taken with reference to the duty of the judge in this respect, it is,· however, at least essential to the efficient performance of his functions that he should understand and recognize what the principles of justice require; for in the great majority of instances, this is the single consideration upon which the decision of the case should rest; and most generally, where it is unjustly decided, the fault is with the judge rather than with the law.

§ 305. It is, moreover, not only with the view to the more perfect development of the law that the scientific method is essential. It is also essential when we have in view only what Bentham calls the cognoscibility of the law; for obviously the only practical way of mastering this extensive and intricate subject is first to investigate the principles of the law in their scientific integrity, and only after we have done this, to enter upon the investigation of the extent and manner in which the operation of these principles is modified and restricted by the *jus civile*.[1] Accordingly, it is the common testimony of

---

[1] In the words of Cicero: "Non a Prætoris edictu neque a Duodecim Tabulis, sed penitus ex intimâ philosophia hauriendum juris desciplinam."

all competent jurists that this is the only practical method of mastering the law; and such in fact has been the method of the better class of law-writers, as nearly as the existing state of jural science would permit.

§ 306. The adoption of this method is especially advisable at this period in the history of our law, in view of the fact already adverted to, that in England and in this country all technical forms of actions have been abolished, leaving in place of them the simple maxim that every right shall have a remedy —*ubi jus ibi remedium.*

§ 307. It is also especially appropriate in treating of American jurisprudence; for in this country the system of laws prevailing in the different states are altogether independent of each other, and with the exception of the federal laws, which relate to an extremely limited class of cases, there is no law of positive institution common to all of them. When we speak of American law, therefore, we speak of a *jus gentium,* and not of a *jus civile;* as the Greeks used to speak of the law or *nomos* of Greece; or as we would now say, that the civil law is the law of Europe. There is, indeed, a similarity approximating to identity in the systems of the several states; but this arises merely from a common origin and common customs and modes of thought, and exists to almost the same extent between those systems and the English law, and, to a great extent, between them and those of all other civilized nations. The American jurist, therefore, in treating of American law, is bound neither by statutory regulations nor by judicial precedents, but is at liberty to follow the scientific method; though of course he should at the same time note the general concurrence and divergence of customs and laws in the several states.

CHAPTER VI.

HISTORICAL DEVELOPMENT OF THE ENGLISH LAW.

§ 308. The English law, as received in America, was mainly developed in the practical administration of justice by four courts, which existed in England from an early period, until abolished by the late judicature act, and which were known as the courts of king's bench, of common pleas, of exchequer, and of chancery.

§ 309. Of these courts, the first three were vested with substantially the same jurisdiction over civil cases, and were known as the courts of law; and the last, the jurisdiction of which differed materially from that of the others, both in its origin and nature, was called the court of equity.

§ 310. Hence it has resulted that the English law is composed of two distinct systems of jurisprudence, known as law and equity; which were developed respectively by the courts of law and the court of equity; and of which the latter may be briefly described as being supplementary to and corrective of the former.

§ 311. To understand the nature of the development of the English law, some account must therefore be given of the origin and growth of these two jurisdictions; and as the courts of law were first in order of time, these will first receive our attention.

§ 312. In Saxon times, justice was ordinarily

administered by the county and other local courts, and this continued to be the case for several reigns after the Conquest; but ultimately, the jurisdiction of these courts was absorbed by the king's court, and the local courts became therefore practically obsolete. It is, therefore, to the jurisdiction originally vested under the Norman régime in the king that we must look for the source of the jurisdiction of the English courts.

§ 313. The early Norman kings exercised an absolute and supreme control over the administration of justice: 1 Spence's Eq. Jur. *101; and it was a received principle that all jurisdiction was vested in the king, and that the jurisdiction of·the courts was a mere delegation of power from him: Id. *120; 1 ·Bla. Com. *266, *267; 2 Id. *24, *31. Indeed, this continued to be a recognized principle of the law, even down to modern times; for Blackstone tells us that the king "is the fountain of justice, ... and . . . . that all jurisdiction of courts are, either mediately or immediately, derived from the crown:" 1 Bla. Com. *66, *67; or, as he otherwise expresses it, "all courts of justice are derived from the power of the crown. . . . . In all these courts, the king is supposed, in contemplation of law, to be always present; but as that is in fact impossible, he is there represented by his judges, whose power is only an emanation of the royal prerogative:" 2 Id. *24; which is but a repetition of the principle asserted by Bracton, and which in his time was substantially true, "that all judicial power flowed from the king; and that the king would have been bound by his

coronation oath himself to administer justice to his
people if such a task could have been performed by
him; but as this was impossible, it was his duty to
appoint competent persons as justices, sheriffs and
ministers, to perform this office:" 1 Spence's Eq.
Jur. *120.

§ 314. This, however, is to be understood as referring only to the historical origin of the jurisdiction of the English courts, and not as implying that
the king still retained, in the latter periods of English history, the extensive jurisdiction with which
he was originally invested.

§ 315. For during the period that elapsed from
the Conquest to the reign of Edward I—when the
three common law courts were finally established—
a gradual and progressive change took place, the
result of which was to vest in those courts, to the
exclusion of the king, the ordinary administration
of justice. Accordingly, we are told by Blackstone
that, although "in very early times, before our constitution arrived at its full perfection, our kings in
person often heard and determined causes between
party and party, yet at present, by the law and uniform usage of many ages, our kings have delegated
their whole judicial power to the judges of the several
courts; which are the grand depositaries of the
fundamental laws of the kingdom, and have gained
a known and stated jurisdiction, regulated by certain and established rules, which the crown itself
can not alter but by act of parliament:" 1 Id. *267.

§ 316. But although the principle that the jurisdiction of the courts is a mere delegation of power
from the king has become, for many ages past, a

mere fiction as applied to the actual state of the law,
it was in fact true with reference to the times immediately succeeding the Conquest; for though the
jurisdiction of the king—like his other functions—
must from the first have been mainly exercised
through subordinate ministers, it is undoubtedly
true that he was originally invested with an absolute and uncontrolled jurisdiction to administer
justice between man and man; and that it was in
his discretion either to exercise it himself, with or
without the advice of his council or other judicial
advisers, or to exercise it through such subordinate
judges as he might think proper from time to time
to appoint; and also that he had and exercised the
power to resume as well as to delegate jurisdiction,
and to abolish as well as to establish courts: 1
Spence's Eq. Jur. *101, *120.

§ 317. Accordingly, it appears that, in the time
of the Conqueror and some of his successors, though
the ordinary administration of justice continued in
the county courts, yet this was altogether by sufferance of the king; and in fact, with regard to a large,
and in those times the most important, class of
cases, they could act only when especially authorized
to do so by the king; for, " as a consequence of the
maxim that all lands were held mediately or immediately of the king, it had become a settled rule that
no one should be put to answer in any court whatever, in regard to his freehold, without the king's
writ. Whether the plea should be decided in the
king's court, or before the sheriff " (the presiding
officer of the county court), " or other person ap-

pointed by the king to act as his justice at one of
the ordinary tribunals, depended on the nature of
the question and the will of the king:" 1 Spence's
Eq. Jur. *111.

§ 318.   Judges were also sometimes appointed by
the king to preside over the county court: 1 Reeves'
Hist. Com. L., Finlayson's ed., 259, note *a;* 1 Spence's
Eq. Jur. *101; and from time to time itinerant justices were also commissioned by the king to hold independent local courts, and these under Henry III,
became a permanent institution under the name of
"justices in eyre:" 1 Spence's Eq. Jur. *101, *115;
but were afterward discontinued.

§ 319.   In the mean time the king himself was
accustomed to exercise a general and constantly increasing jurisdiction in his own court, called the
"aula," or *curia regis;* and ultimately, upon the dis-
continuance of the justices in eyre—the jurisdiction
of the local courts having in the mean time become
obsolete — the general administration of justice
throughout the realm became vested in it; and it
" became the ordinary tribunal for the administration of justice in all questions arising between subjects:" 1 Spence's Eq. Jur. *284.

§ 320.   It is difficult to ascertain from the current
histories of the law the precise nature of the original
constitution of this court; but it seems originally to
have been nothing more than the council, consisting
of the great officers of the palace; and which, though
distinct from the great council or parliament, formed
part of it when assembled.

§ 321.   According to the common account, how-

ever, it seems to have consisted, in the latter part of
the Conqueror's reign, of the king himself, the grand
justiciary, the chancellor, and the other great officers of the palace, " with whom were associated certain persons called justices or *justitiarii*, to the
number of five or six, on whom, with the grand
justiciary, the burden of judicature principally fell.
The justices were the part of this court that was
principally considered, as appears by the return of
writs which was *coram me vel justitiis meis*, unless
that appellation may be supposed to include every
member thereof in his judicial capacity:" 1 Reeves'
Hist. Com. L., Finlayson's ed., 264, 266. It seems,
also, that the great persons who held *in capite* of the
crown, or in other words, the bishops, earls, and
barons, when summoned, were members of this
court, which, however, was then called the *commune
concilium regni*, or parliament: 1 Bac. Abr., tit.
Courts, A; 1 Spence's Eq. Jur. *102, *106, *107,
*119, note. But ordinarily the court consisted
merely of the great officers of the palace and the associated justices, and was presided over by the king
himself, or, in his absence, by the grand justiciary:
1 Reeves' Hist. Com. L., Finlayson's ed., 264. It
was the function of this court originally to advise
the king not only as to judicial proceedings, but also
as to affairs of state and matters of legislation: 1
Bac. Abr., tit. Courts, A; 1 Spence's Eq. Jur. *103;
but in the reign of Henry III the judicial business
of the court was finally separated from the legislative, and "the *curia regis*, for the dispatch of judicial business, was created or finally established:"
Id. *107.

§ 322. From this court, the common-law courts ultimately established were derived in the following order: The first division of jurisdiction took place in the reign of the Conqueror, when a separate division or branch of the court was established, especially charged with matters of revenue, which was called the court of exchequer: 1 Spence's Eq. Jur. *102. This court was composed of the same members as the ordinary court, and seems to have been " very little else than the *curia regis* sitting in another place, namely, *ad scaccarium;* only it happened that the justices, when they sat at the exchequer, were called barons:" 1 Reeves' Hist. Com. L., Finlayson's ed., 269; or, as it is expressed by another writer: "As they sat in the hall, they were a court criminal, and when up- stairs, a court of revenue; civil pleas they heard in either court:" 1 Bac. Abr., tit. Courts, A.

§ 323. A further division of jurisdiction took place in the reign of John, resulting from the provision of Magna Charta, that common pleas should no longer follow the king; and "from this time, chief and other justices were appointed expressly to hear and determine pleas of land and injuries merely civil, which were known as common pleas; and that branch of the king's court was held at Westminster. This is the origin of the court of common pleas:" 1 Spence's Eq. Jur. *103, *104.

§ 324. The court still held before the king, from which the court of common pleas was separated, or the court of the king's bench, as it was afterward designated, continued to be the superior court of law for all criminal matters. . . . . It also held pleas of trespasses accompanied with violence (*vi et armis*), replevin, *quare impedit*, and debt relating to its officers; and it held cognizance of all personal actions where the defendant was already under custody of the court. . . . . This court was the court of appeal from all other courts of record excepting the courts of exchequer. The court of exchequer also continued to be a separate court:" Id. *114, *115.

§ 325. In this way, the king's court was divided into the three courts referred to; namely, the court of king's bench, the court of common pleas, and the court of exchequer, which, in the reign of Edward I, were finally established as they afterward continued to exist until abolished by the judicature act. Of these courts as originally organized, the court of common pleas was the regular court for the transaction of civil business, and had exclusive, or almost exclusive, jurisdiction of civil cases between man and man. The other courts, however, subsequently acquired substantially a concurrent jurisdiction of civil cases.

§ 326. Having thus given an account of the establishment of the common law jurisdiction—the instruments by which the law, as distinguished from equity, was developed—let us now briefly review the development of the law itself from the beginning of the Norman rule down to the period at which the jurisdiction of these courts was finally settled, in the early part of the reign of Edward I.

§ 327. Upon the accession of the Conqueror to the throne of England, there was no formal abrogation of the old Saxon law; but, with some modifications hereafter to be adverted to, the law continued to be the same for some time after the Conquest as before. The positive institutions, or *jus civile* of the Anglo-Saxons, however—like that of all rude societies—related almost exclusively to the political and the criminal law, and hardly touched at all upon matters of private right. "The rules of legal decision among a rude people," says Mr. Hallam, "are always very simple, not serving much to guide, still less to control, the feelings of natural equity. Such were those that prevailed among the Anglo-Saxons; . . . . minute to an excess in apportioning punishments, but sparing and indefinite in treating of civil rights." Hallam's Middle Ages, 347, 348; 1 Spence's Eq. Jur., *86, *282.

§ 328. Nor did even the few and meager provisions as to private rights which did exist long survive the Conquest; for the king's courts—by which, as we have seen, the old local courts were supplanted—were presided over by Norman judges, who were in general ignorant of the laws and customs of the Saxons; and hence it naturally resulted that the Saxon law became obsolete, along with the courts that administered it.

§ 329. This, indeed, is at variance with the theory commonly prevailing with the lawyers, who have always asserted that the English common law is of Saxon origin: 1 Bla. Com. *411, *412. But, however true this opinion may be with reference to constitutional law—which doubtless had its germs in the rude but free institutions of our Saxon ancestors —all competent authorities now agree that with reference to private right the opinion is altogether unfounded. This can be readily verified by a comparison of the provisions of the Saxon codes, as given by Reeves, Spence, or Hallam, with the treatises of Glanville and Bracton, and other early writers on the common law. "The laws of the Anglo-Saxon kings," says Maddox, in a passage quoted by the writers named above, "are as different from those collected by Glanville as the laws of different nations:" Hallam's Middle Ages, Id.; 1 Spence's Eq. Jur. *122, *126; 1 Reeves' Hist. Com. L., c. 4, p. 285. "There is not," adds Reeves, "the least feature of resemblance between them."

§ 330. It must therefore be assumed, as a fact beyond controversy, that the origin of the English common law—by which is here meant the *jus civile* or that part of the law peculiar to the system—is to be sought in the period subsequent to the Conquest. Nor is it difficult, though our records of the period immediately succeeding the Conquest are somewhat scanty, to trace the general course and to understand the precise nature of the development of that law.

§ 331. In the beginning of the Norman rule there was, as we have seen, no developed system of law in England; nor, indeed, with the exception of the few meager provisions of the old Saxon law with reference to private rights, which were soon to become obsolete, was there any law at all other than justice or right, as commonly received in the community.

§ 332. The jurisdiction of the king, therefore,

consisted in the power and duty to administer justice and right, and was, with the exceptions above stated, altogether unrestricted, either by positive regulations or otherwise, except by the nature of the function itself.

§ 333. This jurisdiction was never formally parted with by the king; but was in fact exercised by the king himself, either personally or by judges to whom jurisdiction was temporarily delegated by him; and although in the course of time regular courts came, in the manner we have explained, to be established, they did not as originally constituted, nor did the *curia regis* from which they were derived, have any general jurisdiction to decide all or any particular class of cases; but only a special jurisdiction to determine such particular cases as might be especially referred to them by the king.

§ 334. Hence it became a fundamental principle of the law, and one that exercised a controlling influence in determining the course and nature of its subsequent development, that the king's writ, or, as it was called, "the original writ," was essential in every case to confer jurisdiction upon the court. "This writ was in the form of a precept or mandate from the king, under the great seal, addressed to the sheriff of the county in which the cause of action arose, or where the defendant resided, commanding him to cause the party complained of to appear in the king's court at a certain day to answer the complaint:" 1 Spence's Eq. Jur. *226; 2 Bla. Com. *273. "These writs were made out in the name of the king, but with the teste of the grand judiciary;

for the making and issuing of which (as well as for other offices), the king used to have near his person some great man, usually an ecclesiastic, who was called his chancellor, and had the keeping of his seal:" 1 Reeves' Hist. Com. L., Finlayson's ed., 267.

§ 335. "And for the ease of the chancellor, who, besides having the care of the great seal, had other important duties to perform, there were associated with the chancellor a certain number of clerks, called *præceptores* (afterward masters). . . . . Their duties as regards the issuing of writs were to hear and examine the complaints of those who sought redress in the king's court, and to furnish them with the appropriate writs. . . . . Besides the masters, or superior clerks, there were six other clerks belonging to the chancellor, whose duty it was to engross writs not strictly of course, and junior clerks to write out from the register of the chancery, in which the forms of writs were enrolled, those writs which were of course:" 1 Spence's Eq. Jur. *238, *239. This description of the function of the chancellor and his clerks in the issuing of original writs is to be understood, however, as referring only to latter times, when his jurisdiction, like that of the common-law judges had become established by usage, to the exclusion of that of the king.

§ 336. Hence the form and nature of actions, and the question whether in any particular case an action would lie, were determined by the original writ, or, what amounts to the same thing, by the chancellor, upon whom devolved the function of

.   15

determining the cases in which the writ should issue.

§ 337. This function was strictly judicial in its
nature, and consisted merely in determining whether
in the case presented there was a right for which a
remedy was required. For it was the recognized
function of the king to protect the rights of his subjects, and to administer justice between them.

§ 338. The functions of the chancellor were therefore, in this respect, substantially identical with those
of the prætor in the Roman law—that is to say, in
the one case it was the function of the prætor, and
in the other of the chancellor, to determine whether
upon the facts presented an action would lie, and
the form and nature of the action.

§ 339. In other respects, however, the functions
of the chancellor differed from those of the prætor;
"for, though the chancellor issued all writs, the
judges of the common-law courts assumed exclusive
jurisdiction to decide upon their validity, disregarding the sanction of the chancellor and his college
of clerks. Nor could the chancellor declare what
should be a sufficient defense to an action; indeed,
with this part of the judicial machinery he had no
opportunity to interfere:" 1 Spence's Eq. Jur. *324,
*325.

§ 340. While on the one hand, therefore, the jurisdiction of the common-law courts was limited to
the cases delegated to them by the chancellor, on
the other hand, the jurisdiction of the chancellor to
grant writs was limited by that of the common-law
courts.

§ 341. From this and the strict subserviency to the authority of former decisions, which at this period and for some centuries afterward characterized the common-law courts, it resulted that the forms of writs originally devised (a register of which was kept in the chancery), came to be regarded as precedents beyond which the power of the chancellor to grant writs could not be exercised. On the other hand, in all cases where a precedent could be found in the register, the writ issued as of course, and thus the function of granting writs, originally judicial, ultimately became merely ministerial. The jurisdiction of the common-law courts thus became, in effect, a general jurisdiction over all that class of cases for which precedents could be found in the register, instead of a special jurisdiction in each case delegated to it, but was rigidly limited by the precedents.

§ 342. With this change in jurisdiction a corresponding change also took place in the nature of the law itself. As we have seen in the beginning, the exercise of jurisdiction, whether by the chancellor or judges or by the king, was unembarrassed by positive rules, either statutory or established by precedent, and cases were decided by the principles of natural justice generally received in the community. At that time, therefore, the administration of justice, in so far as the functions of the courts were properly performed, was in fact precisely what its name indicated; which is but to say, in other words, that right or justice constituted the law, and the only law of private right, or *jus*, at that time existing in England. In the end, however, not only had the power of the chancellor to issue new writs ceased, or rather ceased to be exercised, and the jurisdiction of the courts thus come to be limited by the precedents found in the register, but in exercising even this limited jurisdiction, the judges had imposed upon themselves the fetters of an iron rule which bound them rigidly to follow their own prior decisions and those of other judges. Thus the law, or rather the *jus civile*, or positive law, became in the main a mere body of rules established by precedent or the custom of the court; and at this period, therefore, we find very nearly realized the ideal of those jurists who hold that the law consists, or ought to consist, of rigid rules, at once absolutely controlling and limiting the jurisdiction of the courts, and unsusceptible of change except by legislative power.

§ 343. We may also add that it would be difficult to conceive of a more perfect *reductio ad absurdum* of the theory itself than was presented of the law at this time, or a more striking illustration of the truth of Lord Mansfield's remark (*supra*, § 420, subd. 15), that "the law of England would be an absurd science if founded on precedents only." For in establishing the rule that for the future justice should be administered only in those cases in which it had previously happened to be administered, the chancellor and judges to that extent had abdicated the function of administering justice which had been intrusted to them; and thus the law as administered by them had become grossly inadequate to the administration of justice; and the clearest and most obvious rights were often without remedy.

§ 344. It is not, however, to be assumed that the law, though thus modified, had undergone any *essential* change in its nature. Every step in its development had consisted in the application of principles, or supposed principles, of natural right to cases actually presented; and hence in theory, and so far forth as the function of the courts had been well performed in fact also, the law still continued to be natural right; for, as already observed, the fact that principles of natural right were recognized by the courts did not in any way alter their essential nature. Hence the sole question as to the nature of the law at this period is, not whether its principles were recognized and rigidly observed, but whether those principles were or were not in fact rational and just; and upon this question, there is no room to doubt but that an affirmative answer must be given.

§ 345. For though errors and mistakes had occurred, and false principles had thus to some extent become established in the law, the work in the main had been well done; and though the process of development had been checked by the absurd regard at that time paid to precedent and authority, and the remedial part of the law had thus become grossly inadequate to the administration of justice, it was in the main, as far as it went, rational in its character; and the law, as a whole, fairly justified the assertion of Coke and other lawyers that "the common law itself is nothing else but reason."

§ 346. For fortunately for the interests of civilization, the earlier judges and chancellors, who were generally ecclesiastics, were all more or less familiar with the Roman civil law, and did not hesitate to avail themselves freely of its rational principles; and thus there was rapidly developed a system of law or right, consisting, like the civil law itself—from which it was mainly adopted—in principles of natural right, differing from the popular notions of justice only in being more logically developed and expressed.[1]

§ 347. It is also to be observed that the law as then established had not reached anything like the stage of development at which it has now arrived. For at that time, nothing like a complete system of right had been developed; but the positive law consisted mainly of the remedial law, or the law of actions, and it therefore did not to any considerable extent purport to create or to define rights; but assumed their independent existence, and simply provided remedies for their enforcement.

§ 348. The continued existence of the principles of natural right as part of the law was therefore necessarily implied, and without them the law would have been fragmentary and incomplete.

§ 349. Thus the sole remedies of that time for the enforcement of contracts were the actions of debt and covenant; the former of which lay for the recovery of a debt, that is, a liquidated or a certain sum of money alleged to be due, and the latter for

---

[1] For an interesting account of the influence of the Roman upon the early English law, see passages from Mr. Spence's "Equity Jurisprudence," cited in note at the end of this chapter.

the breach of a contract under seal or specialty: 1 Spence's Eq. Jur. *224. These actions, though manifestly inadequate, rested upon, and therefore implied, the principle of contract; and that principle, therefore, constituted part of the law, not only to the extent to which it was actually recognized and enforced by the courts, but in its entirety. For it constituted the reason or ground of the positive rules of the law providing for the establishment and conduct of these actions, and in which, indeed, they originated; and it is a maxim, as well of the law as of reason, that the law consists not in particular precedents, but in the reason upon which they rest; and accordingly, as we shall see, adequate remedies have been gradually introduced, not by legislative enactment, but by the courts acting upon the same principle that gave rise to the original remedy; namely, that every right should have its appropriate action.

§ 350. Accordingly, we find the existence of rights independently of actions clearly recognized by the statute of Westminster 2, 13 Edw. I, c. 24, which was enacted for the express purpose of authorizing the issuing of writs in cases where rights might exist for which there was no appropriate remedy, by which it was provided "that as often as it shall happen in the chancery that in one case a writ shall be found, and in a like case (*in consimili casu*), falling under the same right and requiring like remedy, no writ shall be found, the clerks in chancery shall agree in making a writ, or adjourn the complaint till the next parliament, and write the cases in which they can not _agree, and refer them to the next parliament."

§ 351. Had this act been originally construed as liberally as it has been in modern times, it would have gone far to remedy the evil which it was designed to obviate, and perhaps, as Sir William Blackstone has remarked, "might effectually have answered all the purposes of a court of equity:" 3 Com. *351; but the act itself was defective in conferring power to issue writs *in consimili casu* only, and not in entirely new cases; and the same mental habits in the judges which had caused the original evil prevented them from giving it a liberal construction.

§ 352. Hence the evil remained unabated, and the jurisdiction of the common-law courts continued to be grossly inadequate to the performance of the function for which they had been originally created; namely, the administration of justice.

§ 353. It is to be observed also in considering what the law of England was at this time, that we can not confine our attention to the law as administered by the ordinary courts; for the jurisdiction of those courts was only part of the general jurisdiction to administer justice originally vested in the king; and there still remained vested in him an extraordinary or prerogative jurisdiction, not only to supply the defects in the jurisdiction of the courts, and to administer justice in cases not provided for, but also to relieve against hardship and injustice in the exercise of the jurisdiction delegated to the courts: 1 Spence's Eq. Jur. 326 *et seq.*

§ 354. This jurisdiction had from the first exist-ed, and had been exercised by the king either in person or by referring particular cases to his coun-cil or the chancellor; but in the reign of Edward III, owing to the inadequacy of the ordinary juris-diction to the complete administration of justice, the cases calling for its exercise had become too numer-ous to be conveniently disposed of in this way; and probably in consequence of this, a writ of ordinance was issued in the twenty-second year of that reign, conferring upon the chancellor general jurisdiction of all cases calling for extraordinary or equitable relief.

§ 355. "The establishment of the court of chan-cery as a regular court for administering extraor-dinary jurisdiction is generally considered to have been mainly attributable to this or some similar ordinance:" 1 Spence's Eq. Jur. *338; and the re-sult was, that this court became vested with all the jurisdiction remaining in the king; which, as we have seen, extended not only to supplying the de-fects, but also to relieving against the injustice of the jurisdiction exercised by the common-law courts; and was therefore at once suppletory to and correct-ive of the ordinary jurisdiction.

§ 356. The jurisdiction of the court of chancery, therefore, while limited in one direction by the ju-risdiction delegated to the common-law courts—so far as the same was adequate to the administration of justice—was in other respects unlimited; and it therefore extended to the administration of justice or right between man and man in all cases where the jurisdiction of the common-law courts was inadequate to the purpose.

§ 357. In the exercise of this jurisdiction, the chancellor was avowedly governed by the principles of natural right. This is indicated by the title of the court—which, as we have said, was called the court of equity—and also by various terms, all expressing the idea of natural right, such as conscience, good faith, honesty, reason, justice, right and equity, which were habitually used to denote the principles by which his decisions were determined. That this was true of the court as originally organized, and for several centuries afterward, is agreed upon all sides, and it must therefore be taken as an admitted fact that during this period—which may be roughly defined as extending into the reign of Charles II—justice or right in the ordinary and familiar sense of the terms, or in other words, natural justice or right, avowedly constituted the rule by which the decisions of the chancellor were governed, and therefore constituted the law, or *jus*, of England, so far forth as administered in the court presided over by him: 1 Spence's Eq. Jur. * 339, * 341, *346, *407, *408; 1 Pomeroy's Eq. Jur. secs. 46, 50, 55; 1 Fonbl. Eq., b. 1, c. 1, sec. 3; 1 Story's Eq. Jur., secs. 8, 21. Our proposition, therefore, that it is the function of the courts to administer justice or right in the ordinary and familiar sense of the term, and that there is no essential distinction between positive and natural right, is true at least with reference to the jurisprudence administered by the courts of chancery during the period referred to.

§ 358. Since the time of Blackstone, however, an opinion has prevailed that, prior to the time of that writer, the jurisprudence administered by the court of chancery had undergone, not a mere modification in form, but an essential change in its nature, and that, though still retaining the name of equity, it had become in fact a system of positive law. This change is supposed to have commenced in the reign of Charles II, with the chancellorship of Sir Heneagè Finch (afterward Lord Nottingham), from whose time, says Chancellor Kent (1 Kent's Com. 492), " equity became a regular and cultivated science," and to have been substantially completed during the term of Lord Hardwicke. It is supposed that in effecting this change, those chancellors performed the function of legislators, and, as it were, established a code, after the manner of Solon or Lycurgus; and that equity, as ultimately developed, was no longer in fact equity, but law in the strict sense: 1 Story's Eq. Jur., sec. 52; 1 Pomeroy's Eq. Jur., secs. 47, 57, 58, 59, 62, 63.

§ 359. The first of these propositions, namely, that equity has become positive law, is no doubt true, except in so far as it asserts that, in becoming positive law, it has undergone any essential change in its nature. For it is undoubtedly true that equity as it now exists, and as it has for a long time existed as part of the law of England, is of essentially the same nature as what is technically termed the law, and differs from it only in being more rational and scientific in its development; but the opinion is without foundation that the modification in its form has taken place principally since the accession of Sir Heneage Finch to the bench; and it is also untrue that its nature has undergone any essential change from what it originally was, or that it is now no longer equity, but a body of laws or rules analogous to law established by statute. Even with regard to the law itself, the latter proposition is, as we have seen, untrue, and with reference to equity, its fallacy is still more apparent. For the proposition rests upon the assumption that the courts, in exercising their jurisdiction, not only determine the particular case presented, but also by their decisions establish rules in the nature of laws for future cases—a proposition, as we show elsewhere, in itself absurd, and which, whatever color may be given to it by the doctrine of *stare decisis* as anciently held by the common lawyers, can not at least be affirmed without absurdity of the decisions of the chancellor. For while the chancellors, under the influence of a principle of human nature, which seems to be universal, always observed a due and proper respect for precedent and custom, precedents were never held by them at least until a comparatively late period, to be of binding authority, like decisions at law; and it has been well remarked, "if they had been, ... a court of equity must afterward have been erected to correct the court of chancery:" 1 Spence's Eq. Jur. *416.

§ 360. Indeed, the doctrine of *stare decisis* as originally held at common law has never to this day obtained a footing in equity: 1 Pomeroy's Eq. Jur., secs. 60 *et seq;* and *vide* the opinion of Lord Hardwicke there cited; and though now the maxim is equally observed by courts of law and courts of equity, and no distinction exists in the manner or in the extent to which it is applied by the two respectively, this is because the maxim itself has become modified, and no longer requires a slavish subservience to the mistakes and errors of fallible men. It is difficult to say at what precise time the doctrine of *stare decisis* in its present form became established in equity, but certainly not before the period when it became customary for lawyers to preside over the court of chancery (which commenced in the reign of. Henry VIII), and probably not until much later: Fry *v.* Porter, 1 Mod. 300, 307, 309, 312; and at the commencement of this period, all the leading principles of equity had been developed, and equity itself had already become a system of positive law. ⁓

§ 361. It is indeed true that in latter times equity has undergone a still further development, and that since the reign of Charles II its development has been more rapid and striking than at any other time. But this is the result of the remarkable advance of science and industrial civilization, which commenced shortly before that time; and a similar development has at the same time taken place in the common law, at least one half of which (as is remarked by Story in a passage cited with approval by Spence), " has had its origin since the reign of Elizabeth:" 1 Story's Eq. Jur., sec. 646, cited 1 Spence's Eq. Jur. *714, note. Nor did this development, as seems to have been supposed by Story (1 Story's Eq. Jur., sec. 52) commence with Sir Heneage Finch, or end with

Lord Hardwicke; but it was part of a continuous development which commenced with the first establishment of the jurisdiction, and has gone on without interruption to the present day—a development common both to law and equity, and which is yet in actual progress.

§ 362. Of the nature of this development, we have only to repeat here what has already been said as to the development of law in general and of the old English law in particular. Every step in its progress has avowedly consisted in the application of principles, or supposed principles, of natural right to actual controversies presented, and has therefore been strictly judicial, and not legislative in its character. Hence, precisely to the extent that the function of the judges has been rightly performed, the law, or rather *jus*, consists of principles of natural right, and in fact is natural right.

§ 363. The fact that its principles, or most of its principles, are, and for a long time have been, recognized and observed by the courts—some of them for ages—is not inconsistent with the proposition that they still continue to be principles of natural right, but on the contrary, constitutes the most conclusive proof of their character as such. For it may be stated as a universal proposition that no principle can ever endure in the law unless it is a true principle of right, and that in the law, as elsewhere, the words of the poet are true:

> "Truth crushed to earth shall rise again,
> The eternal years of God are hers;
> But Error, wounded, writhes with pain,
> And dies among its worshipers."

§ 364. Hence the *jus civile* of every system,
though often asserted to be immutable except by legislation, is always constantly though slowly changing, and at the end of different stages in the progress
of the law is altogether different from what it was
in the beginning. "For," as Coke says in a passage
already quoted, "the principles of natural right are
perfect and immutable, but the condition of human
law is ever changing, and there is nothing in it which
can stand forever. Human laws are born, live and
die."

§ 365. Thus, as we have seen, the old Saxon law
—which was, so far as it had become positive, almost.
exclusively *jus civile*—though never formally abrogated, soon became obsolete. So, if we compare the
law as it existed in the time of Edward I, or even
at a much later period, with the law as it exists in
America at the present day, we find that nothing
remains of it but those principles of natural right
which had then become recognized, and that all that
was peculiar to the system, and which ran "counter
to the *jus commune*, or common natural rule of right"
(Kaufman's Mackeldy, 121), or in other words, the
jus civile of that day, has silently and almost spontaneously passed away. Thus the principle—eternal
and immutable—that every man has a right to the
return of his property which he has intrusted to
another, or of which he has been unjustly deprived,
is still and must ever be a principle of the law; but
the inadequate forms of action then provided for the
enforcement of the right, after having been gradually, and without legislative enactment, supple-

mented by others, have finally been abolished. So the principle that the payment of a debt extinguishes the obligation is now, as it was then, a principle of the law; but the arbitrary rule that the action upon a sealed instrument could only be extinguished by acquittance or release under seal (Doctor and Student, cited *supra*) no longer survives. So, too, the principles of natural justice determining the right of property in land are the same now as then, but the technical and sometimes absurd rules which grew out of the feudal system, and so long survived as a reproach to the English law, have in America, by statute or otherwise, all been abolished; and the principles of our real-estate law, though still incumbered by an immense amount of obsolete rubbish, are in the main purely rational, and require only a competent hand to reduce them to the same noble simplicity of form which characterizes the corresponding portion of the civil law.

§ 366. Hence, though errors have occurred and false principles have thus become established, they have never endured, but have ultimately been or will be eradicated; and hence *jus* has constantly approximated to perfection, and as it now stands, is more nearly identical with natural right than ever before; or, what is the same thing, and may perhaps be more readily admitted, the rights of men are now more fully recognized and in theory protected than at any former time. Nor can there be a greater error than to suppose—as it has become too common to suppose—that the logical and scientific method which has effected such great results has become no longer applicable to the law; for the law is still far from being perfect, especially in form, and we must in the future look to the same method for its perfection, and for the ultimate realization of justice and right on earth.

Note to § 346. "In the reign of Stephen, whether from the discovery of a .perfect copy of the Pandects at Amalphi, or from whatever cause, the study of the Roman law was prosecuted at Bologna with great ardor. In the same reign, A. D. 1143, Archbishop Theobald, the predecessor and instructor of the celebrated Chancellor and Archbishop Thomas à Becket, who himself studied the civil law at Bologna, brought Vacarius, a distinguished Italian jurist, to England. Vacarius, shortly afterward, A. D. 1149, established a school of civil law at Oxford, where he taught with great success. Stephen, instigated, as is supposed, by the bishop of Winchester, Theobald's declared enemy, issued an ordinance prohibiting Vacarius from teaching; but this, instead of putting a stop to the study of the Roman law, had, it seems, the opposite effect. Vacarius composed a summary of the Roman law, which comprises extracts from the Pandects and the code of Justinian, to which he added a commentary, and explanatory notes. It seems that he continued in England down to 1170, at which time he had entered into holy orders, but without renouncing his office of teacher. Peter, of Blois, Archdeacon of London, A. D. 1200, and other eminent persons, studied under Vacarius, and the Roman law became well known to, and, as we shall see, the subject of study with the judges and professors of the law of England; it was even occasionally had recourse to, directly, in the civil tribunals down to the time of Richard II; and professors of the civil law were frequently advanced to be judges of the supreme courts of law. (1 Spencer's Eq. Jur. 108-9.) . . . .

In the reign of Edward the First, from whose time, according to Lord Hale, the whole scheme of English law may date its existence, many treatises appeared. The principal of these are that entitled Fleta, which was written by some learned person confined in the Fleet prison, about the thirteenth year of Edw. I; that which was written by Britton, who is supposed to have been a judge; one by Gilbert de Thornton, who was a chief justice; and another entitled the Mirror of Justices. Bracton's work is, in the

16

main, the ground-work of all these productions. The sources from which these several treatises, particularly Bracton's, were compiled, as they exhibit the rudiments of the law of the present day, naturally excite our curiosity.

When these treatises were compiled the German legislation of the codes of the Anglo-Saxons had become wholly superseded; nor are the Conqueror's Anglo-Norman code or the treatise in the Red Book of the Exchequer, entitled the Laws of Hen. I, ever referred to in them. Some, indeed, of the customs which grew up in the Anglo-Saxon times, molded so as to suit the circumstances of society by the decisions of the justices in eyre, are to be recognized; the doctrine of tenure in particular, the sources of which have already been pointed out, which commenced in the Anglo-Saxon times and was made universal at the Conquest, is the foundation of the system of jurisprudence as to property in land which is to be found in these treatises. But a great proportion of the doctrines which we find in them, are there presented for the first time (at least, in the shape in which they appear), if the documents which have been handed down to us are all that had previously existed relating to the law. These doctrines, no doubt, had been long previously recognized in the king's court; new subjects of litigation had, as before observed, been brought before that tribunal, and novel doctrines arose on the change in the tribunal to which litigated questions were now submitted; and the doctrines which governed that tribunal which had then exclusive jurisdiction over these various subjects, necessarily became the common law of the land. For the sources of most of these doctrines we must look to other monuments than the indigenous codes and records of Saxon and Norman Britain.

The school of Vacarius in which Bracton and many others of the judges had studied, had rendered accessible to all a body of laws which contained provisions applicable in specie to most, in principle to all, the questions that could be presented for judicial decision.

To have neglected to take advantage of the assistance which was thus offered, would have argued a high degree of presumption, or gross and culpable ignorance; neither is to be imputed to the founders of our system of jurisprudence.

A reference to the treatise of Glanville, but more especially to the more comprehensive one of Bracton (neither of whom professes to treat of any law then for the first time introduced, or to quote authorities not before referred to), plainly shows that the doctrines of the Roman law had been before, and were then, largely resorted to in the king's court. To this, perhaps, we may attribute the rapid establishment of the scientific system of jurisprudence, which has been remarked by Sir William Blackstone, indeed by almost every writer, as having grown up in the interval including the reign of Henry II and Edward I.

Glanville, indeed, though in stating the principles which govern the important subject of contracts he has evidently borrowed from the Institutes of Justinian, avoids all notice of the sources from which they were obtained. Bracton also introduces from the Roman law, without reference to their source, the great leading principles of justice, and numerous Roman maxims and doctrines, on a great variety of subjects. The Roman doctrines relating to contracts and obligations, which he notices and explains, appear to have been incorporated in the common law as administered in the king's court, and by the justices in eyre, long before his time. Bracto1 adopts the titles, and to a great extent, the method of the Institutes. The term prætor is sometimes used to designate a common law judge. *Jus civile* is distinguished from *jus prætorium*, which, in Bracton's sense, is the law formed by the decisions of the judges. This *jus prætorium* has been continually enlarged by the common law judges, so as to form a very considerable proportion of the common law of England.

But in numerous instances Bracton expressly quotes or refers to the Institutes, the Digest, and the Code, even when treating of assizes of novel disseizin, to which some doctrines were applied, which may be found in the Roman law. Sometimes he has taken the summary or digest of the Roman law compiled by Azo as his guide. Bracton also refers to the technical actions of *condictio rei furtivæ, actio vi bonorum raptorum, actio legis acquiliæ,* etc., as being known forms of action; also to the obligation by stipulation, that is, by interrogation and response. Roman names also are adopted in the illustrations, precisely after the manner of the Roman lawyers. Bracton also adopts from the Institutes, the law *de libellis (carminibus) famosis;* other similar instances might be cited.

The other sources to which the writers, at least from the time of Bracton, referred, were the rolls of the justices in eyre, principally, if not exclusively, of the reign of Hen. III. These justices, in early times, were generally ecclesiastics, and their decisions would no doubt be influenced by the doctrines of the Roman law where they were applicable; indeed, but for the authority of the Roman law having been recognized, to some extent at least, by the decisions of the judges, Bracton, himself a judge, would hardly have ventured directly to cite the books of the *corpus juris*, and that to the extent above described; Ings, chief justice of the common pleas, 5 Edw. II, expressly declared that the law of the land was founded on the Imperial law.

The reverence for the Roman law, which had been traditionally handed down through the clergy, independently of express adoption, must have operated to facilitate its being so largely resorted to when its stores were opened." (Id. 122-4.) . . . .

"Mr. Reeves (vol. ii., p. 88), after eulogizing Bracton's Treatise, notices the exceptions taken to it on account of the quotations from the Roman law. 'But the passages,' says this industrious writer, 'to which such writers take exception, if put together, would perhaps not fill three whole pages of his book, and it may be doubted whether they are such as can mislead the reader.' Again, 'upon a second consideration,' he says, 'of those places where the Roman law is stated with the most confidence, it would seem to be rather alluded to for illustration and ornament than adduced as an authority, though it is visible that Bracton, with all his endeavors to give form and beauty to our own law by setting forth its native strength to advantage, did not refuse such helps as could be derived from other sources to improve and augment it.' (But see p. 54 of the same volume.) My own observation would lead me to say, as indeed will appear from what has already been stated and what follows in the succeeding chapters, that there is scarcely a principle of law incorporated in the treatise of Bracton, that has survived to our times, which may not be traced to the Roman law. Bracton's direct references plainly do not comprise nearly the whole of what he adopted immediately from the *corpus juris*. I am aware that most of our historians, and, with the exception of Civilians, of the writers on the Laws of England, as well before as since the publication of Mr. Reeves' history, have advocated the independence of the law of England. Lord Lyttelton, particularly in his admirable History of the Life and Times of Henry II, which has formed the basis of most of the subsequent histories of that epoch, refers to a solitary decision of Glanville in regard to the law of bastardy (which is cited, evidently with approbation, by Mr. Beames, p. 183, of his edition) as showing ' the entire independence of the law of England on the canon and civil laws in his time '—a large conclusion from such premises. As regards legal authority on the subject, Mr. Cruise observes (v. p. 66-7) that our legal writers, since the time of Bracton, appear either to have been ignorant of the obligations we owe to the Romans, or, from mistaken pride, to have been extremely unwilling to acknowledge them." (Id. 131-2.) . . . .

" The form which was adopted on the introduction of the modern mode of procedure in England was by action; and actions were divided into two classes, *personal* and *real*, as with the Romans. The latter were in England designated by some of the old writers as feudal actions, by reason that they were confined to the recovery of real property, namely, land, houses, etc., and rights connected with land, as rents, commons, and the like; as, indeed, was generally the practice amongst the Romans, though slaves were frequently the subject of this description of action. Personal actions are described to be such whereby a man claims a debt, or personal duty, or damages, in lieu thereof; and likewise whereby a man claims a satisfaction in damages for some injury done to his person or property. The former are said to be founded on contracts, *ex contractu*, the latter upon torts or wrongs, *ex delicto*, or *ex maleficio*, and they are the same which are described as *actiones in personam* in the passages which have been cited in a former chapter. (3 Bla. Comm. 117.) Mr. Justice Blackstone here, as in many other instances, refers expressly to the Institutes of Justinian (iv. 6, s. I, 15, etc.), as was noticed in a preceding chapter, *supra*, p. 186. In truth, the whole of the doctrines as to personal actions were based upon the Institutes, and the Digest through Bracton, as will be evident from the references already made, and from the extracts set out in the additional note to this chapter, which might be largely increased; not that the Roman law was made by statute, or otherwise, of binding authority, in this or any other instance where it was adopted; it had its force solely from usage and common consent, for ' *Sola Anglia usa est in suis finibus, jure non scripto et consuetudine, in ea quidem ex non scripto jus venit quod usus comprobavit.*' Bracton, fo. I, a. The evidence of that consent was the decisions of the judges in the king's courts, and the treatises of Glanville, Bracton, etc." (Id. 224.) . . . .

"*Personales vero actiones sunt quæ competunt* con*t*ra aliquem ex contractu vel quasi, ex maleficio vel quasi, cum quis teneatur ad aliquid dandum vel faciendum; etc. . . . .

It will be seen by reference to the texts cited in the preceding chapter, that these passages are taken almost literally from the Digest and Institutes; many other extracts of a similar nature might be added. Looking to what has been said before, it appears to me that this can only be accounted for in one of two ways; namely, either that the *corpus juris* was so continually referred to by the king's justices—as it was by the Lombards—that Bracton took these passages from the Digest and Institutes, or at least Azo's Commentary, as being part of the *lex non scripta* or customary law of the land, which he professes to collect, or, that these doctrines had become, by constant previous reference, aided by tradition, the settled law of the king's court; so that the common or customary law might be clothed in the language of the Digest and Institutes.

These passages can hardly be said to have been introduced for illustration of the existing law; they are evidently quoted as the existing law." (Id. 234–5.)

"We have seen that, so early as the reigns of Henry II and III, a complete and comprehensive system was formed which, having been perfected in so short time, if we were to look to it as a mere creation, would excite our astonishment. Systematic treatises, in which the principles of the common law were laid down and expounded in a way that rendered them worthy of being referred to as text books by the greatest luminary of the law, Lord Coke, were compiled from recorded precedents, where such could be found; where this resource failed by reference to the *corpus juris* itself—a circumstance that leads to the conclusion that the Roman law, whether as it had been handed down by tradition, or as it was to be found in the Theodosian Code, and the treatises and books which had been from time to time in use amongst the clergy, had been for a long time before largely resorted to by the justices of the king's court, who in the times we are contemplating. were almost universally of the ecclesiastical order.

'Inasmuch as the law of all nations,' says Lord C. J. Holt, 'are doubtless raised out of the ruins of the civil (Roman) law, as all governments are sprung out of the Roman empire, it must be owned that the principles of our law are borrowed from the civil law, and therefore governed by the same reason in many things.' Lord C. J. Holt, 12 Mod. R., p. 482; and see Wood's Institute of the Civil Law, p. XI, Ed. 1721, quoted in Dr. Irving's Introd., p. 95, to the same effect.

The extent to which the principles and maxims of the Roman laws had been adopted in framing the then laws of England, is indicated by the remarkable fact that the whole machinery of common law writs, by which alone the rights of property could be maintained or enforced, in the reign of Edward I, was committed to the discretion and the exclusive superintendence of persons who were doctors of the civil law, and members of the clerical body, with an ecclesiastical dignitary, not a judge of either of the common law courts, at their head.

In the reign of Richard II, as will be particularly adverted to hereafter, all resorts to the Roman law in the common law courts ceased, just as it happened with the Visigoths, whose code was avowedly compiled for the most part from the Roman law. The judges were content with the treatises that had been written by their own countrymen, and the precedents which they found, and which they enlarged so far as their powers extended; the legislature, to some extent, also affording its aid. From this time the common law may be considered as having become really English, that is, founded on decisions in the English courts, and the writings of English judges and jurists, and on the enactments of the English legislature. We look in vain in the records of the common law, which was thus constructed, and which is the basis of the present law of the land, for any remains of the Anglo-Saxon laws embodied in their codes, which can with any certainty be denominated native, excepting perhaps, the succession to personal property in case of intestacy." (Id. 285-6.) . . . .

" In the reign of Richard II, the barons protested that they would never suffer the kingdom to be governed by the Roman law, and the judges prohibited it from being any longer cited in the common law tribunals. Perhaps one object on the part of the judges might have been to exclude the doctrine as to *fidei commissa*, or trusts, which, as we shall see, first came distinctly into notice in this reign. The effect, however, of the exclusion of the Roman law from the common law tribunals, was, as will be more particularly noticed when I come to treat of trusts, that a distinct code of laws was formed and administered in the court of chancery, by which the enjoyment and alienation of property were regulated on principles varying in many essential particulars from the system which those who originated and carried into effect the exclusion of the Roman law, were so anxious to preserve.

Nor were these united endeavors for the exclusion of the Roman law, as it appears to me, less important in fixing the appointment of the office of chancellor in the members of the clerical body.

Notwithstanding all the efforts that were made to repress them, trusts soon became general.   Some rules for their regulation were absolutely necessary; it was from the Roman law they had sprung up; who so proper to introduce and systematize the necessary rules for their regulation, as those who were now exclusively conversant with this law, and who alone, as it was excluded from the common law courts, could resort to it for their guidance? Accordingly, from this time (with some exceptions, which only tend to affirm the general proposition), none but clerical chancellors were appointed, down to the 21st year of Henry VIII." (Id. 346-7.) . . . .

BOOK III.

HISTORICAL AND CRITICAL REVIEW OF THE SEVERAL THEORIES OF JURISPRUDENCE.

CHAPTER I.

STATEMENT OF THE SEVERAL THEORIES OF THE LAW.

§ 367. We have observed (*supra*, § 214) that in every civil suit the immediate question to be determined by the court is whether the force of the government shall be used in behalf of the plaintiff to compel some act or forbearance on the part of the defendant; that this power of coercing another by means of the force of the state is called an action; and that the immediate question, therefore, in such controversies, is to determine whether the plaintiff has an action against the defendant or otherwise; that whether an action exists is to be determined in every case, not by the result of the particular suit, but by general principles applicable to all similar cases, and that of these principles, the fundamental one is, that wherever there is a right there shall be an action; or, as it is expressed in a maxim common to our own and the Roman law, *Ubi jus ibi remedium* (where there is a right there is a remedy); and also that the reverse of this proposition is true—all actions being in theory mere means of enforcing rights. To this extent, all theories of the law must, and in fact do, agree; for it is a fact too obvious to admit of denial that it is the function of the courts to determine and enforce rights, and that the performance of this function constitutes in fact the sole business of courts of civil jurisdiction.

§ 368. With regard to the nature of rights, however, two different and indeed contradictory theories prevail. According to one, the rights which the courts enforce, or assume to enforce, are rights in the ordinary, familiar and proper sense of the term; or in other words (as in this sense, the term connotes or necessarily implies the quality of rightness), they are what are sometimes, though unnecessarily, called *moral* rights. This theory may, therefore, with propriety be called the *jural* theory of rights, and its advocates the *jurists.*

§ 369. The latter term, indeed, seems open to the objection that it has already been appropriated to denote the lawyers or students of the law; and its use in the manner suggested seems, therefore, to imply that these are to be classed among the advocates of jural theory. This, however, as will be shown more fully hereafter, is in fact the case; and hence our use of the term will be found to be doubly appropriate.

§ 370. The jurists are to be divided into two schools, which have been respectively called the historical and the philosophical, but which may with more propriety be termed the practical and the scientific.

§ 371. The former regard the law as consisting of the jural principles, or notions of right or justice,

established in the manners and customs of the
people, without seeking any further foundation for
those principles than the fact that they are so established; or in other words, they regard the law as
resting upon custom. This conception is embodied
in the old definition of the common law of England
as consisting of the general customs of the realm: 1
Bla. Com. *62, *67; and also in one of the definitions of the *jus gentium* of the Roman lawyers, as
being "the law or *jus* commonly observed by all
men;" *jus gentium est quo gentes humanæ utuntur:
Vide infra,* § 403. And this, indeed, is the primitive
conception, not only of justice, but of morality generally; as is indicated by the etymology of that term,
and also by that of the kindred terms "ethics,"
"mores," "*dike,*" etc.

§ 372. We find, however, universally accompanying the principles thus established, the conception
of just and unjust. This is recognized by the historical as well as by the philosophical jurists; but
they differ in this, viz., that the former accept the
received principles of right, or at least the more
fundamental of them, as ultimate facts; while the
latter hold that they are in the main but expressions,
more or less accurate, of necessary truths, which are
susceptible of scientific proof. In other words, the
one asserts and the other denies, or rather fails to
recognize, the scientific nature of the principles of
justice or right, and of morality generally.[1]

[1] This remark is, however, to be understood as applying only to
the fundamental principles of *jus;* for otherwise both schools have
treated the law scientifically, and the former—as, for instance, in
the case of Savigny—with perhaps more success than the latter.

§ 373. The historical theory corresponds precisely with the etymology of the term "*jus*," which is derived from *jur*, to bind: Skeat's Etym. Dict.; Leverett's Lat. Lex.; and originally denoted merely the aggregate of the principles or rules regarded by the community as binding or compulsory on men in their dealings with each other; the philosophical, to the latter signification of the term, and to that of its derivative, *justitia*, and of its modern equivalents, *right*, *recht*, *droit*, etc. And the difference between the two schools is perhaps precisely indicated by the advance from the primitive conception originally denoted by *jus*, to the conception of right or justice as now commonly held.

§ 374. The historical theory is therefore inadequate rather than false, and is in fact included in the philosophical; for in jurisprudence, as well as in morality generally, the practical standard to which rights are habitually referred, and by which they are in fact determined, is the general conscience, or, to use the Greek term *nomos;* or in other words, the concurring moral convictions of the people; and both schools hold this to be the legitimate, and indeed only possible practical standard. The philosophical jurists, however, while they accept received notions as the practical standard, go further, and hold that these notions should be subjected to the test of reason in order that they may be either scientifically vindicated, or, if wrong, gradually corrected.[1] We may

[1] The difference between the two schools may indeed be regarded as one of method only, and these methods, so far from being opposed to each other, are both essential to the investigation of all questions of social philosophy.

therefore class the two schools together, under the common appellation of jurists.

§ 375. Accordingly, we find that jurists pass habitually and unconsciously from one school to the other. Thus, the old common lawyers, while they defined the law as consisting of general customs (*supra*, § 371), also asserted that reason was the life of the law, and indeed, that the law itself was nothing else but reason: *Infra*, § 420. So the Roman lawyers defined the *jus gentium* as the *jus* commonly observed by all peoples, and also as the *jus* which reason has established among all men: *Infra*, § 403. So also Aristotle defines the *nomos koinos*, or common law, as "the unwritten rules which appear to be recognized among all men," and also as "that which is conformable merely to the dictates of nature:" *Infra*, §§ 387 *et seq.*

§ 376. The other theory of rights to which we have referred denies that it is the function of the courts to enforce, or that they have anything to do with, moral rights, or rights in the proper and familiar sense of the term; and asserts that the rights which the courts enforce, or assume to enforce, are mere *legal powers*, or powers conferred by the state. This theory logically follows from the first of the definitions of the law to which we refer at the beginning of our second book, namely, that it is a mere aggregate of laws (*leges*); for as the rules or principles by which rights are determined constitute part of the law, it is obvious, if we assume the definition to be true, that rights are mere creatures of the legislative will. It may therefore be appropriately termed the *legal* theory of rights, and its advocates the *legists*.

§ 377. This theory derives its origin and its plausibility from the ambiguity of the term "law," which, in its proper and familiar sense, denotes a law or statute (*lex*), or an aggregate of such laws, but which is also used to denote the more complex subject which we call *the law*, and naturally in the latter application it has carried with it its original connotation.[1]

§ 378. Hence, the theory is a peculiar growth, or rather excrescence, of English jurisprudence, and has never prevailed among the jurists of other countries: See observations of Maine, *infra*, § 573; and also of

---

[1] This furnishes one of the most striking instances in the history of philosophy of the tyranny of words over the mind, so forcibly described by Bacon:

"There are also idols formed by the reciprocal intercourse and society of man with man which we call idols of the market, from the commerce and association of men with each other. For men converse by means of language; but words are formed at the will of the generality; and there arises from a bad and unapt formation of words a wonderful obstruction to the mind. Nor can the definitions and explanations with which learned men are wont to guard and protect themselves in some instances afford a complete remedy; words still manifestly force the understanding, throw everything into confusion, and lead mankind into vain and innumerable controversies and fallacies:" Nov. Org., b. 1, aph. 43.

" The idols of the market are the most troublesome of all; those, namely, which have entwined themselves round the understanding from the associations of words and names. For men imagine that their reason governs words, whilst, in fact, words react upon the understanding; and this has rendered philosophy and the sciences sophistical and inactive:" Id., aph. 59. " The syllogism consists of propositions, propositions of words; words are the signs of notions. If, therefore, the notions (which form the basis of the whole) be confused and carelessly abstracted from things, there is no solidity in the superstructure; our only hope then is in a genuine induction:" Id., aph. 14.

Mr. Holland, in the preface to his Jurisprudence. For in all other languages, what we term the law is denoted by a term signifying *right* or *justice;* as, for instance, in the Greek by *nomos*, in the Latin by *jus*, in the French by *droit*, in the Spanish by *derccho*, in the German by *recht*, etc.—a usage, indeed, which once prevailed, and is yet not altogether obsolete, in our own tongue; as, for instance, in the term "folc-right," the ancient name of the common law, and its more modern equivalent, *common right.* And in the same way as with us, the use of the term "law" has originated a peculiar conception of the nature of the law, corresponding to the connotation of the term used, the use of the term "*jus*," or its equivalent, has, with other peoples, given rise to a conception of the law corresponding to the connotation of that term.

§ 379. The legal, the historical, and the philosophical theories of rights correspond to the three definitions referred to in the preceding book, §§ 198 *et seq.*, and to the three elements of the law from which these definitions are respectively derived, viz., statutes, customs, and natural reason, and hence exhaust all possible theories as to the nature of the law. As we have explained, however, the last two are not essentially distinct; and we may therefore say that all theories of the law may be reduced to the *legal* or to the *jural* theory, or to some combination of the two.

§ 380. The jural theory of rights and of the law has been fully developed in the preceding books. To complete what is there said, we add in the next chapter a brief historical sketch of the theory from the earliest times. The remainder of the book will be devoted to the explication and discussion of the legal theory.

CHAPTER II.

HISTORICAL SKETCH OF THE JURAL THEORY.

§ 382. The views we have presented as to the nature of rights and of the law seem so obvious that we might, perhaps, could the subject be approached without prejudice, count upon their being readily accepted upon their mere statement; but, unfortunately, in English and American jurisprudence the field is so completely occupied with the opposite or legal theory, and the prejudice—or, we might say, the superstition—in favor of that theory is so inveterate, that we must anticipate that our views will, at first sight, appear to most persons extremely paradoxical. To open the way for their acceptance, therefore, it will be well to show, as we have already asserted, that substantially the same views have been generally, and indeed until a late period universally, held and more or less explicitly asserted by jurists from the earliest periods in the history of jurisprudence.

§ 383. With the Greeks, there was no systematized body of jurisprudence, such as was afterward developed by the Roman lawyers; but, except as to questions to which statutory regulations or rules established by custom applied, the tribunals seem to have been governed by the common notions of justice prevailing among the people.

17

§ 384. Thus, at Athens, which may be taken as a type of the other Greek communities, all civil jurisdiction was vested in a court called the *dikastery*, which was composed of six thousand judges, or *dikasts*, chosen annually by lot from the body of the people, and divided into ten panels or departments of five hundred each, with a reserve of one thousand to fill vacancies in the several panels.

§ 385. These judges, by their oaths, were required, in the absence of any statutory regulation applying to the case, to judge according to their best judgment or conscience; and from this, and also from the popular character of the court, it is evident that, as in the case of the English court of chancery in the earlier period of its history, the principles of equity or natural justice, except in the limited class of questions turning upon statutory regulations, furnished the rule of decision; or in other words, that, with the exception referred to—which, in the Greek as in other systems, embraced but a small proportion of the total number of cases arising— justice or right, as popularly received, constituted the law, or *jus*, of Athens.[1]

---

[1] " The Greek intellect, with all its nobility and elasticity, was quite unable to confine itself within the strait waistcoat of a legal formula; and if we may judge them by the popular courts of Athens, of whose working we possess accurate knowledge, the Greek tribunals exhibited the strongest tendency to confound law and fact. The remains of the orators, and the forensic commonplaces preserved by Aristotle in his treatise on rhetoric, show that questions of pure law were constantly argued on every consideration which could possibly influence the minds of the judges. No durable system of jurisprudence could be produced in that way. A community which never hesitated to relax rules of

§ 386. Hence, with the Athenians, as with the Greeks generally, the law was regarded as identical with justice, and this accordingly was the view taken of it by the Greek philosophers generally. For though we find two different and irreconcilable theories prevailing among them with reference to the nature of justice—namely, the one that it exists naturally, and the other that it is of mere human imposition—yet, whatever view was taken of this question, it seems to have been always assumed that the justice to which it related was the justice actually administered by the state through its tribunals; and the modern notion that there are two separate and independent systems of justice, essentially different in their nature—namely *legal* and *moral*, or natural justice—seems never to have occurred to the Greek mind.

§ 387. The distinction between natural and legal justice was indeed very clearly perceived and explained by Aristotle; but according to his view, these did not constitute two independent systems of justice, but parts of one system, which he called *political* justice; by which term he denoted the justice actu-

written law whenever they stood in the way of an ideally perfect decision on the facts of particular cases, would only, if it bequeathed any body of judicial principles to posterity, bequeath one consisting of the ideas of right and wrong which happened to be prevalent at the time. Such jurisprudence would contain no framework to which the more advanced conceptions of subsequent ages could be fitted. It would amount at best to a philosophy marked with the imperfections of the civilization under which it grew up:" Maine's Ancient Law, c. 4.

This passage is remarkable at once for its acute perception of the facts and of their significance, and for the erroneous con-ally having place between the citizens of the state; and which he defined as consisting in conformity to the law (or *nomos*) of the state. "For," he says, "the term 'just' implies the case of those who have laws (*nomoi*) to which they are subject:" Ethics, b. 5, c. 6, fol. 4; and hence justice can exist only "in the case of those between whom laws exist:" Id., b. 5, c. 6, fol. 7.

§ 388. In his view, therefore, the terms "justice" and "the law" connoted the same essential idea, and differed only in this, that the one denoted the rule, and the other conformity to the rule. Indeed, he expressly asserts that "the administration of law is the determination of the just and the unjust:" Id., b. 5, c. 6, fol. 4; or in other words, the administration of justice; which is in effect to assert the identity of justice and the law.

§ 389. Having thus identified political justice with the justice actually existing in and enforced by the state, or in other words, with the law, he proceeds to say that it is partly *natural* and partly *legal*. To use his own language: "Of the political just, one part is natural and the other legal. The natural

clusions deduced from them. It is true that the administration of the law at Athens consisted mainly in the application of the principles of popular justice to controversies presented for decision, and that the received justice of the community, in fact, constituted substantially the law of Athens; but this is equally true of all systems of law in the earlier periods of their history, and in fact, the development of all systems commences in this way. It is true, also, that a system of law thus developed must consist in the main of " the ideas of right and wrong which happened to be prevalent at the time," or " would amount at best to a philosophy," or, as philosophy has been defined, a body of "reasoned

is that which everywhere is equally valid, and depends not upon being or not being received. But the legal is that which was originally a matter of indifference, but which when enacted is so no longer; as the price of a ransom being fixed at a *mina*, or the sacrificing a goat and not two sheep, and further all particular acts of legislation, as the sacrificing to Brasidas, and all those matters which are the subjects of decrees:" Id., b. 5, c. 7, fol. 1.

§ 390. Again, in the Rhetoric, in treating of the law, a precisely corresponding division is made. "Let the acting unjustly," he says, "be defined as the voluntary commission of hurt in contravention of law. Now, law is either *common* or *peculiar*"— *nomos koinos*, or *nomos idios:* Rhet., b. 1, c. 10, fols. 2, 3.

§ 391. "The peculiar law I call that by whose written enactments men direct their polity; the general, whatever unwritten rules appear to be recognized among all men:" Id.

§ 392. And in another place, the same essential idea is somewhat differently expressed. "Law, now, I understand to be either *peculiar* or *common* (*idios* or

truth;" but this is also true, as is shown elsewhere, of the two great systems of law which regulate the jural relations of the modern civilized world, and must be true of all systems whatever.

It is also true that such a body of laws, or philosophy, will be "marked with the imperfections of the civilization under which it grew up." But this is also true of all law and of all philosophy, until its principles are finally and scientifically determined; and hence in the law arises the necessary distinction between the *jus gentium* and the *jus civile*, the normal and the abnormal part of the law; and hence, also, perhaps, the mythical origin of Themis,

koinos); peculiar, to be that which has been marked
out by each people in reference to itself, and that
this is partly written and partly unwritten. I call
that the *common law* which is conformable merely
to dictates of nature; for there does exist naturally a universal sense of right and wrong, which, in
a certain degree, all intuitively divine, even should
no intercourse with each other, nor any compact,
have existed; which sentiment the Antigone of
Sophocles enters, uttering that it was just, namely,
to bury Polynices, though forbidden, since by nature
this was a deed of justice; for by no means is it for
this or the next day merely that this maxim is
enforced, but forever; nor is there any one that
knows from whom it proceeded. And as Emped-
ocles says, on the subject of not slaying that which
has life; for this is a maxim not right here and
wrong there, but a principle of law to all:" Id., b.
1, c. 13, fol. 2.

§ 393. Political justice, therefore, according to
the view of Aristotle, includes conformity to both
the common and the peculiar law, or in other words,
both natural and legal justice; and on the other

as the daughter of Uranus and Gæa (Heaven and Earth). But,
though this is true, it is true also of the law, as of philosophy, that
these imperfections pass away with the civilization that gave them
birth, and that the truth only ultimately survives. Hence, it is not
true that a system of law thus developed "would contain no
framework to which the more advanced conceptions of subsequent
ages could be fitted;" on the contrary, it is the rational part of the
ancient law only that does constitute the framework upon which
the later law is built, and the *jus civile*, or anomalous part of the
law, was, as it were, the mere scaffolding. Nor is it true that the

hand, injustice consists "in the voluntary commission of hurt in contravention of the law," either
common or peculiar; there being, as he otherwise
expresses it, "two species of things just and unjust,"
the one "of written prescript, the other of unwritten
law."

§ 394. Considering the difficulty of the subject
and the period at which he wrote, perhaps no other
part of the works of Aristotle exhibit more favor-
ably the character of his original and profound
genius than the few brief passages above quoted
from the Ethics and the Rhetoric. But there are
some inaccuracies and some confusion in his views, to
which it is necessary to advert, in order that the
problem under consideration may be fairly presented; and this, the more especially as his errors have
been transmitted along with his better thoughts to
succeeding ages.

§ 395. First, the definition of political justice, as
consisting in conformity to law, involves a confusion
of ideas. For the term "law," itself according to
Aristotle's definition, includes in its signification
two things essentially different in nature, and which

Greek mind was deficient in genius for jurisprudence. In this, as
in other respects, it was pre-eminent, and in it were born the jural
conceptions upon which rests the law or right of modern civilization; for it is to Aristotle, its great exemplar—who was one of the
first, as he was perhaps the greatest of the jurists—that we owe the
true conception of the nature of law and of justice—the first, as it
was the greatest, step in the development of jural science; from
which conception, as we shall see, the development of the Roman
law commenced, and was, in fact, but little more than a logical
consequence.

coincide, where they coincide at all, only accident-
ally, namely, the *nomos koinos*, or natural law used
by the state in common with the other states, and
the *nomos idios*, or portion of the law of the state
peculiar to itself. Hence, according to the definition,
political justice includes two significations essentially different, and even irreconcilable, namely, that
of natural justice, or justice in the ordinary sense,
and conformity to the peculiar laws of the state,
whether just in the ordinary sense or not. For if
there is such a thing as natural justice, it is obvious
that the laws themselves, like all other human acts,
are determined by its principles to be just or unjust;
hence, in the case of an unjust law, conformity to it
would *ex vi termini* be just, and at the same time, if
such conformity violated natural justice, unjust,
which is absurd; unless, indeed, we use the term
"justice" in two essentially different and independent senses, which is contrary to the hypothesis.
Hence, to present a distinct and single idea, political
justice should have been defined as consisting exclusively, either in conformity to the *nomos koinos*
or in conformity to the *nomos idios*.

§ 396. The latter was the theory of the sophists,
who held that justice was purely of human imposition; and is the theory asserted in modern times by
Hobbes and Bentham, and in effect by Austin and
his followers, and is in fact the legal theory now
generally prevailing in English and American jurisprudence; for though some of the advocates of this
theory admit the existence of a moral or natural
justice, yet they assert that it is something essen-

tially different and distinct from political justice, with which alone the jurist is in any way concerned; and they hold the latter to be altogether a creature of the legislative will.

§ 397. But this theory is manifestly opposed to the universal conception of the nature of justice, according to which legislation as well as all other human acts are judged to be just or unjust according to their character. Thus it would seem absurd to say that the laws were just under which Socrates was poisoned and Christ crucified, or those under which other martyrs were put to death, or that their execution was just in any sense of the term. So it would be absurd to say that the laws against witch-craft were just, or that the myriads of wretches executed in obedience to those laws were justly condemned, or to say (to put a less extreme case) that justice ceases to require the payment of a debt or the performance of any other obligation as soon as it is barred by the statute of limitations; or that we may justly refuse to perform a contract or execute a trust because not reduced to writing, as required by the statute of frauds. Justice may indeed require of us, as a necessary condition of the peace and security of society, to submit to the will of the government, whether just or unjust—at least to the extent of surrendering our own rights; but it will not in any case permit us to enforce an unjust power which the law gives us over another, or to evade our own obligations because the law does not enforce them; nor, as we have already observed, is there any reason why we should corrupt our language and debauch our conscience by calling the unjust just, whether conformable to law or not. It may indeed be convenient, in order to reconcile a preconceived theory with actual facts, to say that conformity to law is legally just though morally unjust; but this not only violates the universally received sense of the term "justice"—clothing injustice with that venerable name—but produces an unnecessary confusion of ideas; for the theory that the law is merely an expression of the will of the state is at least clear and readily understood; and it can not but be productive of confusion to apply to it a term the usual connotation of which is altogether different: *Vide infra*, c. 4.

§ 398. It seems, however, that the theory to which Aristotle actually inclined, and which really represented his conception of justice, was that justice consists in conformity to the natural law, or *nomos koinos;* for in the Ethics, in dividing justice into natural and legal, he confines the latter to matters morally indifferent (*supra*, § 389), and thereby implies that it can not include anything naturally unjust; and the definition of legal justice in the Rhetoric, as consisting merely in conformity to the *nomos idios*, seems to be a mere expedient for reconciling his definition of justice with the existence of that portion of the law.

§ 399. Adopting then, this conception of justice, namely, that it consists in conformity to the *nomos koinos*, or natural law, it follows that the definition of legal justice last referred to is too broad; for to constitute justice of any kind, conformity to the *nomos koinos* is required; and therefore, to constitute legal justice, conformity to that, as well as to the *nomos idios*, is essential. Hence the use of the terms "natural" and "legal" to distinguish the two parts of political justice is not proper; for according to the definition assumed, all justice is natural, and there can not be a justice of any other kind; for if in any case conformity to the statutory law constitutes justice, it must be by virtue of some principle of natural justice that requires in that case conformity to the legislative will.

§ 400. There also seems to be some confusion in Aristotle with reference to the distinction between the statute or written and the unwritten law; for according to two of the passages quoted above, he seems to consider this as corresponding to the distinction between the *nomos koinos* and the *nomos idios: Supra,* §§ 389, 391; while in another he says that the *nomos idios* is partly unwritten and partly written: *Supra,* § 392. The latter is the correct view, for obviously the *nomos idios*, or peculiar law of the state, includes not only statutes, but also all customs which are peculiar to it.

§ 401. The division of the law into written and unwritten, therefore, does not correspond with the division into the *nomos idios* and *nomos koinos;* but the unwritten law includes the whole of the latter and part of the former.

§ 402. The views of Aristotle as to the identity of the law with justice, and as to the distinction between the rational and accidental parts of the law, or in other words, between the *nomos koinos* and the *nomos idios*, were adopted in their integrity by the Roman lawyers, and in fact constituted the starting-point from which the rational development of the Roman law commenced.

§ 403. A reference to the following passages from the Pandects and the Institutes will make this apparent:

1. "First of all, it is necessary to understand what is justice, what *jus*, and what jurisprudence."

"Justice is the constant and perpetual will to render to every one his right." *Jus* is so called from *justitia;*[1] for, as Celsus elegantly defines it, "*jus* is the art of the good and the equal"—*ars boni et æqui.*

"Of which some one deservedly calls us the priests; for we cultivate justice, and profess the knowledge of the good and the equal, separating the equal from the unequal, and distinguishing the right from the wrong; . . . . following, unless I am deceived, a true and not a pretended philosophy."

"Jurisprudence is . . . . the science of the just and the unjust, *justi atque injusti scientia.*"[2]

2. "The precepts of *jus* are to live decently, to hurt no one, and to give every one his due."

3. "*Jus civile* is distinguished from *jus gentium* because every people ruled by laws and customs, *legibus et moribus*, uses partly its own peculiar *jus* and partly a *jus* common to all men."

---

[1] Or rather, *justitia* from *jus:* Skeat's Etym. Dict.

[2] The full text is: *Jurisprudentia est divinarum atque humanarum rerum notitia, justi atque injusti scientia.* The meaning of the clause omitted has given rise to much controversy; but it is simply used as the equivalent of the last clause, and may be omitted without changing the sense.

"For that *jus* which each people has established for itself is peculiar to the state, and is called the *jus civile*, as belonging peculiarly to the state; but that which natural reason has established among men, that is observed generally among all peoples, and is called the *jus gentium*, as being the *jus* which all nations use."

"*Jus civile* is that which neither recedes altogether from the *jus naturale* or *jus gentium*, nor altogether follows it. Therefore, when we add anything to or detract anything from the common law (*jus communis*), we make a peculiar law, *jus proprium* or *jus civile.*"

"The Roman people, therefore, uses a law or *jus* partly peculiar to itself, partly common to all men."[1]

[1] "In an excerpt from Ulpian, placed at the beginning of the Pandects, and also inserted by Justinian in the second title of his Institutes, a fancied *jus naturale*, common to all animals, is distinguished from the *jus naturale* or *gentium*, which I have adverted to above. . . . . I must, however, remark that the *jus quod natura omnia animalia docent* is a conceit peculiar to Ulpian; and that this most foolish conceit, though inserted in Justinian's compilations, has no perceptible influence on the detail of the Roman law. The *jus naturale* of the classical jurists generally, and the *jus naturale* occurring generally in the Pandects, is equivalent to the *natural law* of modern writers on jurisprudence, and is synonymous with the *jus gentium*, or the *jus naturale et gentium:*" Austin's Jur. 214, 215; see, also, to same effect, Maine's Ancient Law, 50, and Lindley's Introd. to Jur., app. 5.

"It was stolen by the jurists, styled classical, and by them imported into the Roman law, from certain muddy hypotheses of certain Greek philosophers touching the measure or test of positive law and morality:" Id. 39. Among the philosophers referred to must be numbered Socrates, Plato and Aristotle.

Sir Henry Maine strangely mistakes the origin of the conception

4. "Almost all contracts were introduced from this *jus gentium;* as, for instance, buying and selling, letting, hiring, partnership, deposit, loan, and others innumerable."

5. "This law of ours is partly written, partly unwritten; as with the Greeks the laws (*nomoi*) were written or unwritten."

"The written law (*jus scriptum*) consists of the several kinds of statutes (*legis plebiscita, senatus consulta, principum placita*), of the edicts of the magistrates or judges, and the opinions of the learned in the law (*responsa prudentum*)."

"The unwritten law is that which custom has approved."

6. "The principles of natural right (*naturalia jura*) which are observed equally among all peoples,

of the *jus gentium* or *naturale,* of which he says: "The Roman juris-consults . . . . borrowed from Greece the doctrine of a natural state of man, a natural society, anterior to the organization of commonwealths governed by positive laws:" Ancient Law, 54, 68, 70, 71. The conception, however, was directly derived from Aristotle, who defined man to be a political animal (*zoon politikon*), and conceived his natural state to be that of political society, and the *jus gentium,* or *nomos koinos,* to constitute a part of the actual law by which he was governed in that state. His original conception was precisely that of the Roman lawyers, which is thus well described by Maine himself: "Natural law, for all practical purposes, was something belonging to the present, something entwined with existing institutions, something which could be distinguished from them by a competent observer. The tests which separate the ordinances of nature from the gross ingredients with which they were mingled was a sense of simplicity and harmony:" Id. 70, 71. To which he adds, however: "It was not on account of their simplicity and harmony that these finer elements were primarily respected, but on the score of their descent from the aboriginal right of nature."

being established by a certain divine providence, remain always firm and immutable, but those which each state has established for itself are often changed, either by the tacit consent of the people or by some later law."

7. "Inveterate custom is rightly observed as law (*pro lege*), and that is what is called the law established by manners or customs (*jus moribus constitum*)."

"For since laws (*leges*) themselves bind us from no other cause than that they are received by the judgment of the people, those also which the people have approved without any writing will bind all; for what difference does it make whether the people declare their will by vote or by acts? Wherefore it is also rightly received that laws may be abrogated not only by the vote of the legislator, but also by the tacit consent of all evidenced by disuse:" Pandects, 1, 3, 28.

"Nevertheless, with reference to the authority of custom, this limitation is to be observed as enacted by Constantinus; the authority of custom and of long use is not to be despised, but it is not to be extended to such a point as to overcome reason or law (*ut aut rationem vincat aut legem*):" Id. 1, 3, 30.[1]

§ 404. It was to this conception of *jus* that the Roman law owed the rational character of its development; which in fact commenced with, and was in a large measure due to, the reception of the Greek philosophy by the Roman lawyers.[2]

[1] The passages cited, with the exception of the last two, will all be found either in the first title of the Institutes, or in that of the Pandects, Pothier's edition.

[2] "On the whole, the progress of the Romans in legal improve-

§ 405. This development, as we have observed, was essentially the same as that of the common law, and consisted simply in the logical definition and development of the principles of natural right. The process in either case was indeed modified by the arbitrary and accidental rules constituting the *jus civile* or *nomos idios* of each system respectively; but these rules, as we have explained (*supra*, § 254)—except where they relate to matters jurally indifferent—stand to the rest of the law in the relation of mere anomalies or exceptions to the application of its principles; and therefore do not enter into the development of the law, or in any way affect it except to a certain extent to embarrass and obstruct it.

§ 406. This is clearly recognized, as we have seen, in the distinction made in our law between reasoning from principle and reasoning from authority: *Supra*, § 253; and it is recognized, also, with equal clearness by the civil lawyers, in the distinction made by them between the *jus commune* and *jus singulare;* the latter of which included all rules running counter to the common and natural rule of right; and with reference to the latter, the same principle is held by the civil as by the common lawyers, viz., that it is to be treated strictly, and not to be extended by way of analogy: *Supra*, § 263, note.

ment was astonishingly rapid as soon as stimulus was applied to it by the theory of natural law:" Maine's Ancient Law, 54, 55. "I know of no reason why the law of the Romans should be superior to the laws of the Hindoos, unless the theory of natural law has given it a type of excellence different from the usual one:" Id. 75.

§ 407. Hence the Roman law, like our own, is, as Celsus says of it, "a true philosophy," or in other words, a "body of reasoned truth," differing, as we have already remarked, from justice, as popularly received, simply in being a more scientific, and therefore a truer, expression of natural right.

§ 408. To this proposition we may cite the opinion of Leibnitz, perhaps the most competent of all men to speak upon the subject.

"I have often said that, after the writings of the geometricians, there exists nothing which, in point of strength, subtilty, and depth, can be compared to the works of the Roman lawyers; and, as it would be scarcely possible from intrinsic evidence to distinguish a demonstration of Euclid's from one of Archimedes or Apollonius (the style of each of them appearing no less uniform than if reason herself were speaking through her organs), so also the Roman lawyers all resemble each other, like twin brothers; insomuch, from the style alone of any particular opinion or argument, hardly any conjecture could be formed about its author; nor are the traces of a refined and deeply meditated system of natural jurisprudence anywhere to be found more visible or in greater abundance. And even in those cases where its principles are departed from, in compliance with the language consecrated by technical forms, or in consequence of new statutes or of ancient traditions, the conclusions which the assumed hypothesis renders it necessary to incorporate with the external dictates of right reason are deduced with a soundness of logic and with an in-

18

genuity that excites admiration. Nor are these deviations from the law of nature so frequent as is commonly supposed."[1]

§ 409. It is this view of the nature of the Roman law, and of law in general, that can alone explain the spontaneous acceptance of that law by the modern civilized world, which on any other hypothesis is utterly inexplicable.

§ 410. Nor is England to be taken as an exception to this remark; for it is a notorious fact that, in spite of the avowed hostility of the English people to the civil law, the English lawyers have, from the time of Glanville to the present day, freely borrowed its principles; and to this, undoubtedly, is mainly

---

[1] This passage is quoted by Dugald Stewart (Philosophy of the Human Mind, 2, 3, 3), with the following remarks: "In those branches of study which are conversant about moral and political propositions, the nearest approach I can imagine to a hypothetical science, analogous to mathematics, is to be found in a code of municipal jurisprudence; or rather, might be conceived to exist in such a code, if systematically carried into execution, agreeably to certain general or fundamental principles. . . . . This consideration seems to me to throw some light on the following very curious parallel which Leibnitz has drawn (with what justness I presume not to decide) between the works of the Roman civilians and those of the Greek geometers. Few writers, certainly, have been so fully qualified as he was to pronounce on the characteristical merits of both. . . . . I have quoted this passage merely as an illustration of the analogy already alluded to between the systematical unity of mathematical science and that which is conceivable in a system of municipal law. How far this unity is exemplified in the Roman code I leave to be determined by more competent judges. . . . . Making all due allowance for the exaggeration of Leibnitz, it is difficult to conceive that his opinions on a subject which he had so profoundly studied should be so very widely at variance with the truth."

due the rational development which the English law has undergone.[1] Nor can any one even slight-

---

[1] The most striking illustration of this fact is furnished by the treatise of Bracton, with reference to which Mr. Maine observes: " That an English writer of the time of Henry III should have been able to put off on his countrymen as a compendium of pure English law a treatise of which the entire form and a third of the contents were directly borrowed from the *corpus juris*, and that he should have ventured on this experiment in a country where the systematic study of the Roman law was formally proscribed, will always be among the most hopeless enigmas in the history of jurisprudence:" Maine's Ancient Law, c. 4. It must, indeed, be hopeless to reconcile this fact with Mr. Maine's (or rather, Austin's and Bentham's) theory of the law; but in the light of the true theory, there is nothing in it to surprise us. It was the function of the judges to administer justice, and their duty, at least in the then condition of the law, to seek the principles of justice where they could best find them, namely, in the Roman law. " What is good sense in one age must be good sense, all circumstances remaining, in another, and pure, unsophisticated reason is the same in Italy and in England, in the mind of a Papinian and of a Blackstone:" Sir William Jones, cited *infra*, § 421, note.

" To have neglected to take advantage of the assistance which was then offered would have argued a high degree of presumption, or gross and culpable ignorance; neither is to be imputed to the founders of our system of jurisprudence:" 1 Spence's Eq. Jur. *123.

The same process took place on the continent, and resulted in the establishment of the civil law as the common law of Europe—a fact, it would seem, more calculated to surprise than its partial adoption in England. In the latter country, the process was, at a period subsequent to the time of Bracton (Id. *346), checked by the hostility of the English people to the civil law; but the only result was, that the process was transferred from the common-law courts to the court of chancery, where it went on unchecked. In modern and more enlightened times the common-law judges again commenced to borrow freely from the civilians: See *supra*, § 346, note. It is related of one of the greatest of our jurists, Sir Matthew Hale, that " he applied himself with great avidity to the

ly familiar with the two systems fail to perceive the entire identity of principle and method in that portion of each system that deals with the determination of rights, and the substantial identity of rights themselves, as realized in all civilized nations.

§ 411. The Roman law has also furnished to moral philosophy the principles and method of scientific jurisprudence, or of that department of morality which deals with rights. For not only can this be verified by an actual reference to the books of morality, and especially to those which treat of international right, but it is in fact as impossible to devise a science of rights differing radically from that already developed by the jurists as it would be to devise a new science of geometry.

§ 412. Nor is it possible upon any other theory to account for the development of international right, and the ready acceptance of its principles by the civilized world upon the publication of the works of Grotius and other writers upon the subject. For nations have no common political superior, and it is therefore impossible that there should be any law, in the sense of *lex*, governing their jural relations; and hence Austin was clearly right in asserting that international law is merely a branch of morality;

contemplation of the Roman law; "and that " he often affirmed that the principles of jurisprudence were so well delivered in the Digests that law could not be understood as a science without first resorting to them for information: " Hale's History of the Common Law, Runnington's ed., iii.

For a fuller account of the influence of the Roman upon the English law, see observations of Spence, cited in note to § 346. Mr. Markby, in his late work, Elements of Law, takes a different view, but in this he is clearly wrong.

though wrong in asserting that on that account it is not also law in the same sense as is the internal law which determines the rights and obligations of the citizens of a state.

§ 413. For nothing can be more certain than that the *jus gentium*, which in the main determines the rights and obligations of individuals in particular states, is essentially the same in method and principle as the *jus gentium* which determines the rights and obligations of states; and the necessity imposed by their theory on the legists of asserting the contrary, and of denying to international right the title of law, is a clear *reductio ad absurdum* of the theory itself.

§ 414. With regard to the modern civilians, we have not the space nor the requisite information to give anything like an adequate account of their views as to the nature of the law and of jurisprudence. We are therefore reluctantly compelled to pass them by with the remark that they may, with some inconsiderable exceptions, be classed either with the historical or the philosophical school of jurists, to which we elsewhere refer; and that we find among them all shades of opinion, from that which regards jurisprudence as a pure science, to that which regards it as a mere collection of rules owing their force to the fact that they are historically established.

§ 415. One other remark may, however, be hazarded: the Roman law was inherited by modern Europe from a corrupt and degenerate age, after its spirit had fled and the rational method by which it

had been developed had ceased to operate; and its
general reception on the continent in its completed
form, as part of the positive law, has given to it an
undue authority. Hence the genius of the conti-
nental jurists seems to a certain extent to have been
cramped, or fettered, by the authority of Justinian's
collections, in the same manner as in other branches
of philosophy thought was once dominated by the
authority of the church; and accordingly it has
been well remarked that "the fruits to be obtained
from the study of the Roman law . . . . can be
reaped to their full extent only in countries where it
is not allowed the force of law:" Kaufman's
Mackeldy, translator's preface, 7.[1]

---

[1] To the same effect, Professor Meyers (in his treatise Ueber
Romisches Recht, etc.) remarks, in reference to the study of the
Roman law in Germany: "When its provisions shall have ceased
to have the force of law, its study will produce greater fruits, and
the peculiar method employed by the so-called classical jurists in
treating the law will be better estimated and turned to practical
account." Like views are expressed by Professor Falck and Professor Beseler. "Had we attempted," says the latter, "to master
the art of the Roman jurists, to thoroughly explore what is sound
in the ancient Roman law, and to ascertain what is injurious in
the additions of ruder times; had the powers of that long period,
thus strengthened by precept and example, been applied to the
national law—can it be doubted that its regeneration would have
been happily effected? But a different course was adopted. Most
of the Germanic nations, who required assistance in struggling
through a dangerous crisis of their development, had this foreign
law thrust upon them, not as a model, but as a direct source of law;
and Europe still suffers from the consequences of this unnatural
union. England alone succeeded, after a protracted struggle, in
subduing the political elements of the Germanic Middle Ages,
which most other nations were unable to cope with, and in raising
upon them the lofty and elaborate structure of the English consti-

§ 416. This has been, and still is, to a considerable extent illustrated in the case of the English law; for while the Roman law has never been regarded as authoritative in England, the English jurists have never hesitated, and do not now hesitate, to borrow its principles when conceived to be rational and just; and it is perhaps not too much to anticipate that their growing familiarity with the writings of the civilians, ancient and modern, will ultimately result in establishing theoretical jurisprudence, or the science of rights, upon a purely rational and scientific basis.

§ 417. Our jurists also have this great advantage, that our law has been developed in the practical administration of justice, and is still in the process of development. Hence, as we have shown elsewhere, the method of its development has been in the main rational and scientific; and this method, though somewhat checked by the prevalence of a false theory, is still in actual operation. Our jurists, therefore, have perhaps inherited to a larger extent than those of other countries, not indeed the formulated principles, but the method and spirit of the classical Roman jurists.

§ 418. It must, however, be confessed that they have in general concerned themselves but little with the scientific investigation of the nature of the law and of the nature of its method and principles; and

tution. . . . . From the constitution of England no unprejudiced man could withhold his admiration. Yet the English law, considered in itself, is far from having attained an equal completeness, and the remedy for the imperfections under which it labors is to be found in the use of the ancient spirit as a model: " Id.

that their notions upon these subjects are often not only loose and ill-defined, but also sometimes inconsistent and contradictory.[1]

§ 419. The rational nature of the law has, however, at all periods in its history, been constantly, if not consistently, asserted by the most eminent authorities, as will appear by the following citations. These will perhaps appear unnecessarily copious, but the importance of the subject, and the inveterate prejudices with which it is surrounded, will serve as an excuse.

§ 420. 1. "England alone uses in her boundaries unwritten law (*jus*) and custom; in it *jus*, indeed, has come without written enactment (*ex non scripto*), because use has established it:" Bracton, b. 1, c. 1, § 2.

"Since all laws (*jura*) emanate from justice as

[1] "All who have written concerning laws have written either as philosophers or lawyers. The philosophers lay down many principles fair in argument, but not applicable to use; the lawyers being subject and addicted to the positive rules, either of the laws of their own country, or else of the Roman or pontifical law, have no freedom of opinion but, as it were, 'walk in fetters:'" Bacon's De Aug. 8, 3. Pantagruel expresses the same opinion of the French lawyers, in somewhat more forcible language. "Seeing," says he, "that the law is excerpted from the very bowels of moral and natural philosophy, how should these people know the law?— who, by . . . . have read no more in philosophy than my ass"—a remark generally true of our own lawyers, of which a striking illustration is furnished by the following extract from a notice of this work appearing in a leading law journal: "This is not in any proper sense a law book, although it purports to treat of law and of jurisprudence; it is really a philosophic treatise on these subjects; and as such, we recommend it to those persons who have the leisure and inclination to devote themselves to studies of that description."

from a fountain, and what justice demands that *jus* seeks to effect, let us see what is justice, ... what *jus*, what *lex*, and what custom; without which no one can be just so as to do justice and to make a just judgment between man and man."

"Justice is the constant and perpetual will to give to every one his right."

" *Jus* is derived from justice, and has various significations. It is sometimes put for the art itself, or for that which we have in writing concerning *jus;* because *jus* is said to be the art of the good and the equal, of which some one deservedly calls us the priests; for we cultivate justice, and administer the principles of sacred right."

" Also *jus* is sometimes put for the natural law (*jus naturale*), which is always the good and the equal; sometimes for the civil law (*jus civile*) only; sometimes for the whole law, which commands us to live decorously, to injure no one, and to give to every one his right."

" Jurisprudence is a knowledge of things divine and human, the science of the just and the unjust."

" Jurisprudence differs much, therefore, from justice; for jurisprudence recognizes, and justice gives, what is due to every one.

Justice, therefore, is the virtue, jurisprudence the science; justice the end (*summum bonum*), jurisprudence the means."

" *Jus civile* is used in several ways; in one, for the statute law of any state; in another sense, *jus civile* is that which sometimes detracts from or adds to the *jus naturale* or *jus gentium*. . . . . Also the whole law which the state uses, whether natural or civil, or *jus gentium,* may be called *jus civile:* " Bracton, b. 1, c. 4, §§ 1–4.

2. "Not only deuteronomical, but also all human laws are sacred; the definition of a law being thus: it is an holy sanction, commanding whatever is honest, and prohibiting the contrary. . . . . The law (*jus*) is also defined to be the art of the good and the equal, of which we are deservedly called priests:" Fortescue's De Laudibus Legum Angliæ, c. 3.

" All human laws (*jura*) are either the law of nature, customs, or statutes, which are also called constitutions; but the two former when they are reduced into writing, and commanded to be observed, are changed into the nature of constitutions or statutes, and afterward bind the subjects to their observance more penally than before:" Id., c. 15.

"The laws of England, as far as they agree with and are deduced from the law of nature, are neither better nor worse in their decisions than the laws of all other states or kingdoms in similar cases. For, as the philosopher says in the fifth of the Ethics, 'the law of nature is that which has the same power with all men:'" Id., c. 16.

3. In the following pages from St. Germain's Doctor and Student, it will be understood that the dialogue is between a doctor of the civil law and a student of the common law, the former of whom applies to the latter "to know whereupon the law of England is grounded;" to which the student consents, but first desires the doctor to show him "somewhat of other laws that pertain most to this

matter, and that doctors treat of," which he does as follows:

"DOCTOR. The law of nature, ... which is also called the law of reason, pertaineth only to creatures reasonable, that is, man. . . . . And this law ought to be kept as well among Jews and gentiles as among Christian men; . . . . and because it is written in the heart, therefore it may not be put away, ne it is never changeable by no diversity of place ne time; and therefore, against this law pre-scription, statute, nor custom may not prevail; and if any be brought in against it, they be not statutes, prescriptions, nor customs; but things void and against justice.

"The law of man (the which sometimes is called the law positive) is derived by reason as a thing which is necessary and probably following of the law of reason and of the law of God. . . . .

"For every man's law must be consonant to the law of God. And therefore the laws of princes, the commandments of prelates, the statutes of common-alities, ne yet the ordinances of the church, is not righteous nor obligatory but it be consonant to the law of God.

"And of such a law of man that is consonant to the law of God it appeareth who hath right to lands and goods, and who hath not; for whatsoever a man hath by such laws of man, he hath righteously; and whatsoever he hath against such laws is un-righteously had.

"For laws of man not contrary to the law of God, nor to the law of reason, must be observed in the law of the soul, and he that despiseth them despiseth God and resisteth God.

"STUDENT. . . . . The law of England is grounded upon six principal grounds: 1. It is grounded upon the law of reason; 2. On the law of God; 3. On divers general customs of the realm; 4. On divers principles that we call maxims; 5. On divers particular customs; 6. On divers statutes made in parliament by the king and by the common council of the realm. . . . .

" The first ground of the law of England is the law of reason whereof thou hast treated before; . . . . the which is kept in this realm, as it is in all other realms, and as a necessity it must needs be (as thou hast said before).

"DOCTOR. But I would like to know what is called the law of nature after the laws of England.

"STUDENT. It is not used among them that be learned in the laws of England to reason what thing as commanded or prohibited by the law of nature, and what not; but all the reasoning in that behalf is under this manner:

"As when anything is grounded upon the law of nature, they say that reason will that such a thing be done; and if it be prohibited by the law of nature, they say it is against reason, or that reason will not suffer it to be done:" Doctor and Student, 11, 12.

" The second ground of the law of England is the law of God. . . . . If any general custom were directly against the law of God, or if any statute were made directly against it—as if it were ordered that no alms should be given for no necessity—the custom and statute were void:" Id. 15.

"The third ground of the law of England standeth upon divers general customs of old time used through all the realm which had been accepted and approved by our sovereign lord the king, and his progenitors and all his subjects; and because the said customs be neither against the law of God nor the law of reason, and have always been taken to be good and necessary for the commonwealth of all the realm, therefore they have obtained the strength of a law insomuch that he that doth against them doth against justice; and these be the customs that properly be common law:" Id. 17, 18.

"And it is understood that there is no statute that treateth of the beginning of the said customs, ne why should they be holden for law; and therefore after them that be learned in the laws of the realm, the old custom of the realm is the only and sufficient authority to them in that behalf—and I pray thee show me what doctors hold therein, that is to say, whether a custom only be a sufficient authority of any law.

"DOCTOR. Doctors hold that a law grounded upon a custom is the most surest law; but this thou must always understand therewith, that such a custom is neither contrary to the law of reason nor the law of God:" Id. 25.

"STUDENT. The fourth ground of the law of England standeth in divers principles that be called in the law maxims, the which have always been taken for law in this realm. . . . . And it needeth not to assign any reason why they were first received for maxims, for it sufficeth that they be not against the law of reason nor the law of God, and that they have always been taken for law:" Id. 25, 26.

"The fifth ground of the law of England standeth in divers particular customs, used in divers counties, towns, cities, and lordships in this realm; the which particular customs, because they be not against the law of reason nor the law of God, though they be against the said general customs or maxims of the law, yet, nevertheless, they stand in effect and be taken for law:" Id. 34.

"The sixth ground of the law of England standeth in divers statutes made by our sovereign lord the king and his progenitors, and by the lords spiritual and temporal, and the commons in divers parliaments, in such cases where the law of reason, the law of God, customs, maxims, ne other grounds of the law seemed not to be sufficient to punish evil men and to reward good men:" Id. 35, 36.

"Doctor. . . . . Forasmuch as it appeareth that thou hast said before that the learned of the law of England pretend to verify that the law of England will nothing do ne attempt against the law of reason nor the law of God, pray thee answer me some questions grounded upon the law of England, how thou thinkest the law may stand with reason or conscience in them:" Id. 36.

The balance of the book is devoted to answering the objections put by the doctor, and to establishing the thesis that the law of England, taken together with the law of equity, administered by the court of chancery, was in fact consonant with reason or conscience.

4. "And Fleta saith: *Est autem jus publicum et privatum quod ex naturalibus præceptis, aut gentium aut civilibus est collectum; et quod in jure scripto, jus appellatur, id in lege Angliæ rectum esse dicitur.* And in the mirror and other places of the law it is called *droit* as *droit defend*—the law defendeth:" Co. Lit. 158 b.

" And it is to be observed that the common law of England is sometimes called right, sometimes common right, and sometimes *communis justitia.* In the Great Charter the common law is called right. *Nulli vendimus, nulli negabimus, aut differemus justitiam vel rectum."*

" In the statute Wm. I, c. 1, it is called common *droit. En primes voet le roy et commande . . . . que common droit soit fait a touts, aussi bien a poers come aux riches, sauns regard a nullay;* which agreeth with the ancient law in the time of King Edgar . . . . *Primum publici juris beneficio fruitur quisquam idque ex æquo et bono, sive is dives sive inops fuerit, jus reddit."* And Fleta saith: " *Quod communis justitia singulis puriter exhibeatur.* " And all the commissions and charters for execution of justice are *facturi quod ad justitiam pertinet secundem legem et consuetudinem Angliæ:* " Id. 142 a.

" The law of nature is part of the law of England. . . . . The law of nature is that which God at the time of the creation of the nature of man infused into his heart for his preservation and direction; and this is *lex æterna,* the moral law, called also the law of nature, and by this law, written with the finger of God in the heart of man, were the people of God a long time governed, before the law was written by Moses, who was the first reporter or writer of the law in the world.

" The apostle, in the second chapter to the Romans, saith: *Cum enim gentes quæ legem non habent naturaliter ea quæ legis sunt facerent.* . . . . And Aristotle, Nature's secretary, lib. 5, Æthic., saith that *jus naturale est quod apud omnes homines eandem habet potentiam.*

"Seeing, then, that faith, obedience, and ligeance are due by the law of nature, it followeth that the same can not be changed or taken away; for albeit judicial or municipal laws have inflicted and imposed in several places, and at several times, divers and several punishments and penalties, for breach or not observance of the law of nature (for that law consisteth in commanding or prohibiting without any certain punishment or penalty), yet the very law of nature itself never was nor could be altered or changed, and therefore it is certainly true that *jura naturalia sunt immutabilia.*

" And herewith agreeth Bracton, lib. 1, c. 5, and Doctor and Student, c. 5, 6.

" And this appeareth plainly and plentifully in our books: " Calvin's Case, 7 Co. 12, 13.

" For *leges naturæ perfectissimæ sunt et immutabiles; humani vero juris conditio semper in infinitum currit, et nihil est in eo quod perpetuo stare possit; leges humanæ nascuntur, vivunt, et moriuntur:* " Id. 25.

"*Sequi debit potentia justitiam non præcedere:* " 2 Inst. 454.

" And this is another strong argument in law,

nihil quod est contra rationem est licitum; for reason is the life of the law, nay, the common law itself is nothing else but reason; which is to be understood of an artificial perfection of reason gotten by long study, observation, and experience, and not of every man's natural [*i. e.*, uncultivated] reason; for *nemo nascitur artifex.*

"This legal reason is *summa ratio*, and therefore, if all the reason that is dispersed into so many several heads were united into one, yet could he not make such a law as the law of England is; because by many successions of ages it has been fined and refined by an infinite number of grave and learned men, and by long experience grown to such a perfection for the government of this realm, as the old rule may be justly verified of it, *Neminem oportet esse sapientiorem legibus;* no man out of his own private reason ought to be wiser than the law which is the perfection of reason:" Co. Lit. 976.

"An argument drawn from an inconvenience is forcible in law, as hath been observed before, and shall be often hereafter—*nihil quod est inconveniens est licitum.*

"And the law that is the perfection of reason can not suffer anything that is inconvenient:" Id. 97 b.

"And judges by the authoritie of our author are to judge of inconveniences as of things unlawful:" Id. 279 a. But, "here note three things: 1. That whatsoever is against the rule of law is inconvenient: 2. That an argument *ab inconvenienti* is strong to prove it is against law, as often hath been observed; 3. That new inventions (though of a

19

learned judge in his own profession) are full of inconvenience. *Periculosum est res novas et inusitatas inducere; eventus varios res nova semper habit:*" Id. 379 a.

"Because it would be against common right and reason, the common law adjudges the said act of parliament as to that point void, ... and the opinion of the court was that this statute was void:" Bonham's Case, 8 Co. 118.

5. "Even an act of parliament made against natural equity—as to make a man judge in his own case—is void in itself, for *jura naturalia sunt immutabilia* and they are *leges legum:*" Hobart, 87; see also Bishop's First Book of the Law, c. 9, § 90.

6. "The proceedings in our courts are founded upon the law of England, and that law is again founded upon the law of nature and the revealed law of God.

"If the right sought to be enforced is inconsistent with either of these, the English municipal law can not recognize it. I take it that that principle is acknowledged, indeed, by the laws of all Europe.

"It appears to have been recognized by the French court in the celebrated case alluded to by Mr. Hargrave in his argument in Somerset's Case. Mr. Blackstone in his Commentaries, vol. 1, p. 42, says: 'Upon the law of nature and revelation depend all human laws; that is to say, no human law should be suffered to contradict them.'

"Now if it can be shown that slavery is against the law of nature and the law of God, it can not be recognized in our courts:" Forbes *v.* Cochrane, 2 Barn. & Cress. 471.

7. "Let us consider the reason of the case, for nothing is law that is not reason:" Powell, J., in Coggs *v.* Bernard, 2 Ld. Raym. 911.

8. "I do not recollect that any case was cited which proves such a position; but if there were any such to be found, I should not hesitate to say that it could not be law; for I have so great a veneration for the law as to suppose that nothing could be law which is not founded in common sense or common honesty:" Ashurst, J., in Pasley *v.* Freeman, 3 T. R. 62.

9. "Private justice, moral fitness, and public convenience, ... when applied to a new subject, make common law without a precedent:" Willes, J., in Millar *v.* Taylor, 4 Burr. 2312.

10. "The common law now so called is founded on the law of nature and reason. Its grounds, maxims, and principles are derived from many different principles: from natural and moral philosophy, from the civil and the canon law, from logic, from the use, custom, and conversation among men, collected out of the general disposition, nature, and condition of human kind. . . . . It had an ancienter original than Edward the Confessor and was first called the *folc-right,* or the people's right. . . . . The common law so founded and named is universally comprehensive, *jubens honesta prohibens contraria;* its precepts are *honeste vivere, alterum non lædere suum cui que tribuere:*" Aston, J., in Id. 2343, 2344.

"Upon the whole, I conclude that upon every principle of reason, natural justice, morality, and common law, ... the right of an author to the copy of his works appears to be well founded:" Id. 2354.

11. "One rule can never vary, viz., the eternal rule of natural justice. This is a case that ought to be looked on in that light:" Lee, C. J., in Omychund v. Barker, 1 Atk. 46.

"When the nature of things changes, the rules of law must change too. When it was holden that deer were not distrainable, it was because they were kept principally for pleasure, and not for profit, and were not sold and turned into money as they are now.

"But now they are become as much a sort of husbandry as horses, cows, sheep, or any other cattle. Whenever they are so, and it is universally known, it would be ridiculous to say that when they are kept merely for profit they are not distrainable as other cattle, though it has been holden that they were not so when they were kept merely for pleasure :" Willes, C. J., in Davis v. Powell, Willes, 48–51.

12. "It has been the constant labor of judges, through all changes of society, to keep the common law consistent with reason and with itself:" Sir James Mackintosh, cited Ram's Leg. Judg. 26.

13. " *Quicquid agant homines* is the business of courts, and as the usages of society alter, the law must adapt itself to the various situations of mankind:" 3 Doug., ed. Frere & Rox, 373.

14. "It is one of the noblest properties of the common law that, instead of molding the habits, the

manners, and the transactions of mankind to inflexible rules, it adapts itself to the business and circumstances of the times, and keeps pace with the
improvements of the age:" Gibson, C. J., in Lyle
v. Richards, 9 G. & R. 351.

15. "The common law, which works itself pure
by rules drawn from the fountains of justice, is superior to an act of parliament:" Lord Mansfield,
cited Austin's Jur. 686.

"The law of England would be an absurd science
were it founded upon precedent only:" Lord Mansfield, cited by Kent, 1 Kent's Com. *477.

16. "The science of jurisprudence, the pride of
the human intellect, which with all its defects, redundancies and errors, is the collected reason of
ages, combining the principles of original justice
with the infinite variety of human concerns:"
Burke, cited supra, § 257.

17. "By the absolute rights of individuals, we
mean those which are so in their primary and strictest sense; such as would belong to their persons
merely in a state of nature, and which every man is
entitled to enjoy, whether out of society or in it. For
the principal aim of society is to protect individuals
in the enjoyment of those absolute rights which
were vested in them by the immutable laws of
nature; but which could not be preserved in peace
without that mutual assistance and intercourse
which is gained by the institution of friendly and
social communities. Hence it follows that the first
and primary end of human laws is to maintain and
regulate these absolute rights of individuals. And

therefore the principal view of human law is, or
ought to be, to explain, protect, and enforce such
rights as are absolute, which in themselves are few
and simple. The absolute rights of man, considered
as a free agent, endowed with discernment to know
good from evil, and with power of choosing those
measures which appear to him to be the most desirable, are usually summed up in one general appellation, and denominated the natural liberty of mankind. This natural liberty consists properly in a
power of acting as one thinks fit, without any restraint or control, unless by the law of nature; being
a right inherent in us by birth, and one of the gifts
of God to man at his creation, when he endued him
with the faculty of free-will:" 1 Bla. Com. 123–125.

§ 421. The opinions of different jurists, and
often even those of the same jurist as to the nature
of the law are, however, as we have often remarked,
extremely contradictory, and many expressions of
opinion inconsistent with those cited above might
be quoted. This inconsistency results from a conflict between two principles—namely, those of reason and authority—which prevails in the law as it
has at some periods prevailed in all other branches
of knowledge; and which, from the nature of things,
must always prevail with reference to every subject
until scientific knowledge takes the place of mere
opinion.[1]

---

[1] A striking and also typical illustration of this is furnished by
Sir William Jones, in his Essay on the Law of Bailments. This
work, the author intimates, may " be considered merely as a commentary on the argument of Chief Justice Holt, in *Coggs* v. *Bernard*," 2 Ld. Raym., 909; with reference to which Judge Story

§ 422. Rightly construed, indeed, the latter principle is not inconsistent with the former; for the force of authority rests upon the presumption that the opinions of men skilled in any particular branch of study are the most likely to be right; and hence, in all matters affecting the practical conduct of men, it is reasonable, in the absence of actual knowledge, that we should be governed by authority, or, as it is expressed in the maxim, *Cuilibet in sua arte perito est credendum.* This presumption is, however, merely a *prima facie* one, and must fall to the ground when actual knowledge intervenes. Hence, while great respect is always due to author-

says, in his work on bailments, § 8: "These divisions [referring to the classification of bailments made by Holt], it will at once be perceived, are borrowed from the civil law; and they have been transferred into our law by the elaborate opinion of Lord Holt, in the case of *Coggs* v. *Bernard,* and by the elegant genius of Sir William Jones, in his Essay on Bailments." The method and spirit of the essay will appear from the following passages:

"I propose to begin with treating the subject analytically, and having traced every part of it up to the first principle of natural reason, shall proceed historically to show with what perfect harmony those principles are recognized and established by other nations, especially the Romans, as well as by our English courts, when their decisions are properly understood and clearly distinguished:" Jones on Bailments, 4, 5. "The rescripts of Severus and Caracalla, which were laws, it seems, at Rome, have certainly no kind of authority at Westminster; but in questions of rational law no cause can be assigned why we should not shorten our own labor by resorting occasionally to the wisdom of ancient jurists, many of whom were the most ingenious and sagacious of men. What is good sense in one age must be good sense, all circumstances remaining, in another, and pure, unsophisticated reason is the same in Italy and in England, in the mind of a Papinian and of a Blackstone:" Id. 16. "Highly as I venerate his

ity, it is, as we have seen, in general the duty of the jurist to disregard it where it is clearly erroneous.

§ 423. This is the true doctrine, and, as we show elsewhere, is also the doctrine which most generally prevails among jurists, and especially among those of our own country: *Supra,* § 283, and note. It is, however, natural that the two principles should carry with them different force with different minds; and hence, while we find the greatest masters of our law asserting in the strongest terms the supremacy of reason, we find others asserting in equally strong terms the supremacy of authority, and indeed, we often find the same jurist asserting with equal emphasis at different times each of these two proposi-

[Sir John Holt's] learning and singular sagacity, I shall find my-self constrained, in some few instances, to differ from him, and shall be presumptuous enough to offer a correction or two in part of the doctrine which he propounded in the course of his argument : " Id. 40. " If law be a science and really deserves so sublime a name it must be founded on principle, and claim an exalted rank in the empire of reason; but if it be merely an unconnected series of decrees and ordinances, its use may remain though its dignity be lessened, and he will become the greatest lawyer who has the strongest habitual or artificial memory :" Id. 144.

It would be difficult to find more elegant and forcible illustrations of the main positions asserted in our text; and yet, in the brief space of the same little book, we find the following inconsistent assertions: "Nothing," said Mr. Justice Powell emphatically, "is law that is not reason"—a maxin in theory excellent, but in practice dangerous, as many rules true in the abstract are false in the concrete; for since the reason of Titius may, and frequently does differ from the reason of Septimius, no man who is not a lawyer would, in many instances, know how to advise, *unless courts were bound by authority as firmly as the pagan deities were supposed to be bound by the decrees of fate:"* Id. 70.

tions, without any apparent conception of their inconsistency.[1]

§ 424. The prevailing view of the profession is unquestionably that reason is to be held superior to authority; but at the same time, it is perceived that this is a dangerous principle in the hands of incompetent judges; and it is due to this perception that the principle of authority is so strongly insisted upon. The latter may therefore be said to be the *exoteric* and the former the *esoteric* doctrine of the profession.

§ 425. Whatever conflict has existed, it is, however, at least clear that at most periods in the history of the law the English jurist has been at liberty, as a general rule, to determine all or most questions arising by principles of reason and justice.

§ 426. This has been the practice of our greatest jurists, and to this is unquestionably due every step that has been made in the progressive development of the law.

[1] " Here we find two parties opposed each to the other, each of which takes as its device the sacredness of the law: the one, that of the historical law, the law of the past; the other, that of the law which is ever coming into existence, ever renewing its youth, the eternal, primordial law of mankind:" Ihering's Struggle for Right.

CHAPTER III.

EXPLICATION OF THE LEGAL THEORY.

§ 427. We pass now to the consideration of the legal theory. This we will briefly state in the form of propositions or aphorisms, which for convenience of reference are numbered, and to distinguish them from explanatory matter, also italicized. With one or two exceptions, these propositions will be found to be logically deduced the one from the other, and ultimately from the definition of the law as given by the legists.

§ 428. In order, however, that we may not be suspected of attempting to refute the definition upon which the theory rests, by drawing from it absurd consequences, it may be well to premise that these propositions have all been asserted; and—if we assume the definition—all, with the exceptions referred to, successfully maintained by the intrepid logic of Bentham and Austin; and that they have been generally received by later writers of their school.

§ 429. 1. *The fundamental principle of the legists is contained in their definition of the law, as being the command, or expression of the will, of the sovereign.*

§ 430. It is, however, a fact too obvious to admit of denial, that the greater part of the law is not of statutory origin, but has been developed, or, as the legists say, made by the courts in their judicial decisions.

2. *Hence, to meet this point, it is asserted that judicial decisions are in effect laws, or expressions of the will of the sovereign through the judges as its officers; and that, in the development of the law, the judges have in fact performed the functions of legislators.*

§ 431. It is also a well known historical fact that in all stages of society the jural relations of men are, to a large extent, determined by custom; and accordingly, it is the common opinion of the jurists of our own as well as of the Roman law, that custom has the force of law, or in other words, is law; and that in fact, as we have seen, it constitutes the most considerable element of the law.

3. *Austin, however, asserts, and in this he has been generally followed by later writers of his school, that, custom does not in fact constitute a part of the law until it has been recognized by the courts.*

§ 432. 4. *It follows from the definition that what is called international law is not law in the proper sense, but merely a branch of positive morality.[1]*

[1] Mr. Amos, indeed, seems disposed to recede from the position stated in this and the following proposition. Speaking of international law, which he describes as a "code of practical regulations closely analogous to a system of positive law," he says: "Some eminent writers, indeed, have rather insisted upon the analogy of this code to a body of mere moral prescriptions; but this analogy is far less close and real than the other one, inasmuch as the moral duties of states toward each other reach infinitely further than can or ought to be attempted by the most beneficial international code. Furthermore, the way in which such a code has in fact grown up, the form in which it is couched, the methods of its interpretation, and every other feature short of that of a political authority competent to enforce it, bear the

§ 433. 5. *The same proposition is also true with regard to constitutional law:* Seę note to preceding section.

§ 434. 6. *It follows, also, as we have already explained, that rights are mere legal powers created by the will of the government, or, as the jurists would call them, actions.*

§ 435. 7. *Hence, as is expressly asserted by Bentham, there can be no such things as natural rights, or rights other than those created by the government.*

§ 436. 8. *It also follows—since the state is the source of all rights—that it can not itself have any rights or be subject to obligations, either toward foreign states or its own citizens:* Austin's Jur. 73.

§ 437. 9. *The theory also involves the denial of moral distinctions as commonly understood.* For the term "rights," as we have seen, in its ordinary and proper sense connotes the quality of rightness, and there-

closest possible resemblance to the phenomena of positive law:" Jur. 46. Again, speaking of constitutional law, he says: "These rules, resting as they do on a more adamantine foundation than the passing caprice of the government of the hour, which indeed to them owes its very existence and authority, have been called by some writers 'constitutional morality.' . . . . As a matter of ethical or historical research, the use of the word 'morality' is here neither unappropriate nor uninteresting, but, just as in the parallel case of international law, the rules in question are as unlike as possible to moral principles and maxims, and are as like as possible to genuine laws:" Id. 104, 105. The qualified nature of these observations shows that the author recognizes their logical inconsistency with his fundamental theory—an inconsistency too obvious, indeed, to be formally denied. For as Maine well observes: "Whenever you introduce any one of the legal conceptions determined by the analysis of Bentham and Austin, you introduce all the others by a process which is apparently inevitable:" Village Communities, 69.

fore refers to and implies some standard of right
and wrong by which the existence of rights is to be
determined. To assert, therefore, that rights rest
for their existence exclusively upon the will of the
government (unless we abandon the ordinary use of
terms) is to identify that will with the standard referred to and to assert that conformity or non-conformity to it of itself constitutes right and wrong;
which is in effect to deny the existence of any natural standard; for whatever the standard of right
may be, it must necessarily be paramount to and
exclusive of any other. Indeed, apart from this
consideration, it is impossible to conceive of any
ground upon which the principles of justice, or
those principles which relate to rights, can be denied,
and at the same time any other moral principles
admitted; for these are, of all moral convictions, the
most clear and definite, and apparently the most
certain; and it would therefore seem that they must
constitute the last stronghold of morality to be sur-
rendered; and that if the conception of rights so universal and profound is a delusion, *a fortiori* our
other moral convictions must be so.

§ 438. Accordingly, Hobbes expressly asserts
that the will of the government is the supreme
standard of right; and that the terms "right" and
"wrong," "just" and "unjust," signify nothing
more than conformity or non-conformity to its will;
and Bentham and Austin in effect assert the same
proposition. For though they hold that utility constitutes the essence of right, yet they also assert that
it is too uncertain and indefinite to serve as a prac-

tical standard; and that of necessity, therefore, the government must be the sole and supreme judge of what utility may require.

§ 439. The difference, therefore, is only in the manner in which they arrive at the same conclusions; Hobbes for that purpose inventing the fiction of a social compact, and Bentham and Austin making use of the theory of utility; for they both in the end assert that the will of the sovereign is the supreme rule, and that the obligation of conforming to it is paramount to every other.

§ 440. So paradoxical, however, is this, and the conclusion stated in the seventh proposition, that the legists generally, since the time of Austin, have found it necessary to recede somewhat from the extreme but logical views of Hobbes and Bentham upon the subject, or at least to explain and modify them in such a manner as to be less shocking to the common sense of ordinary persons.

10. *Accordingly, Austin and the later writers of his school assert a distinction between legal and moral rights, and thereby seem to admit the existence of natural rights of a certain kind.*

They are careful, however, to explain and to insist that such rights are not rights in a proper sense, but mere moral claims, which the party interested is not at liberty to enforce, and which all, including the state, are at liberty to violate. In effect, therefore, they assert equally with Bentham that there are no rights but legal rights, and that it is these alone which the courts undertake to enforce, or with which the jurist is in any way concerned.

§ 441. A legal right, according to this theory, may be unjust and oppressive; or in other words, a man may have a legal right to violate what are commonly called the rights of others. Thus a man has a legal right to appropriate land conveyed to him on a parol trust, but not to appropriate personal property so conveyed; for in the former case the law expressly declares the trust to be void, and in the latter it does not. So a man may acquire a legal right to the property of another by holding it adversely for the period prescribed by the statute of limitations, though he originally obtained it by force or fraud, or even by larceny or robbery; and in the same sense at Rome, the master had the right to kill his slave, or the father his child.

§ 442. 11. *In the same way, a corresponding distinction is asserted between legal and moral right or justice; and it is asserted that an act may be at the same time legally right and morally wrong, and vice versa.*

§ 443. According to this theory, the terms "right" and "wrong," "just" and "unjust," do not denote conformity to a single paramount standard of right, but refer indifferently to several. These, according to Austin, are the will of God, the principle of general utility, the will of the sovereign, and common opinion. Of these, the first can be known to us only by means of the principle of utility, and is therefore in effect identical with that standard. The principle of utility itself, however, is, he asserts, so far uncertain and indefinite as to require, in matters of general concern, an interpreter, whose judgment shall be final and conclusive; and from the necessity of the case this interpreter can be no other than the government, or organized sovereign power. Practically, therefore, the will of the government is the paramount and supreme standard of right and wrong, or at least, of that species of right and wrong which is denoted by the terms "just" and "unjust." Persons, however, think for themselves, and form opinions as to their moral relations, and thus there is generated a body of moral principles, which by the force of custom and authority came to be generally accepted, and to which men in thought and speech habitually refer.

§ 444. There may, therefore, be distinguished three several standards to which the terms "right" and "wrong" refer, viz., the principle of utility, the will of the sovereign, and received notions of right. Of these, the first and last are denoted by the common term "morality," a distinction being made, however, between *theoretic* and *positive* morality; the former of which corresponds to the standard of utility, and the latter to that of common opinion, or received notions of right.

§ 445. When we say, therefore, of anything that it is right or wrong, just or unjust, we may mean either that it is conformable or otherwise to the principle of utility or to received moral notions, in which case we call it morally right or wrong, just or unjust; or we may mean that it is conformable or not conformable to the will of the state, in which case we say it is legally right or wrong, just or unjust, as the case may be.

§ 446. An act may therefore be right in one of

these senses and wrong in another. Thus, as is re-marked elsewhere, we may say that the poisoning of Socrates or the crucifixion of Christ was legally right; or we may say the same of the innumerable executions of innocent people for religious opinions, or for the imaginary crime of witchcraft; or, to put less extreme cases, we may say it is legally right to repudiate an admitted debt, or to refuse to restore property to another where the action of the creditor or owner is barred by the statute of limitations, or to refuse to perform a trust or a contract because it is not evidenced by writing; or generally, we may say, in every case where the law gives one man the advantage over another, however unjust or uncon-scientious it may be, that it is legally right and just that he should have it.

§ 447. 12. *It also follows, and the legists uniformly assert, that the power of the government is in its nature unlimited and absolute;* for the term "rights" includes every possible claim that men can have, either to the ownership of property, the enjoyment of the family relations, or the possession of liberty, or even life; and therefore to assert that these depend alto-gether upon the will of the government for their existence is to assert the absolute control of the government over the entire destinies of its citizens.

§ 448. 13. The last proposition is thus stated by Austin in a qualified form: "*Every supreme govern-ment is free from legal restraint;*" or "*(what is the same thing dressed in different phrase)*, ... *is legally des-potic;*" or, as he still otherwise expresses it, "*the*

20

power of the sovereign is incapable of legal limitation:"
Austin's Jur. 264, 283.

§ 449. It will be observed that in Austin's vocabulary, the terms "legal" and "legally" refer to
the whole law, and not to statutes only; and the
proposition therefore means that the power of the
supreme government or sovereign is not, and can
not be, limited by the law, or *jus.*

§ 450. Most of these propositions have already
been referred to and discussed, and are repeated here
in order that a complete and connected view of the
legal theory may be presented. They will, therefore, require only a few additional remarks at this
place.

§ 451. The second and third propositions are, as
we have remarked, mere expedients devised for the
purpose of reconciling the assumed definition of the
law with obvious and undeniable facts. Both are
the invention of Austin. With reference to the
second proposition, Bentham had indeed asserted
before him that the judges, under the pretense of
administering the law, did in fact make laws; but
this he regarded—and assuming it to be true, justly
regarded—as a gross and reprehensible usurpation;
but Austin, with a clearer perception of the logical
exigency, asserts that the judges not only exercised
but are in fact vested with legislative power; and
that the exercise of such power is therefore perfectly
legitimate and proper.

§ 452. The fourth and fifth propositions are necessary deductions from the definitions. The former
is obviously untrue; for nothing can be more certain
than that international and private right are essen-

tially identical in their nature. The fifth proposition will be discussed in connection with the thirteenth. The sixth and the seventh have been fully discussed.

§ 453. The eighth proposition is also a necessary deduction from the definition, but is obviously untrue. For in addition to the ordinary powers of government, there are other rights vested in the state which can not be distinguished in any essential particular from private rights; as, for instance, the right which the state has to its public buildings, and to the land on which these are situate, or to such personal property as it has occasion to own, and also the right to enforce contracts entered into with private individuals. Nor, though the state can not be sued without its own consent, it is less obvious that obligations are imposed upon it by its own contracts. It is also obvious that, with regard to foreign nations it has rights, and is subject to obligations, essentially identical in their nature with those existing between private individuals. Thus a state has a right to its independence, a right of essentially the same nature as that of personal liberty; and it also has a right of property in its territory, a right to restitution, and to compensation in case of injury, and a right to the observance of contracts made with it; and it is subject to all the corresponding duties and obligations.

§ 454. With reference to the ninth proposition, it is sufficient to say that not only does the reality of moral distinctions rest upon the universal consciousness of mankind, but it has been recognized by the jurists of all ages and of all systems of law;

and if—as is admitted, and indeed asserted as a fundamental proposition, by the legists—statutory and judicial authority can establish any principle, the existence of an inherent and necessary distinction between right and wrong, and the just and unjust, may be considered as an established principle of the law.

CHAPTER IV.

OF THE SUPPOSED DISTINCTION BETWEEN LEGAL AND
MORAL RIGHT, OR JUSTICE, AND BETWEEN LEGAL
AND MORAL RIGHTS.

§ 455. The assertion of a distinction between the
legally and the *morally* right or just clearly involves
an illegitimate use of terms. For if there are any
terms in our language that have a perfectly definite
signification, they are the terms "right" and
"wrong," "just" and "unjust;" and whatever difficulty there may be in determining the nature of
moral distinctions, it is at least certain that these
terms refer to one supreme standard, by which all
acts are judged to be right or wrong, just or unjust,
accordingly as they conform or fail to conform to it.

§ 456. There are, indeed, several standards to
which the question of right or wrong in particular
cases, or classes of cases, may be referred, but of
these, one is supreme and all others are subordinate.
Thus the command of a parent is, within certain
limits, the standard of right for the child; and
where the parties are bound by contract, the will of
the one is to the other, to the extent of his obligation, the standard of the just and the unjust.

§ 457. But in these and in other like cases, the
standard is confessedly subordinate, and conformity
to it is right or just merely because conformity to
some higher standard requires it.

§ 458. So, too, with reference to a vast range of subjects, the rectitude of actions is determined by their conformity or non-conformity to the will of the state, or to custom, or to utility; but when we assert that an act is right or wrong from its conformity or non-conformity to one of these standards, we do not merely assert such conformity or non-conformity, but also that the standard referred to either conforms to a higher standard, or is itself the supreme standard. Hence, the assertion that mere conformity to the will of the state constitutes right in any sense involves the assertion that that will is the paramount standard of right and wrong. In this matter, we can not serve two masters, but must declare our allegiance to one or the other. If the will of the state is, as Austin asserts, the supreme rule of justice, it is treasonable to that will to assert that anything can be just which conflicts with it, or unjust which conforms to it. On the other hand, if it be assumed that there is a higher standard than the will of the state, it is a direct attack upon the principle of morality to recognize any species of right and wrong, or just and unjust, that is not determined so to be by that standard; for, upon this assumption, the term "legally right," or just, connotes, as we have observed, both legality and rightness, or justness, and can not properly be affirmed of anything that lacks either quality. To say, therefore, that anything can be morally wrong and legally right, or *vice versa*, is as much a contradiction in terms as to say that a crooked line can be straight in any sense, or an uneven surface a plane.

§ 459. Thus (referring to an illustration already

used), according to received notions, it is absurd to
say of the execution of Christ or of Socrates, or any
other innocent person, that it was right or just in
any sense of the term; or to say that it is right or
just in any sense for a man to repudiate an honest
debt, or to appropriate the property of another, because the action of the creditor or of the owner is
barred by the statute of limitations; or to refuse to
perform a contract or a trust because not reduced
to writing as required by the statute of frauds. So,
upon the assumption that the will of the state is the
supreme standard, it would be equally a contradiction in terms to assert the converse of these propositions; and to do so would be as subversive of the
assumed standard as the assertion of the propositions themselves is subversive of all received notions of morality.

§ 460. The same remarks apply to the term
"legal rights," which in its ordinary sense denotes
merely rights which are recognized by the courts,
or in other words, *actionable* as opposed to *non-actionable* rights, but which is used by the legists in a sense
peculiar to themselves, viz., as denoting rights
created or existing by the will of the state.

§ 461. In whatever sense we use the term, however, it connotes not only the quality of legality, but
also that of rightness, and therefore can not be truly
affirmed of a power which, though legal, is unjust.
To speak of an unjust legal right is therefore as much
a contradiction in terms as to speak of a square circle
or a four-sided triangle.[1]

---

[1] V. Ihering severely criticizes Portia's judgment in Shylock's
case, and seems to be of opinion that she ought to have given the

§ 462. The term "rights" is indeed often applied to powers which are in fact ordinarily conceded to be unjust; as, for instance, in the case of many of the supposed rights which it was formerly asserted the husband had with reference to the wife. But in all such cases, what we mean to assert is, not that there can be a right which is unjust, but that the power referred to is in fact not unjust—an untrue, but not an absurd, proposition; and accordingly, although there has been no formal change of the law, many supposed rights, formerly exercised by the husbands, are no longer asserted.

§ 463. The supposed right of a master in his slave is referred to by Austin as an instance of a legal which is not a moral right; and he severely criticises Blackstone for asserting that such a right can not exist: Austin's Jur. 221, 222. It may be well therefore, to test the correctness of the two propositions by an analysis and examination of the rights, or supposed rights, growing out of the institution of slavery.

§ 464. To this end, it is necessary to revert to the distinction between rights *in personam* and *in rem;* the essential distinction between which is that the former avail or operate against some particular per-

---

Jew his pound of flesh (Struggle for Right). And indeed it must be admitted that sounder reasons might have been given for her judgment. It is absurd, however, to assert that Shylock had a right to what he demanded; and the judgment though based on insufficient reasoning, was obviously correct.

Indeed this seems to be the chief point of V. Ihering's objection; but surely the main point is to have the conclusion right; and if one's premises are wrong, it is better to be illogical.

son or persons, while the latter do not, but avail only against the world generally. In either case, as we have explained, the essence of the right consists in the jural relation existing between the owner of the right and some other person or persons ; viz., in the case of a right *in personam*, the relation of obligation upon the particular person or persons subject to the right; and in the case of a right *in rem*, the relation of duty upon third persons generally not to interfere with the free action of the owner of the right with reference to its object.

§ 465. Thus, in the case of the right of property, it is not the power of the owner over the thing owned that is denoted by the term, but the jural relation between the owner and third persons which prohibits interference on their part with the thing owned; for the exclusive object of the law is to regulate the relations between men, and, except so far as is implied by this object, it has no concern with the relations between men and things—as is implied by the term "property" itself, which, as we have observed, denotes merely· that the use of the thing owned is or should be appropriated, or exclusively confined, to the owner; or in other words, that it should be proper (in the sense of the Latin *proprium*), or peculiar to him, and not common to others.

§ 466. So in the case of the right of a husband in his wife, or of a parent in his child, or *vice versa*, the essence of the right consists not in the power which the one has over the other—for such a power, where it rightfully exists, constitutes, *ex vi termini*, a right *in personam*—but in the power to exact from

third persons non-interference with the relation.
Thus, a child has, in general, no power over his
father, but has, with reference to him, rights against
the rest of the world that they shall not interfere in
such a way as to deprive him of the benefits which
he otherwise would receive from the relation.

§ 467. In all cases of rights *in rem*, where the
object of the right is a person, there may, as we have
explained, also exist rights *in personam*, as between
the parties; and hence the rights arising out of the
family relation may be either rights *in rem* or rights
in personam. Thus the wife has a right *in rem* in
her husband as against the world generally, and also
a right *in personam* against him for her support; and
the same is true of the child with reference to its
parents, and of the family relations generally; but
the two classes of rights, though arising out of
the same relations, and often included under a common term, are essentially different in their nature
and are to be carefully distinguished from each
other.

§ 468. The same remark is also true of the rights
or supposed rights arising out of the relation of
master and slave; that is to say, they may be either
in rem or *in personam;* and if, as is generally assumed,
this classification is exhaustive, must be of the one
kind or the other.

§ 469. When we speak of the rights of the master, however, we generally have in view his rights
in rem only, or rights of the master as against third
persons, and not rights *in personam* which he may
have against his slave; and in this connection there
is no impropriety in the use of the term.

For as against third persons, that is to say, against all the world except the slave, and those acting in his behalf, and with his authority, express or implied, the rights of the master are true rights; for the injustice of the relation is a matter which concerns him and the slave alone; and there is no principle of right or morality that would authorize any one to interfere with another in this or any other respect, unless by virtue of some right in himself. Hence, though the relation be iniquitous, true rights *in rem* arise out of it as against third persons; and from these rights, rights *in personam* may also arise, as, for instance, the right of compensation for the killing or injury of the slave, or of restitution where he is appropriated by another, or the purchase money in case of a sale on credit: Chamberlain *v.* Harvey, 1 Ld. Raym. 477; 5 Mod. 186; Smith *v.* Brown, Salk. 60.

§ 470. In the same way, in many other cases, true rights may arise out of unjust acts or unjust relations. Thus the man who by force or fraud has acquired the property of another acquires as against all the world but the owner a right to it, with which justice and the law forbids interference; and so in countries where polygamy exists, the parties have rights *in rem* essentially identical with those which exist with us.

§ 471. It is obvious, therefore, whether we define a right as a *rightful* or merely as a legal power, that the master may have true rights *in rem* in his slave; that is, rights against all the world but the slave; for it is not only the will of the state, but also just and right that he should have them.

§ 472. The only question to be considered therefore is, whether the power which the master has over the slave himself can be termed a right; and with regard to this, it seems clear that it can not; for such a right, if it could exist, would be a right *in personam*, and would, therefore, imply an obligation upon the slave to submit to the will of his master, and in no sense of the term can the existence of such an obligation be affirmed. For an obligation implies a duty, or rather it is a species of duty; and it is impossible to conceive of any principle upon which it can be asserted that it is the duty of the slave to submit to the unjust power of his master; or upon which it can be denied that it is right for him to escape from it if he can.

§ 473. And this proposition is true, even though we should adopt Mr. Austin's own definition of duty or obligation; for according to him the very essence of a legal duty, or such a duty as can give rise to a right, is that it is imposed by the sovereign, and enforced by liability to punishment by the sovereign. But the state does not in general attempt to regulate the conduct of the slave to his master by its laws or commands, or to punish him for disobedience, but simply abandons him to his master's power. His position, therefore, so far as the law can make it so, is simply that of a chattel, as, for instance, a horse or a cow; and it would seem as proper to attribute the duty of obligation or obedience to the one as to the other.

§ 474. The last argument, however, carries with it but little weight, except so far as it demonstrates the absurdity of Austin's definition of duty; for if we could assume the relation of master and slave to be just, it would doubtless follow that the former would have rights *in personam* against the latter, precisely similar to those which, for instance, a father has against his child.

§ 475. The question as to the right, therefore, resolves itself into the question whether the relation between the master and the slave is a just or a righteous one; and as it is clear that in the ordinary sense of the term it is not, the affirmation of the master's right must rest upon the proposition of Hobbes, that whatever the state wills is right; for so long as terms are used in the ordinary sense, the enlightened reason of mankind will concur in the reasoning of Blackstone: 1 Bla. Com. *423–425; which, it may be added, has uniformly been sustained by the English courts: Forbes *v.* Cochrane, 2 Barn. & Cress. 448, cited *supra;* Smith *v.* Brown, Salk. 60; 2 Ld. Raym. 1274; Chamberlain *v.* Harvey, Id. 147, more fully reported 5 Mod. 186; Somerset's Case, Loft. 1; 11 St. Tr. 340.

§ 476. It is clear, therefore, that the use of the term "legal rights," as well as of the term "legally right," or just, in the sense in which they are used by Austin and writers of his school, is too great an innovation upon ordinary and established usage to be admissible.

§ 477. Nor is there any excuse for retaining them presented by the lack of appropriate terms to express the idea intended to be conveyed. For the term "legal " by itself expresses all that is expressed by the term "legally right" or just, as understood by the legists; and in the terms "action" and "legal power," we have terms which convey precisely the idea of a right as understood by them.

§ 478. It is, moreover, inconsistent in the legists —who, of all men, insist most strenuously upon the entire separation of law from morality—to make use of the terms "right" and "wrong" "just" and "unjust" or even of the term "right;" for however they may seek by definitions to eliminate from these terms their ordinary and familiar sense, they will always consciously or unconsciously, carry with them a meaning entirely inconsistent with their theory, and must therefore necessarily tend to confuse ideas which, whether tenable or not, would otherwise at least have the merit of simplicity.

§ 479. Without the use of these misleading terms, the whole theory can be clearly and unambiguously stated in a few words, for in effect it consists in the proposition that jurisprudence or the science of *jus*, or the law, is the science or doctrine of legal powers or actions only; and that rights, and right and justice, as ordinarily understood, are things either non-existing, which is in effect the proposition of Hobbes and Bentham, or at least non-existent so far as the law is concerned, which is the doctrine of the modern legists.

§ 480. Of these propositions, the former, as we have observed, is the most logical; for if it may be assumed that there are any principles of right or justice naturally existing, they must be as applicable to political rulers as other men; and, as we have already observed, it would be a monstrous proposition to assert that it is within the legitimate functions of the government to invent and enforce, in the comparatively limited class of cases which are referred to it for determination, a set of artificial principles, different from and inconsistent with those by which the intercourse of mankind is habitually regulated.

§ 481. We conclude, therefore, that the hypothesis of two kinds of right and justice and two kinds of rights, viz., legal and moral, is inadmissible; and that the legal theory of rights must rest for its vindication, if it can be vindicated at all, upon the proposition that the will of the state is at once the source and standard of right and justice, and that nothing can be right or just that does not conform to it.

CHAPTER V.

OF THE PROPOSITION THAT THE POWER OF THE GOVERNMENT IS ABSOLUTE OR UNLIMITED.

§ 482. The term "power" is extremely ambiguous, and from this chiefly has resulted the almost inextricable confusion of ideas which prevails with reference to the nature and extent of the powers of government. It will be necessary, therefore, at the outset clearly to distinguish the different senses of the term.

§ 483. In its ordinary and proper sense, the term denotes mere *might*, or ability to act, or, as it is sometimes called, actual power. It is also used to denote rightful power, or right; as when we say that the owner of property has the power to dispose of it as he will, or that the child is subject to the power of the parent: Puffendorf, b. 1, c. 1, § 19. It is in this sense we generally use the term when we speak of the power of government; as, for instance, in the following passage, quoted from 2 Rutherford's Inst. 393: "Civil power is in its own nature a limited power; as it arose first from the social union, so it is limited by the ends and purposes of such union;" and also where we say that the government has the power to defend itself against external enemies, or to maintain the peace. The term is also used to denote power existing by virtue of the law, or *jus*, and which may be called either jural or legal power, which terms, however, are themselves ambiguous, and require explanation. The term "jural" may refer either to *jus* or right, or in other words, either to positive or theoretic right; and though, in ordinary thought, the two senses are conceived to be identical in fact, as they are in theory, accuracy requires that they should be distinguished. The term is, however, most generally used as correlative to right, and we will therefore, in this chapter, make use of the term "legal power" exclusively to denote power conferred by *jus*, or the law. The term "legal" is also ambiguous, as it may refer either to *jus* or *lex*, and in the latter case would denote merely power conferred by law, in the strict sense, or statute; as, for instance, the powers vested in a municipal corporation by its charter, or in the federal or a state government by its written constitution. The latter sense is, however, exactly expressed by the term "statutory," and it will therefore be unnecessary to use the term "legal" for that purpose.

§ 484. The proposition that the power of the government is unlimited may therefore mean—according to the sense assigned to the term "power"—either that the government has, in fact, unlimited power, which is in effect to say that its power is unsusceptible of actual limitation (for otherwise the proposition would not be universally true), or that it has an unlimited right to control the liberty and to dispose of the lives and the fortunes of its subjects, or that it has the unlimited legal power to do so.

§ 485. These three propositions differ altogether
21

in effect, and will therefore each require a separate discussion. Pursuing this course, it will be found that the several problems presented admit of an easy and obvious solution.

§ 486. With regard to the actual power of government, the proposition is manifestly untrue; for all human power is in its nature necessarily limited, and the power of government, though generally great and even tremendous, is, like all other human powers, susceptible of successful resistance.

§ 487. The most obvious instance of such resistance is that of revolution, or, as it is called until successful, rebellion, the evil consequences of which are so obvious that it is not wonderful that it is often asserted to be unjustifiable; but whatever theory may be adopted as to what the power of government ought to be, or however great may be its actual power, revolutions in fact occur, and the power of government is thus successfully restrained; and to a still greater extent is its power restrained by the fear of revolution—a restraint as real, and as constant and steady in its operation, as the fear of the prison or gallows is to the would-be thief or murderer.

§ 488. The power of government is also often successfully resisted, and still more frequently evaded, by individuals. In this respect, despotic governments have no advantage over constitutional; in the latter of which the safety of rulers and the observance of the laws are enforced not only by fear, but by the intelligent sentiment of the community; while in the former not only are the laws in general less observed, but the sovereign himself is frequently assassinated.

§ 489. By means of these instrumentalities, namely, by fear of force, and by evasion, a real and powerful restraint is imposed upon the government by the manners and customs, or moral convictions, or, as it may be otherwise expressed, the positive morality, of the people; or in other words, by the force of public opinion;[1] for no fact in the history of mankind is more obvious than that beyond a certain point the power of government is unavailing against the quiet but resistless operation of this force; and that, when opposed by it, laws in general are dead letters—either failing originally to take effect, or becoming obsolete as manners and customs change.

§ 490. Of these moral convictions, as we have already observed, and can not too often observe, the strongest and most universal are those which relate to right; and whether this is a mere superstition or

[1] " Nothing appears more surprising, to those who consider human affairs with a philosophical eye, than the easiness with which the many are governed by the few; and the implicit submission with which men resign their own sentiments and passions to those of their rulers. When we inquire by what means this wonder is effected, we shall find that, as *force* is always on the side of the governed, the governors have nothing to support them but *opinion*. It is therefore on opinion only that government is founded; and this maxim extends to the most despotic and most military government, as well as to the most free and most popular. The soldan of Egypt, or the emperor of Rome, might drive his harmless subjects, like brute beasts, against their sentiments and inclinations; but he must at least have led his mamalukes, or pretorian bands, like men, by their opinion:" Hume's Essays, 4.

not, the fact is certain that in all ages and states of society their existence is asserted, and accepted with implicit faith, by all; as, for instance, the right to life, to liberty, and to property, and the right of a husband and father over his family, and in case of injury the consequent rights to compensation and restitution; and while in different periods and states of society, the opinions, or rather the moral convictions, of the people have varied, not as to the nature and existence, but as to the extent, of these rights, yet in all countries at any given time such rights are clearly and sharply defined by the manners and customs of the people, and in general are subject to no doubts or differences of opinion either as to their existence or extent. Accordingly, the sentiment of rights, and the corresponding notions of justice as established in the general conscience, or concurring moral convictions of the people, impose an insuperable resistance to the power of government; and all governments in fact hold their very existence upon the condition that they shall substantially observe them.[1]

§ 491. This resistance, indeed, varies in different political societies, but it is real and powerful everywhere, and may be safely affirmed to be greatest in those which are most advanced in civilization—a fact strikingly illustrated in the modern civilized nations of the world, in none of which could any government long exist if the rights to

[1] This is pithily expressed in the old Visigothic code: *Rcy seras si fecieres derecho, et si non fecieres derecho non seras rey* (thou shalt be king if thou doest right, and if thou doest not right thou shalt not be king).

life, liberty or property, or those arising out of the family relation should become insecure, either by reason of the inefficiency of the government or its own positive interference; and indeed the most characteristic distinction of the modern civilization consists in the clearer and more definite conception of rights generally prevailing, and the controlling power of this conception over government.

§ 492. It is *Nomos*, therefore, (to use a familiar illustration), who is the only absolute king (*nomos ho panton Basileus*), and *Leviathan* is but his vicegerent, who, like other subordinate ministers, may often, within certain limits, abuse the powers intrusted to him, but who, if he undertakes to resist and defy the will of the true king, is sooner or later made to know and to submit to his power.

§ 493. The proposition that the government has an unlimited right as against its subjects is equally untenable. Government exists for certain specific purposes, and its rightful powers are limited to such as are necessary and proper to the exercise of its function: 2 Rutherford's Inst. 393. Beyond this the exercise of political power is a usurpation, to which a regard to our own or the public welfare may require us in some cases to submit, but which in others may be rightfully resisted.

§ 494. Thus it is obvious—and indeed is admitted by Bentham and Austin with the legists generally—that circumstances of such extreme oppression may occur as to justify revolution or organized resistance to the government; and at the present day it is perhaps generally conceded that every state has a right to abrogate or to alter its existing government, and that the sole question involved with reference to such a change is that of expediency.

§ 495. Hence the proposition under discussion, as qualified by the legists, merely asserts that the power of government can not rightfully be resisted except in extreme and anomalous cases, and then only by the extraordinary remedy of revolution. But even this proposition is obviously untrue; for the same reason that would justify revolution in extreme cases would also justify resistance to or evasion of the will of government in any case of extreme oppression, where it can be made available, without producing greater evil than submission. This is expressly admitted by Bentham, and in effect by Austin, and is, indeed, too clear to be denied.

§ 496. Thus it can not be wrong, or opposed to utility, for a man condemned under an unjust law, as, for instance, for heresy or witchcraft, to escape if he can from death or imprisonment,[1] or for a slave to escape from his master; and indeed, it is extremely doubtful whether in any case there is any principle of right or utility which would forbid a man to resist any unjust law which wrongs him, provided he can do it without violating some principle of right or utility other than that which enjoins submission to the will of the government.

§ 497. It is also clear that the rightful power ·of the government is limited by the principles of justice established in the morality of the people and recognized by the general conscience. These constitute,

---

[1] The reasoning of Socrates (or Plato) on this point, in the Crito, is not very sat·sfactory.

as we have seen, a limit by which all governments are in fact restrained; nor can it be doubted that, in this, human nature is wiser than any theory, and that it would be contrary to the welfare of mankind for the fact to be otherwise.

§ 498. For the power of government, though essential to the good and even to the existence of society, is nevertheless dangerous and terrible in its nature, and in all ages has been the source of the most serious evils with which mankind has been afflicted. Hence every limitation upon its power, which is consistent with its existence, and with the performance of its essential functions, is a blessing to mankind; and in this case we have a natural limitation universally operating, which has not been productive of any serious inconvenience, and against which no objection can be urged, except that it is inconsistent with a newly invented theory as to the nature of rights and the power of government, which is neither definite in its expression nor susceptible of any rational demonstration.[1]

§ 499. The proposition that the government is vested *by law* with unlimited power over its subjects

---

[1] "Moreover, he who bids the law to be supreme makes God supreme; but he who intrusts man with supreme power gives it to a wild beast, for such his appetites sometimes make him; passion, too, influences those who are in power, even the very best of men; for which reason the law is 'intellect free from appetite:'" Aristotle, Politics, b. 3, c. 16.

"How sublime is Guizot's metaphor, and how welcome the word (sovereignty,) as he uses it. Justice, reason, law, as embodying its dictates, is alone sovereign. Let the notion of any other sovereign be trampled under foot:" Bliss on Sovereignty, 175.

;s also untenable. According to the legal theory, indeed, the term "legal power," as applied to the government, is, indeed, inadmissible; for to assert that the government derives its powers from the law is but to say that it derives them from its own will, which is meaningless and absurd. Hence, according to this theory, it is equally absurd to say either that the legal power of the government is limited or that it is not.

§ 500. It is, however, beyond dispute that in general the power of the government is, in fact, derived from the constitution of the state; for it is this alone, as Austin himself says, "which fixes the constitution and structure of the government," and "which determines . . . . the person or . . . . the persons in whom, for the time being, the sovereignty shall reside—and supposing the government in question an aristocracy, or government of a number —which determines, moreover, the mode wherein the sovereign powers shall be shared by the constituent members of the sovereign number or body:" Austin's Jur. 274. Which is, in effect, to say that the sovereign derives not only its powers, but its corporate existence, from the law. And this is true, even of the most absolute governments; for in such governments, unless there were some law or principle to determine the succession, the government itself would dissolve upon the death of the reigning sovereign.

§ 501. Thus in the European monarchies the succession is universally determined by established and well defined rules of descent, identical in their nature with those which determine the succession to private property, and which are equally part of the law; and it is by virtue of these alone that upon the death of the reigning monarch his heir succeeds. In the same way, in popular or mixed governments, the succession of the different members of the supreme government is determined either by the rules of descent, as in the case of the king and the house of lords in England, or by some other fixed and established principles; and without these society would be continually reduced to a state of anarchy. Nor would the case be different even if we should assume with Austin (Austin's Jur. 275) that where the monarch is sovereign he has the power to abrogate the existing rules of descent and to establish a different order of succession, or even to designate a particular successor. For in this case, also, the new sovereign would derive his power from the law as established by his predecessor, and it would therefore come within the description of legal power.

§ 502. There is no impropriety, therefore, in saying that the sovereign derives his power from the law, or that he is vested with legal power. On the contrary, it may in fact be asserted that his power in all cases, except in that of usurpation, is thus derived; and accordingly we find this, in effect, asserted by Bracton: "*Ipse autem rex non debit esse sub homine, sed sub Deo, et lege, quia lex facit regem:*" 1 Spence's Eq. Jur. *125.

§ 503. It seems obvious, also, that the power given by the law is necessarily limited to what is given. This, in different cases, may be greater or less, but in no case, at least in civilized countries, can it be considered unlimited. For in all such countries, as we have seen, the power of government is in fact limited, to a greater or less extent, by the principles of private right, which in fact constitute, in part, the law of the land, and the observance of which is, in fact as in theory, an implied condition of political power.

§ 504. In all constitutional governments especially, not only are the powers given by the constitution clearly defined, but universally there are special provisions limiting and restraining the powers granted. Thus the powers of the United States government are limited to the general powers granted by the constitution, either expressly or by necessary implication, and are subject also to various special restrictions; and this is true also of the state government, whose powers, though more general than those of the federal government, are also derived from their written constitutions, and are therefore not only limited to the powers granted, but also by numerous restrictive provisions. So, also, in England, the powers granted are not only defined with equal clearness by the unwritten constitution, but are restricted by numerous well established and fundamental principles.

§ 505. It is, however, asserted by Austin that constitutional law, as against the sovereign, " is positive morality only, or is enforced merely by moral sanctions," and he therefore infers that, like international law, it is not law in the proper sense. The conclusion, however, does not follow from the premises; for, as we have seen, the law generally is in the main nothing more than positive morality;

and it is also true with reference to some of its most
clearly established principles, that the means for
their enforcement are inadequate. Thus in England the right of personal liberty was clearly a valid
right; and it was declared in Magna Charta, and in
other statutes, that it should not be infringed; but
as against the king no adequate legal remedy existed
until the passage of the *habeas corpus* act. So in
other cases, as we have shown elsewhere, rights may
exist, though remedies to enforce them, or to enforce
the principles upon which they rest, may be lack-
ing. The conclusion that constitutional law is not
law is therefore no more tenable than the similar
proposition with reference to international law.

CHAPTER VI.

OF THE PROPOSITION THAT THE POWER OF THE SOVER-
EIGN OR SUPREME GOVERNMENT IS NOT SUSCEPTIBLE
OF LEGAL LIMITATION.

§ 506. The conclusion at which we arrived in
our last chapter, that the sovereign power is susceptible of legal limitation, and that it is in fact generally so limited, was based upon the assumption
that the law is not a mere expression of legislative
will, but consists in the main of principles established in the manners and customs of the people;
and the conclusion reached, therefore, does not
touch the argument of Austin, which is based upon
the contrary assumption. It remains, therefore, to
inquire whether his proposition can be sustained
upon his own assumption, *i. e.*, whether the sovereign power is susceptible of being limited by law in
the strict sense, or statute.

§ 507. The proposition as stated by Austin would
seem, in fact, to assert two propositions, viz., one as
to the power of *the supreme government*, and the
other as to that of *the sovereign;* but these terms are
properly used by him as synonymous, and the two
propositions are therefore to be taken as identical.

§ 508. The term "sovereign" is, however, sometimes used to denote the state considered independently of the political organization existing at any
given time—a notion essentially different from that

of supreme political government: *Supra*, § 91. For
though, for instance, it may be said without impropriety that England has existed as a sovereign state
from the time of the Saxons, this can not be affirmed
of the supreme government, which, besides being
frequently revolutionized, has been constantly under-
going a gradual but radical change, and which has
never at any two considerably removed epochs continued to be the same. Hence, if we use the term
"sovereign" as equivalent to supreme government,
no proposition as to the location of the sovereignty
can be affirmed, which will be true of all periods of
English history. Immediately after the Conquest,
it was in the king, afterward in the king and lords,
then in the king, lords and commons, and now,
perhaps, as is asserted by a recent writer, in the
commons alone: Pollock's Hist. of Pol. 288, note.

§ 509. The two senses of the term are, however,
extremely liable to be confounded; and have, in fact,
been confounded by Austin in the argument used
by him to support his proposition, and which we
here reproduce in his own language.

§ 510. "It follows," he says, "from the essential
difference of a positive law, and from the nature of
sovereignty, and independent political society, that
the power of a monarch properly so called, or the
power of a sovereign body in its collegiate and sovereign capacity, is incapable of legal limitation. A
monarch or sovereign number bound by legal duty
were subject to a higher or superior sovereign, that
is to say, a monarch or sovereign bound by a legal
duty were sovereign, and not sovereign. Supreme
power limited by a positive law is a flat contradic-

tion in terms. Nor would a political society escape from legal despotism, although the power of the sovereign were bound by legal restraint. The power of the superior sovereign immediately imposing the restraints, or the power of some other sovereign superior to that superior, would still be absolutely free from the fetters of positive law. For unless the imagined restraints were ultimately imposed by a sovereign not in a state of subjection to a higher and superior sovereign, a series of sovereigns ascending to infinity would govern the imagined community— which is impossible and absurd. Monarchs and sovereign bodies have attempted to bind themselves or to oblige the successors to their sovereign powers. But in spite of the laws which sovereigns have imposed on themselves, or which they have imposed on the successors to their sovereign powers, the position that sovereign power is incapable of legal limitation will hold universally, or without exception. The immediate author of a law or any of the sovereign successors to that immediate author, may abrogate it at pleasure. And though the law be not abrogated, the sovereign for the time being is not constrained to observe it by a legal or political sanction; . . . . a departure by a sovereign or a state from the law of the kind in question is not illegal. If a law which it sets to its subjects conflicts with a law of the kind, the former is legally valid or legally binding:" Austin's Jur. 270, 271.

§ 511. Obviously, the apparent force of this argument is due to a confusion of the two senses of the term "sovereign." For, keeping this ambiguity in view, there is nothing absurd in asserting that the supreme government may be at once " sovereign, and not sovereign :" *i. e.*, sovereign as being the supreme political organization, but not sovereign as being the state.

§ 512. Nor is there at least any absurdity in the proposition that the government, though sovereign in one sense, may be "subject to a higher or superior sovereign," namely, the state; or that its powers may be limited by organic laws imposed by the state, or in other words, by the expressed will of the state.

§ 513. Indeed, this, though its possibility is sometimes denied by those familiar only with the political organizations of the Old World, is in fact, realized by the governments of the American states, and in that of the United States. For the powers of all the American governments, state and federal, are in fact limited by written constitutions which come within the definition of law in the strictest sense; and it is, as we have seen, a familiar principle of the American law that any law enacted by the legislature or congress in excess of its constitutional power is invalid.[1]

[1] In England, also, the power of the government is limited to a certain extent by written laws; for in that country, not only have the fundamental rights of life, liberty and property been universally recognized and asserted by the courts as well as by the community generally, but their existence has been affirmed, and their protection provided for by numerous acts of parliament, which have been universally considered to be fundamental or constitutional in their character; and at least on one memorable occasion, we have seen a king deposed and the succession altered by the lords and commons on the ground that he had " endeavored to subvert the constitution of the kingdom by breaking the original

§ 514. The only question, therefore, that can arise is, whether these governments are supreme governments; and this again turns upon the definition of that term. The term "supreme," when applied to a government, denotes merely that it is the highest government in the state and has no reference to the degree of power with which it may be vested. And the meaning of the term "government" is itself equally obvious; it denotes the permanent political organization by which the people of a state are governed, and does not include in its signification such bodies as constitutional conventions, which are only occasional in occurrence, and temporary in continuance. Hence, in the proper sense of the term, the only governments that exist in the United States, except municipalities, are those of the several states and the federal government; and these are, therefore, unquestionably supreme governments.

contract between the king and the people," and had "violated the fundamental laws:" 1 Bla. Com. *211. It may, indeed, be said that the act was in violation of the principle of the constitution, which required the concurrence of the king, and that it was, therefore, revolutionary in its character. But this is merely to say that an ordinary remedy did not exist to vindicate the fundamental law to which the government owed "its very existence and authority:" Amos' Jur. 104. It may therefore be said, without any impropriety, that Magna Charta † the petition of right, the *habeas corpus* act, and the other statutes by which the rights of life, liberty and property have been asserted and their protection provided for, are, in fact, fundamental or constitutional laws, identical in their nature with the bills of rights of the American constitutions.

† "Magna Charta 'neath whose sheltering wings
    Kings are but subjects, subjects kings."
                        Schiller, *Bowring's Translation.*

§ 515. Nor is it a sufficient answer to this reasoning to say that a constitutional convention is itself a legislative assembly, or, as Mr. Austin expresses it, "an extraordinary and ulterior legislature:" Austin's Jur. 254. This is undoubtedly true; but it is not true that it can be called a government, even when in session; or, still less, after it has adjourned and ceased to exist.

§ 516. Nor can it be said, with any propriety, that the body of electors by whom the constitution is adopted constitutes a government or political organization; for it is only an unorganized mass, incapable of spontaneous movement, and which can be called into action only by a power from without; for, by all the American constitutions, a constitutional convention can be called, or a constitutional amendment submitted to the people, only by an act of the legislature; and hence, until such a law is enacted, the electoral body is without power to act, and constitutes no part of the government.

§ 517. In America, therefore, at least, the case is presented of governments whose powers are defined and limited by organic laws, imposed upon them by the state, acting by a temporary organization, which ceased with the enactment of such laws; and these governments are unquestionably supreme in the same sense that other governments are; for in them is vested the highest organized political power in the state; and apart from them, there is in the state no other political power, except that which exists as in other countries, in the unorganized mass of the people.

22

§ 518. It will be observed, however, that the argument of Austin does not rest exclusively upon the definition of the law as being an expression of the will of the sovereign, but in part upon the proposition that constitutional law is not susceptible of "a legal or political sanction," or in other words, is not susceptible of being legally enforced; hence he asserts it is not law in the true sense, but positive morality only.

§ 519. It is obvious, however, as we have observed, that if by the term "power" either right or legal power is meant, the power of the sovereign is limited by the organic law, to which it admittedly owes its existence; and this proposition is in no way affected even though it should happen that there should be no legal remedy provided for the enforcement of the limit.

§ 520. Thus it is a well established principle of the American law, that an act of congress in excess of the constitutional powers of the federal government is absolutely void; and so far as the direct infringement of private rights is concerned, this principle is in fact enforced by the courts; but in questions merely political, there is in general no practical means of restraining the execution of the law. Nevertheless, such a law is void, and not only affords no legal justification to any one seeking to enforce it, but every subordinate officer, and indeed every private individual, has the right to disobey it, and will be vindicated in doing so by the courts.

§ 521. The proposition, therefore, must be construed as asserting only that it is impossible by means of law or statute to impose any restraint upon the actual power of the sovereign.

§ 522. We are here met, however, by another ambiguity in the term "sovereign,"[1] to which, in fact, all the plausibility of this proposition is due. For the term "sovereign," or "supreme government," is used indifferently to denote either the government of a single individual or that of a number— two senses of the term assumed by Austin to be identical, but which are in fact essentially different. For in the former the term denotes an actual human being, and in the latter, a corporation or body politic —a fictitious or ideal being—different and distinct from the individuals that compose it.

§ 523. Hence the proposition that the power of the sovereign, or the sovereign power, is incapable of legal limitation, when predicated of a corporate sovereign, affirms nothing with reference to the powers of the individual human beings that constitute it.

§ 524. But this is in fact the real question involved. For the struggle for human liberty is not against an imaginary leviathan, but against the power of actual human beings; and the only question of material interest is to determine whether any legal means can be devised to restrain individual political rulers from abusing the formidable power with which it is necessary to intrust them. For the power we have under consideration is human power,

---

[1] Mr. Bliss justly complains of the dangerous uses that have been made of this word, and with much reason recommends its disuse: "As used by some, though intangible, it is not deceptive or dangerous; but it will not be so used, and in the future, as in the past, will breed disorder and tyranny:" Bliss on Sovereignty, 175.

which can exist only as an attribute or quality of some actual human being; and there are, therefore, in reality as many different powers as there are officers in whom power is vested; nor is there in fact any other power than the power vested in such officers. Hence if the power of each constituent member of the corporate sovereign can be effectually limited, the power of the sovereign, which is but the resultant of such several powers, will necessarily be limited, also, in the only sense which it is material to consider; that is to say, it will necessarily be less than the sum of the natural powers of all the individual members of the government, or less than the power of a single sovereign. For the same rule will apply here as in mechanics, that the resultant of several forces must be less than their sum, except where they all happen to act in the same direction.

§ 525. The proposition is, however, stated by Austin in another form, which avoids this ambiguity, viz., that "sovereign power is incapable of legal limitation;" and we will therefore adopt this as the proposition to be discussed. It is to be observed, however, that the proposition is to be distinguished from the proposition that "the sovereign power is incapable of legal limitation;" for the term "the sovereign power" is simply equivalent to "the power of the sovereign;" and in using it, we fall back into the ambiguity from which we are seeking to escape.

§ 526. To avoid confusion, therefore, we will define sovereign or supreme power as power existing in a political officer who has no superior in the government.

§ 527. It follows from the definition that where

there is but one officer or monarch in whom sovereign power is vested, his actual power can not be restrained by any legal means; for such would imply, in order to impose it, an officer superior to the monarch, which is contrary to the hypothesis.

§ 528. But where there are several officers vested with sovereign power, it is equally obvious that the power of each is limited or restrained by the others; and even though we contemplate the several powers of the different members of the government as one aggregate, the same limitations will still exist; that is to say, the power of each constituent part of the whole will be limited by that of the others, and there will be nowhere in the government a power such as that of a single sovereign. It may, therefore, be laid down as a proposition, true absolutely and without exception, that any distribution or division of the sovereign powers necessarily operates to limit and restrain them; and, as a practical corollary, that the maxim, *Divide et impera,* is as obvious a principle in the art of political organization as it is of war or of diplomacy.

§ 529. The proposition thus stated is too obvious to be denied, and in fact does not conflict with the proposition of Austin, which refers not to the power of individual rulers, but to that of a body or corporation conceived to be constituted out of such individual rulers. The two propositions, therefore, being affirmed of different subjects, can not be contradictory.

§ 530. It remains, therefore, to inquire, with reference to this corporate sovereign, whether its power is susceptible of legal limitation.

§ 531. We have defined sovereign power as power vested in an officer who has no superior in the government. Modifying this definition to meet the present case, sovereign power may be defined as power vested in an officer or political organization which has no superior; and the term "sovereign" itself may be defined as being such an officer or political organization—definitions which neither admit nor deny the unity of the sovereign and of the sovereign power, and which are therefore consistent with either hypothesis.

§ 532. The term "political organization," or "body politic," may be defined as any aggregate of individuals united by the possession of a common power, and capable of joint or combined action. The mere possession of common power, as, for instance, in the case of joint tenants or tenants in common in property, is insufficient to constitute such a body; but there must also be some sort of an organization by which the corporate powers may be exercised.

§ 533. It is assumed in the proposition under discussion that there can be but one sovereign or sovereign organization in a state, and that sovereign power is therefore necessarily a unit. Our inquiry therefore is resolved into the question whether this assumption is in fact true of all possible forms of political organization; and, unless this is universally true, the proposition must fall to the ground.

§ 534. In every state, the sovereign powers may be vested or distributed in various modes, of which at least five may be distinguished.

§ 535. First, it may be vested in a single sovereign; in which cases it may be admitted that the actual power of the sovereign is unsusceptible of legal limitation.

§ 536. Secondly, the sovereign powers may be vested in several individuals or organizations, in such a way that neither can act without the concurrence of the others, or of some majority of the others; as, for instance, in an assembly, or, to put an actual case, as in the constituent members of the British government, viz., the king, the lords and the commons. In governments of this class, there is no individual invested with complete power, or who can properly be called a sovereign; it is natural, therefore, that we should regard the members of the government in the aggregate as constituting a body politic or corporation; and for the sake of argument, it may be admitted in this case that thè actual power of the sovereign is unsusceptible of legal limitation.

§ 537. Thirdly, there may be several officers or organizations, each vested with general sovereign powers, which may be exercised by each without the concurrence of the others. Thus, on more than one occasion, the Roman empire was amicably ruled by two or more monarchs or emperors, and during a considerable portion of its history the Roman republic, by two independent and co-ordinate organizations or bodies politic, each vested with general sovereign powers.[1] In cases of this kind, there are

---

[1] That is, in the *comitia centuriata* and *comitia tributa;* for an account of which, see Hume's Essays, 10. The Roman constitu-

in fact two or more sovereigns, and it can not with propriety be asserted that there is any other; for there is nowhere in the government any individual or any organization of superior power to either.

§ 538. This, indeed, seems to be admitted by Austin, who asserts that in such a case "the given political society .... is split into two or more independent political societies;" Austin's Jur. 228. But in no admissible sense can it be asserted that the Roman republic was ever anything else than a single state, or that the Roman empire ceased to be such upon every occasion that it happened to be ruled over by more than one sovereign.

§ 539. Fourthly, the sovereign power may be divided between two independent governments, each of which may, within a limited and defined sphere, act independently of the other. Thus, in each of the American states, the federal and the state government, each within its appropriate sphere, exercises sovereign powers over the same people and territory, and are yet altogether independent of each other. In this case, also, there are in fact two sovereigns; for neither has any superior, nor can it be said that there is any other sovereign, either individual or corporate. And accordingly, it has been uniformly so held by the American courts, both state and federal.

§ 540. Upon this point, indeed, Austin is of the opinion that neither government is supreme, but

tion also furnishes a striking illustration of the case stated, in section 541, viz., the institution of the tribunate, with reference to which, see Mr. Calhoun's Disquisition on Government.

that the sovereignty is vested in the states jointly: Austin's Jur. 219; or in other words, that the states, considered as a body politic, constitute the real sovereign. But this is obviously incorrect; for the states can not act at all except upon the initiative of congress. Nor can they act without the concurrence of three fourths of their number: Const., art. 5; and hence if they be regarded as sovereign, the case is presented of a sovereign whose power is limited by a law of its own making.

§ 541. Fifthly, the sovereign powers may be divided between several departments or organizations of the same government, each of which may, within its appropriate sphere, act independently of the others; as, for example, in the legislative, executive and judicial departments of the government of the United States, or of any of the state governments.

§ 542. In this case, each department is sovereign, and, though the expression is unusual, may be said in fact to constitute a sovereign; for each is an independent and complete organization, vested within its appropriate sphere with sovereign power, and there is not anywhere in the government any individual organization superior to it in power.

§ 543. It is, indeed, more in accordance with common speech to consider the several departments as part of one government; and it may therefore be said that the three together constitute one corporate sovereign; but the sovereign thus constituted is a mere abstraction, which has no powers other than those vested separately in its separate departments, and is incapable of acting in any way except through them. Hence it can not be affirmed that its power is unlimited, for such a proposition could only mean that the powers of its several departments are unlimited, which is untrue.

CHAPTER VII.

HISTORICAL REVIEW OF THE LEGAL THEORY.

§ 544. The conception of the law upon which the legal theory rests seems to have originated in the definition of Blackstone, viz., that the law " is a rule of civil conduct prescribed by the supreme power in a state" [1]—a definition which itself owes its origin, as we have explained (*supra*, § 197, note), perhaps mainly to the ambiguity of the term, but immediately to the blunder of the commentator with regard to the nature of the *jus civile*, which he erroneously conceived to be the whole law, instead of being, as the Roman lawyers conceived it, a comparatively small and inconsiderable part of it.

§ 545. From Blackstone this conception was transmitted to Bentham, who derived his first notions of the law from the Commentaries of that author, and, among others, this conception.

§ 546. Bentham, however, being a man of great acuteness and independence of thought, and singularly emancipated from the influence of authority, quickly perceived the confused and contradictory nature of Blackstone's views; and especially the in-

---

[1] We are perhaps a little inaccurate in this, and should say only that it owes its reception to Blackstone's definition. The conception itself is coeval with despotic power, of which it exactly expresses the essential principle.

consistency of his definition with the conception of
natural rights, which he, in common with lawyers
generally, emphatically asserted. Hence, to escape
this inconsistency, it became necessary for him
either to abandon the definition or the hypothesis of
natural justice; and accordingly, after a period of
confusion and doubt, from which he seems to have
been relieved by consulting the works of Helvetius,
and perhaps of Hobbes, he embraced the latter alternative.[1]   .

§ 547. This diffculty having been removed,
there remained to him only this conception of the
law, as being a mere expression of the will of the
legislative power in a state, and from this, as a single first principle, all the tenets of the legists are
historically, and in the main logically derived.
Such is a brief and accurate account of this remarkable theory—a theory which, as we have shown,
denies the existence of human rights and the inherent difference between the just and the unjust; and,
as it were, deifies human force; which, as we now
see, was the joint offspring of the ambiguity of a
term and the blunder of a lawyer called from the
beaten tracks of his profession to discourse upon a
subject with which he was but little familiar, and
which, also, though thus ridiculous in its origin,
and absurd in its consequences, has yet come to be

---

[1] "The first ray of light which struck the mind of Bentham in
the study of the law was the perception that *natural right*, the
original pact, the *moral sense*, the *notion of just and unjust*,
which are used to explain everything, were at bottom nothing but
those innate ideas of which Locke has so clearly shown the falsity."
Dumont's Introd. to the Principles of the Civil Code.

almost universally received by English-speaking peoples.

§ 548. But though it is true that this conception of the law constitutes in fact the foundation and the sole first principle of the prevailing theory of juris- prudence, it is not to be supposed that this is in fact admitted by its authors. For though, since the time of Austin, this definition of law is assumed without proof by the writers of his school, this is done upon the supposed grounds that the definition has already been so fully established by Bentham and Austin as to preclude the necessity of further discussion; and they, in fact, hold that it is logical- ly deducible from ulterior first principles, and has, in fact, been thus rigidly demonstrated by the writ- ers referred to. It becomes necessary, therefore, in order to complete our review of the subject, to ex- amine the reasoning by which the definition is sup- posed to be established.

§ 549. The argument of Bentham is extremely popular in its character, and though expressed in nervous language, is so loose and even inconsistent that it is difficult to give it an adequate statement. The following propositions, however, will, we think, give a fair expression of his views, and are arranged in such a manner as to give them the greatest con- sistency of which they admit.[1]

§ 550. 1. The principle of utility may be assumed as a self-evident proposition or axiom.

---

[1] We append at the end of this chapter a statement of Mr. Ben- tham's argument in his own language (as found in the Theory of Legislation), and arranged in the same order as in the text of this work.

2. Utility is the tendency to produce pleasure or to prevent pain.

3. The notions of just and unjust, moral and immoral, good and bad, may all be resolved into that of utility and the opposite.

4. Men are incapable of any motive other than the desire to attain pleasure or to avoid pain; or in other words, a regard to self-interest is the only possible motive by which men can be actuated.

5. Virtue consists in a due regard to one's own utility; or in other words, in an enlightened regard to self-interest.

6. To a certain extent, self-interest naturally impels men to regard the interests of others; but this is not universally or even generally true.

7. Hence artificial motives must be created, which can only be effected by means of legislation, the function of which is to supply the feebleness of the natural interest which men have in the general good, by adding to it an artificial interest more steady and more easily perceived.

8. Such artificial motives can in general be created only by the creation of rights and obligations; and these in turn can be created only by the creation of offenses; or in other words, by penal legislation; that is to say, rights are created by the creation of obligations, and obligations by the imposition of penalties for failing to conform to the law. An obligation may therefore be defined as consisting in the apprehension of punishment threatened by the law; and rights and obligations are, therefore, mere creatures of the legislative will. Law, therefore, or

the expressed will of the legislature, is the source
and the sole standard of justice.

9. The law of nature, natural right, and natural
rights are mere figurative expressions, and the supposition of their actual existence a mischievous
delusion.

§ 551. It will be observed that the assumed first
principle of Bentham consists, in fact, of two distinct
propositions, one ontological, the other psychological; namely, the third and fourth of the propositions above stated, the former of which relates to
the abstract nature of right, and the latter to the
nature of the motive by which men are impelled to
pursue it.

§ 552. The argument of Bentham as above stated
is precisely identical with that of Hobbes, who indeed expresses it much more logically and forcibly,
and who also at least attempts, by an exhaustive
psychological analysis, to demonstrate the premises
which Bentham merely assumes.

§ 553. As far as it goes, the argument is consistent, and the conclusion follows legitimately and
necessarily from the assumed premises; for if it be
assumed that men are incapable of any motive other
than that of self-interest, it must follow, as Hobbes
has graphically demonstrated, that the organization
of a political force is essential to the interest of each
man, in order to save him from the state of universal and never-ending warfare that would otherwise
ensue; and upon this assumption, the necessity of
government would be even more apparent than, in
view of the actual constitution of human nature, it
in fact is.

§ 554. There are, however, several other consequences which would equally follow, and which must
be considered, viz.:

First, there would be no duty or obligation upon
any one to submit to the will of the government, any
further than impelled by the fear of punishment; or
in other words, every man would be at liberty to
resist or evade its will whenever he deemed it to
his interest to do so.

Secondly, there would be no obligation or duty of
any sort upon the government to regard the interest
or welfare of its subjects, any further than the individuals who compose it should deem it to their own
interests to do so; for according to the hypothesis,
these individuals are incapable of being actuated by
any other motive than a desire to secure their interests as understood by them.

Thirdly, there would also be no obligation or duty
upon any man toward his neighbor, either to benefit
him or to refrain from injuring him, except such as
might be imposed by the fear of evil consequences;
and every man would be at liberty, or, as Hobbes
puts it, would have the right, to act toward his
neighbor—even to his injury or destruction—in such
manner as he should deem his own interest required.

Hence Hobbes' state of universal and never-
ending war would still exist, in a modified form;
the only differences being that there would be added
to the warfare of every man against his neighbor
·the warfare of Leviathan against him, and of him
against Leviathan; and that fraud would be in
general substituted for force.

.§ 555. These consequences inevitably flow from

the premises assumed. For, from the nature of the case, the motive of self-interest can operate only through the perception of it existing in the mind of the party upon whom it operates; and the motive, therefore, must consist in the desire to secure, not his real interest, but his interest as understood by himself; and hence obligation or duty is defined as consisting merely in the apprehension of evil or fear of punishment. It is here, therefore, that the theory of Hobbes and Bentham breaks down; for it is utterly impossible to deduce the idea of duty, or moral responsibility, from the principle of self-interest, which is in fact a negation of that idea.

§ 556. Hence, in order to reach the proposition of duty or obligation on the part of the subject to the government—which was the main point at which he aimed—Hobbes was compelled to invent the fiction of a social contract, and thus by deliberate self-delusion to reach the conclusion he had in view.

§ 557. Bentham justly criticises this apparent artifice; but the method adopted by him to bridge over the gap in the argument is perhaps even more reprehensible. For this consists simply in taking advantage of the ambiguity of a term to assume a new first principle as identical with that originally assumed; that is to say, he quietly assumes the general utility, or interest of the community, as the test or standard of right, instead of private utility, or the interest of the individual—two principles not only distinct, but apparently irreconcilable; for the former, though perhaps not true, at least asserts the reality of the distinction between right and wrong;

23

while the latter in effect denies the reality of any moral distinctions whatever.[1]

§ 558. The two principles may indeed be reconciled by either of two hypotheses; namely, the one, that of Paley—which Bentham, indeed, would have repudiated—that the will of God is the supreme rule of right, and that by that will conformity to the general good is enjoined, and punishment denounced for a contrary course of conduct; the other, that self-interest, well understood, equally requires such conformity, or in other words, that a man's own happiness imperatively requires of him a due regard to the happiness of ·his fellows.

§ 559. The latter proposition is asserted by Bentham, not perhaps expressly, but impliedly, for he says, in the course of his argument : "Our own interest, well understood, will never leave us without motives to abstain from injuring our fellows ; " and also, "independently of religion and the laws, we always have some natural motives—that is, motives derived from our own interest—for consulting the happiness of others."

---

[1] Bentham seems to have been completely deceived by the ambiguity of the term, and to have been altogether unconscious of the difference and even inconsistency between the principle of general and that of private or individual utility. This appears, not only from the general way in which he uses the term, but from his definition of utility itself: *Vide,* § 583. His confusion of the two principles is clearly pointed out by Mr. Jouffroy, in his work on Ethics, and is, indeed, too obvious to require remark.

What is stranger than the original blunder is, that Mr. Bain, in the restatement of his theory, should fail to observe it: *Vide infra* § 583; and that it should also have escaped the attention of Austin (Jur. 167) and of Mill (Utilitarianism).

§ 560. Accordingly, the remainder of the argument may be stated in the following propositions, which we number as part of the original series:

10. Individual utility, or self-interest, well understood, imperatively requires of us conformity to the general good, and the motives of self-interest and of a regard to the general good can not in any case really conflict.

11. It therefore requires of us conformity to the will of the government, this being essential to the general welfare.

12. "The public good ought to be the object of the legislature," being necessarily included in the private good of the legislator as an individual.

13. "Morality" (or general, and therefore individual, utility) "commands each individual to do all that is advantageous to the community, his own personal advantage included."

§ 561. It seems, therefore, that Bentham's first principles, instead of being one only, in fact amount to four; namely, 1. That to every man right consists in conformity to his own private utility or interest; 2. That a regard to his own interest is his only possible motive; 3. That right consists in conformity to public utility, or the general welfare; and 4. That self-interest, well understood, requires conformity to the last standard.

§ 562. Of these, the first is inconsistent with a fundamental conception of human consciousness and the second with obvious psychological facts, and the third and fourth, while perhaps true, are certainly unprovable if the first two are admitted.

§ 563. It is to be added, also, that even if all

these distinct and apparently irreconcilable first principles are assumed, the practical difficulty would still remain, that there would be no motive corresponding to the standard of general utility other than that of self-interest, which consists in the desire to secure, not our true interest, or self-interest well understood, but our interests as understood by us. Hence were there no sentiment of moral responsibility or other altruistic motives to enforce it, the theory would be a mere barren abstraction, and all that could be said of it would be that, like the lever of Archimedes, it might move the world if we could find a fulcrum for it to rest upon.

§ 564. It is, indeed, obvious that the principle of general utility, like Hobbes' social compact, performs no other function in his system than that of filling a gap in his argument; and that his theory, like that of Hobbes, really rests upon the proposition that self-interest is the supreme end and the sole possible motive of human conduct. It is in fact, therefore, a mere rehash made up of the base and sensual morality of that philosopher, with the careless definition of Blackstone; and it may be said that it lacks the merits and combines the faults of both. For it lacks on the one hand the profound insight, the rigorous method, and the logical power of Hobbes; and on the other, the loyalty to the common sense or conscience of mankind, and to the notions of right and wrong, of just and unjust, and of rights, which characterizes Blackstone in common with lawyers generally.

§ 565. The fortune of his speculations presents a striking contrast to that of Hobbes, and illustrates at

once the lack of logic and the strength of the conception of right in the popular mind. For Hobbes'
logical consistency, and the aphoristic clearness of his
style, rendered his meaning too clear to be misunderstood, and his theory of human nature and of government was consequently received with general
execration; while Bentham was able to deceive himself and the world by the ambiguity of a term, and
to vail the deformity of his real views, by coupling
with them the altogether inconsistent theory of general utility.

§ 566. Austin's argument is somewhat different
from that of Bentham, and is more fully and logically expressed. His psychological theory, though
stated in a manner less shocking to the moral
sensibilities of mankind, is substantially identical
with that of Hobbes and Bentham. For like
them, he holds that men are unsusceptible of any
but self-regarding motives; and accordingly, he
resolves duty or moral obligation into the fear
of punishment. The following is a brief account of his theory on this point: "A command is a
signification of a desire. But a command is distinguished from other significations of desire by this peculiarity: that the party to whom it is directed is
liable to evil from the other, in case he comply not
with the desire. Being liable to evil from you, if I
comply not with a wish which you signify, I am
bound or obliged by your command, or I lie under a
duty to obey it:" Austin's Jur. 91. "Command,
duty, sanction, are inseparably connected terms.
. . . . When I am talking directly of the chance of
incurring the evil, or (changing the expression) of

the liability or obnoxiousness to the evil, I employ the term ' duty,' or the term ' obligation : '" Id. 94.

§ 567. He, however, does not fall into the error of Bentham in confounding the principle of individual with that of general utility, but clearly perceives and recognizes, and attempts to reconcile, the difference between the two.

§ 568. His argument is, that the ultimate standard of right is the will of God, and that the principle of general utility is to be inferred from his known benevolence. "God," he says, "designs the happiness of all his sentient creatures. Some human actions forward that benevolent purpose, or their tendencies are beneficial or useful; other human actions are adverse to that purpose, or their tendencies are mischievous or pernicious. The former, as promoting his purpose, God has enjoined; the latter, as opposed to his purpose, God has .forbidden. The benevolence of God, therefore, with the principle of general utility, is our only index to his unrevealed will:" Id. 109. " It is assumed further that God will punish those who disobey his will, and hence it follows that there is an obligation upon every man to conform to the principle of utility; or in other words, if he believes in a God, that he will be impelled to do so by the fear of anticipated punishment."

§ 569. It is, however, held by Austin that the will of God is not sufficiently known to us, either by revelation or the principle of utility, to serve as a practical standard, and consequently, that in matters of common concern the will of the government must be adopted for that purpose. Hence he concludes, with Bentham and Hobbes, that that will is the source of rights and obligations and the paramount standard of justice.

Upon this point we give his own language. "If the laws of God are certain," he says, "the motives which they hold out to disobey any human command which is at variance with them is paramount to all others. But the laws of God are not always certain. All divines, or at least all reasonable divines, admit that no scheme of duties perfectly complete and unambiguous was ever imparted to us by revelation. As an index to the divine will, utility is obviously insufficient. What appears pernicious to one person may appear beneficial to another. And as for the moral sense, innate practical principles, conscience, they are merely convenient cloaks for ignorance or sinister interest; they mean either that I hate the law, and can not tell why, or that I hate the law, and the cause of my hatred is one that I find it inconvenient to avow."

Accordingly, he draws the inference that "if we take the principle of utility as our index to the divine commands, we must infer that obedience to established government is enjoined generally [*i. e.*, as the general principle] by the Deity. For without obedience to the powers that be, there would be little security and little enjoyment." And hence, he further asserts, as a necessary consequence of this high function, that "the power of a sovereign is incapable of legal limitation," or, what is the same proposition dressed in a different phrase, "every supreme government is legally despotic:" Id. 221.

§ 570. His argument, however, is obviously inconsequential, and presents, indeed, one of the most familiar logical fallacies. For his major premise is that "no law which is uncertain can constitute a practical standard of right;" his minor, that all of God's laws are not certain; and his conclusion that none of them can constitute such a standard, which is a clear *non sequitur*. It is, however, clear, assuming either the authority of revelation or the principle of utility, that some of God's laws are certain; as, for instance, "Thou shalt do no murder;" and this is, in fact, admitted by Austin when he is defending the principle, instead of attempting to pervert it to the establishment of an inconsistent conclusion: Id. 127. It would seem clear, therefore, that the will of God, so far as known, should be paramount to all human authority; and that Blackstone's argument to that effect, which is severely criticised by Austin and Bentham, is incontrovertible:" 1 Bla. Com. *41.[1]

§ 571. In effect, the conclusion of Austin denies the existence of any revealed law, and, what is more significant, denies the sufficiency of his fundamental principle of utility as a standard of right. For if there be any such thing as right, whatever be its abstract nature—whether it consists in conformity to the divine will, or in conformity to utility, either considered as an index to the divine will or as an independent standard—it can not be denied that there are some moral principles which are certain, and therefore paramount to all human authority; and to assert the supremacy of the will of the state is to deny this patent and indisputable fact.

---

[1] Considering the prevailing character of human rulers, we should therefore say, with honest Dogberry, "Write God first. For God defend but God should go before such villains."

§ 572. It is obvious, therefore, that, like Bentham, Austin uses the principle of' utility merely as an argument to establish the moral supremacy of the government, and that both of them are, as we have elsewhere observed, mere *Hobbists* disguised as *utilitarians.*

§ 573. We conclude our brief review of the theory of Bentham and Austin with the following striking observations of Sir Henry Maine, the most distinguished and one of the most earnest of their followers. They indicate on the part of their author a profound consciousness of the inadequacy of the theory to which he professes to adhere, and which he asserts with perhaps the more earnestness as he feels it to be slipping from his grasp ; and at the same time they exhibit a commendable candor in stating the apparently insurmountable objections by which it is opposed.

" There is such wide-spread dissatisfaction with existing theories of jurisprudence, and so general a conviction that they do not really solve the question they pretend to dispose of, as to justify the suspicion that some line of inquiry necessary to a perfect result has been incompletely followed, or altogether omitted, by their authors: " Ancient Law, c. 5.

" Bentham . . . . and Austin . . . resolve every law into a command of a law-giver, an obligation imposed thereby on the citizen, and a sanction threatened in case of disobedience; and it is further predicated of the command, which is the first element of a law, that it must prescribe not a single act, but a series or number of acts of the same class or kind. The result of this separation of ingredi-

ents tallies exactly with the facts of mature jurisprudence; and with a little straining of language they
may be made to correspond in form with all law, of
all kinds, at all epochs. It is not, however, asserted
that the notion of law entertained by the generality
is even now quite in conformity with this dissec-
tion; and it is curious that the further we penetrate
into the primitive history of thought, the further
we find ourselves from a conception of the law
which at all resembles a compound of the elements
which Bentham determined. It is certain that in
the infancy of mankind no sort of legislator, nor
even a distinct author of law is contemplated or
conceived of.[1] Law has scarcely reached the footing
of custom; it is rather a habit. It is, to use a French
phrase, 'in the air.' The only authoritative statement of right and wrong is a judicial sentence after
the facts, not one presupposing the law which has
been violated, but one which is breathed for the
first time by a higher power into the judge's mind
at the moment of adjudication." Id. c. 1.

"So long as that remarkable analysis of legal
conceptions affected by Bentham and Austin is not
very widely known in this country (and I see no
signs of its being known on the continent at all), it
is perhaps premature to complain of certain errors
into which it is apt to lead us on points of historical jurisprudence. If, then, I employ the Indian
legal phenomena to illustrate these errors, I must
preface what I have to say with the broad assertion

---

[1] "Zeus, or the human king on earth," says Mr. Grote in his
history of Greece, "is not a law-maker but a judge:" Ancient
Law, c. 1.

that nobody who has not mastered the elementary part of that analysis can hope to have clear ideas either of law or of jurisprudence. Some of you may be in a position to call to mind the mode in which these English jurists decomposed the conception of the law, and the nature and order of the derived conceptions which they assert to be associated with the general conception. A law, they say, is a command of a particular kind. It is addressed by political superiors or sovereigns to political inferiors or subjects; it imposes on those subjects an obligation or duty, and threatens a penalty or sanction in the event of disobedience. The power vested in particular members of the community, of drawing down the sanction on neglects or breaches of the duty, is called a right. Now, without the most violent forcing of language, it is impossible to apply these terms 'command,' 'sovereign,' 'obligation,' 'sanction,' 'right,' to the customary laws under which the Indian village communities have lived for centuries, practically knowing no other law civilly obligatory. It would be altogether inappropriate to speak of a political superior commanding a particular course of action to the villagers. The council of village elders does not command anything, it merely declares what has always been. Nor does it generally declare that which it believes some higher power to have commanded; those most entitled to speak on the subject deny that the natives of India necessarily require divine or political authority as the basis of their usages; their antiquity is by itself assumed to be a sufficient reason for obeying them. Nor in the sense of the analytical jurists is there *right* or *duty* in an Indian village community; a person aggrieved complains, not of an individual wrong, but of the disturbance of the order of the entire little society. More than all, customary law is not enforced by a sanction. In the almost inconceivable case of disobedience to the award of the village council, the sole punishment or the sole certain punishment, would appear to be universal disapprobation. And hence, under the system of Bentham and Austin, the customary law of India would have to be called morality—an inversion of language which scarcely requires to be formally protested against:" Village Communities, 66–68. " Whenever you introduce any one of the legal conceptions determined by the analysis of Bentham and Austin, you introduce all the others by a process which is apparently inevitable. No better proof could be given that, though it be improper to employ these terms, ' sovereign,' ' subject,' ' command,' ' obligation,' ' right,' ' sanction,' of law in certain stages of human thought, they nevertheless correspond to a stage to which law is steadily tending, and which it is sure ultimately to reach:" Id. 69, 70.

§ 574. In the above remarks, Sir Henry Maine demonstrates conclusively that Bentham's and Austin's conception of the law has never in fact been even approximately realized in the history of the law; and he is therefore compelled to regard it merely as an ideal toward which the law is tending, and which it must ultimately reach;[1] which, in plain

---

[1] This has been seriously attempted in Spain, which may be emphatically described as a code-cursed country, having *in theory*

language, is simply to say that the legal theory is
not a true conception of the law as it is, or as it
ever has been, but of the law as the legists think it

been governed by written codes since the beginning of its history.
"No country of modern Europe can furnish so complete a collec-
tion of laws as Spain:" Schmidt's Civil Law of Spain and Mexico,
Hist. Outline, 88.

It may be added that the attempt has been altogether a failure,
there being perhaps no other country in Europe in which the law
is in so unsatisfactory a condition. There are, however, in the
fuero jusgo (one of the old Spanish codes, all of which are still
supposed to be law), some provisions, admirable at least in sentiment, to which it may not be uninteresting to refer. " Book I . .
. . provides, among other things, that the law-maker should be
mild and good, not only in words but in deeds and at heart, and
that he should also be merciful, and have God constantly before
his eyes, always aiming at public utility. . . . . The law . . . .
should restrain the bad from doing evil, and permit the good to
dwell in peace:" Id. 30, 31. "It expressly declares that the
people have the right to depose their kings when the latter fail to
do their duty. . . . . The doctrine of the Visigothic code on this
head was both pithy and brief: *Rey seras si fecieres derecho, et
si non fecieres derecho non seras rey*—thou shalt be king if thou
doest right, and if thou doest not right, thou shalt not be king.
In the administration of justice, we also find doctrines recognized
calculated to insure its prompt and efficient execution. . . . .
The responsibility of the judge was strictly enforced, and if he
gave an erroneous judgment, he was bound to pay the party cast
double the amount; and if he was unable to do so, he was pun-
ished with fifty lashes. . . . . The severity of the judicial responsibility was, however, mitigated in this, that the judge could
always exempt himself from the ignominious punishment of whip-
ping by making oath that the error arose from ignorance:" Id.
34–36. In this last provision, the Spanish law has the advantage
of any other with which we are acquainted. It is, indeed, related
of Alfred, that at the commencement of his reign, in order to purify the administration of justice, he hung some fifty or more of
the judges. But this was a mere temporary expedient, which,
fortunately for the judges, did not become a precedent.

ought to be. That such a consummation would be disastrous to the welfare of the human race, and that it is in fact as impracticable as it would be disastrous, has already, we trust, been made sufficiently clear. One other remark, however, may be added. Assuming that the law ought to be reduced to statutory rules, it must be assumed, also, as a necessary preliminary condition, that it should be first determined what those rules ought to be; and this it is the function of theoretical jurisprudence to determine. Even from this point of view, therefore, the study of the principles of natural right is of supreme importance, and ought to be insisted upon by the legists. Unfortunately, however, those principles are, as we have shown, utterly inconsistent with, and therefore necessarily destructive of, the fundamental conception upon which their theory rests; and hence they are compelled by the logical exigency of the case to deny the existence of such a science, and also the truth of the fundamental notions of just and unjust, right and wrong, upon which it rests; and to assert the will of the state as the paramount moral standard—at least, with regard to all matters of common concern.

Note to § 549. 1. "A principle is a first idea which is made the beginning or basis of a system of reasonings. To illustrate by a sensible image, it is a fixed point to which the first link of a chain is attached. Such a principle must be clearly evident; to illustrate and explain it must secure its acknowledgment. Such are the axioms of mathematics; they are not proved directly; it is enough to show that they can not be rejected without falling into absurdities. The logic of utility consists in setting out, in all the operations of the judgment, from the calculation or comparison of pains and pleasures, and in not allowing the interference of any other idea."

2. "Utility is an abstract term. It expresses the property or tendency of a thing to prevent some evil or to procure some good. Evil is pain, or the cause of pain. Good is pleasure, or the cause of pleasure. That which is conformable to the utility or the interest of the individual is that which tends to augment the total sum of his happiness."

3. "I am a partisan of utility when I measure my approbation or disapprobation of a public or private act by its tendency to produce pleasure or pain—when I employ the words 'just,' 'unjust,' 'moral,' 'immoral,' 'good,' 'bad,' simply as collective terms including the ideas of certain pleasures and pains; it being understood that I use the words 'pleasures' and 'pains' in their ordinary signification, without inventing any arbitrary definition for the sake of excluding certain pleasures, or denying the existence of certain pains. . . . . He who adopts the principle of utility esteems virtue to be a good only on account of the pleasures which result from it; he regards vice as being an evil only on account of the pains it produces. Moral good is good only by its tendency to produce physical good. Moral evil is evil only by its tendency to produce physical evil; but when I say physical I mean the pains and pleasures of the soul as well as the pains and pleasures of the senses. I have in view man, such as he is, in his actual constitution."

4. "The will can not be influenced except by motives; but when we speak of motives, we speak of pleasures and pains. . . . . Nature has placed men under the governance of two sovereign masters, pain and pleasure. It is for them alone to point out what we ought to do as well as to determine what we shall do. On the one hand, the standard of right and wrong ; on the other, the chain of causes and effects—are fastened to their throne. We owe to them all our ideas, we refer to them all the judgments and all the determinations of our life. He who pretends to withdraw himself from this subjection knows not what he says. His only object is to seek pleasure and to shun pain, even at the very instant that he rejects the greatest pleasures and embraces pains the most acute. . . . . The principle of utility subjects everything to these two motives."

5. "Virtue is the sacrifice of a less interest to a greater, of a momentary to a durable, of a doubtful to a certain, interest. Every idea of virtue that is not derived from this notion is as obscure in conception as it is precarious in motive; . . . . *sic præ-*

sentibus utaris voluptatibus ut futuris non noceas—so use present
pleasures as not to lessen those which are to come. . . . . It is
easy to reduce to a calculation of good and evil (*i. e.*, pleasures and
pains) all the acts of the most exalted virtue. . . . . The obligation which binds men to their engagements is nothing but the conception of a superior interest, which prevails over an inferior
interest. A man is bound not only by the particular utility of such
and such an engagement, but when the engagement becomes onerous
to one of the parties, he is still bound by the general utility of engagements; by the confidence in his word, which every sensible man
desires to inspire, in order that he may be considered a man of
truth, and enjoy the advantages incident to a reputation of probity.
. . . . This is a sort of a calculation of trade, speaking truth to
obtain confidence ; serving to be served. It is thus we must
understand the saying of a wit, that 'if there were no such thing
as honesty, it would be a good speculation to invent it, as a means
of making one's fortune.' "

6. " Private morality regulates the actions of men, either in
that part of their conduct in which they alone are interested, or
in that which may affect the interests of others. The actions which
affect a man's individual interest compose a class called, perhaps
improperly, duties to ourselves ; and the quality or disposition
manifested in the accomplishment of those receives the name of
prudence. That part of conduct which relates to others composes
a class of actions called duties to others. Now, there are two
ways of consulting the happiness of others ; the one negative, ab-
staining from diminishing it ; the other positive, laboring to augment it. The first constitutes probity ; the second is beneficence.
. . . . The rules of prudence are almost always sufficient of themselves. If a man fails in what regards his particular private interest, it is not his will which is at fault, it is his understanding.
If he does wrong, it can only be through mistake. . . . . It is
true, also, that there is a natural connection between prudence and
probity ; for our own interest, well understood, will never leave
us without motives to abstain from injuring our fellows. . . . .
Independently of religion and the laws, we always have some natural motives, that is, motives derived from our own interest, for
consulting the happiness of others. But in order that the individual should perceive this connection between the interests of others
and his own, he needs an enlightened spirit and a heart free from
seductive passions. The greater part of men have neither sufficient

light, sufficient strength of mind, nor sufficient moral sensibility to place their honesty above the aid of laws."

7. "The legislature must apply the feebleness of this natural interest by adding to it an artificial interest more steady and more easily perceived."

8. "The primitive sense of the word 'law,' and the ordinary meaning of the word, is the will or command of a legislature. The word 'rights,' the same as the word 'law,' has two senses, the one a proper sense, the other a metaphysical sense. Rights properly so called are the creatures of law properly so called ; real laws give birth to real rights. . . . . Rights and obligations, though distinct and opposite in their nature, are simultaneous in their origin and inseparable in their existence. In the nature of things, the law can not grant a benefit to one without imposing at the same time some burden upon another. How confer upon me the right of property in a piece of land? By imposing upon all others the obligation not to touch its produce. . . . . The principal function of government is to guard against pains. It fulfills this function by creating rights—rights of personal security, rights of protection for honor, rights of property, rights of receiving aid in case of need. To these rights correspond offenses of different kinds. The law can not create rights except by creating corresponding obligations. It can not create rights and obligations without creating offenses."

9. "The law of nature is a figurative expression, in which nature is represented as a being; and such and such a disposition is attributed to her which is figuratively called a law. Natural rights are the creatures of natural law; they are a metaphor which derive their existence from another metaphor. Real rights are always spoken of in a legal sense; natural rights are often spoken of in a sense that may be called anti-legal; when it is said, for example, that law can not avail against natural rights, the word 'rights' is employed in a sense above the law; for in this use of it, we acknowledge rights that attack the law, which overturn it, which annul it. In this anti-legal sense, the word 'right' is the greatest enemy of reason, and the most terrible destroyer of governments. There is no reasoning with fanatics armed with natural rights, which each one understands as he pleases, and applies as he sees fit; of which nothing can be yielded nor retrenched; which are inflexible at the same time that they are unintelligible;

24

which are consecrated in dogmas, from which it is a crime to vary."

10, 11. Propositions 10 and 11 as given in the text are, in fact, assumed by Bentham, but not expressly stated. The former is hinted in the passage quoted in paragraph 6; the latter is implied in that quoted in paragraph 13.

12. "Legislation ought to have precisely the same object [as morality]. The public good ought to be the object of the legislators; general utility ought to be the foundation of his reasonings. To know the true good of the community is what constitutes the source of legislation; the art consists in finding the means to realize that good."

13. "That which is conformable to the utility or the interest of a community is what tends to augment the total sum of happiness of the individuals who compose it. Morality, in general, is the art of directing the actions of men in such a way as to produce the greatest possible sum of good. . . . . Morality commands each individual to do all that is advantageous to the community, his own personal advantage included."

CHAPTER VIII.

OF THE THEORY OF UTILITY.

§ 575. It is perhaps unnecessary to examine the theory of utility itself, as it manifestly not only fails to establish the conclusions reached by Bentham and Austin, but is actually inconsistent with them. As, however, it is the principle upon which those conclusions are asserted, a few words with regard to it will not be inappropriate.

§ 576. The principle of general utility seems at first glance to be plain and easily understood, and also obviously true; but in reality, it is difficult to determine what it is; and, in the form in which it is asserted by the utilitarians, it is not only manifestly untrue, but even nonsensical.

§ 577. In its ordinary sense, the term "utility" denotes that which has a use for some end or purpose beneficial to men, and which, therefore, tends to prómote their well-being. The term, therefore, is relative, implying some man or men whose well-being is promoted; and so long as we confine our attention to a single individual, it is sufficiently clear. When, however, we proceed to use the term with reference to a number of men, or to mankind in general, the meaning becomes liable to be confused. Properly speaking, to say that anything is useful to two or more or any number of men is to say that it is useful to each and all of them; and if this is not the case, the proposition is not true; and we should say, not that it is useful to them, but that it is useful to some of them, or to the most of them, as the case may be. In the same way, to say that anything will be useful to a community, or to mankind, is to say, if we speak properly, that it will be universally useful; i. e., useful to every individual of the community or race. Accordingly, it is in this sense we use the term when we say that conformity to right is essential to the well-being of mankind; meaning thereby that in such conformity must consist each man's greatest good, or, in homely language, that honesty is the best policy. Thus when we say that murder or robbery or fraud can not be useful, we mean not only that it will be pernicious in general, but to every one, including the guilty party himself. So, too, in asserting the negative proposition, that nothing which is pernicious, or contrary to utility, is right, we mean that nothing which is contrary to the utility of any individual can be right.

§ 578. This is the conclusion that should follow from the argument used by Austin to establish the principle of utility. "God," he says, "designs the happiness of all his sentient creatures." And from this he should have inferred that whatever detracted from the happiness of any of his sentient creatures is wrong; but the inference actually drawn is, that "the benevolence of God, with the principle of general utility, is our only index to his unrevealed will."

§ 579. And this brings us to examine the meaning of the term "general utility," as used by Bentham and Austin, and utilitarians generally. Used properly, it would denote that which is universally useful; but according to a very common, and therefore allowable usage, it might also denote only that which is useful in most cases. Manifestly, the term can have no other sensible meaning; for, as we have seen, utility is that which tends to promote the happiness or welfare of men or other sentient beings; and it therefore can only exist as a quality in the men or other sentient beings whose happiness is promoted.

§ 580. If the principle of utility is to be understood as asserting only that whatever is universally useful is right, it can not well be denied, and is in fact admitted by all theories of morality.

§ 581. But if it is to be táken as asserting that whatever is generally useful is right, the proposition is altogether indefinite; for the term "generally" is itself unsusceptible of precise definition; and therefore in order to assert the proposition, it is necessary to determine the proportion of individuals whose útility is to be considered—whether a mere majority is sufficient, as is asserted in the execrable maxim that the greatest good of the greatest number is to be observed,[1] or whether three fourths or nine

---

[1] "Greatest happiness of the greatest number." This expression is used by Beccaria in the introduction to his Essay on Crimes and Punishment (1764). The following are additional examples of its use:

"That action is best which procures the greatest happiness for the greatest numbers:" Hutcheson's Inquiry concerning Moral Good and Evil (1720).

tenths, or a still greater proportion, is required;
and until this is done, the proposition has no definite meaning.

§ 582.   Nor even if this difficulty could be met
would it be possible to admit the proposition.   For
it seems impossible to assert as a general proposition
that the advantage of any number of men is a sufficient justification for the infliction of injury even
upon one innocent individual.   There may, indeed,
possibly be some cases in which this may be done,
where, for instance, the safety of the state or of the
community may absolutely require it; but these cases

" Priestley was the first (unless it was Beccaria) who taught my
lips to pronounce this sacred truth—that the greatest happiness of
the greatest number is the foundation of morals and legislation: "
Bentham's Works.

Mr. Spencer in his Social Statics (Introduction) very forcibly
argues that Bentham, in asserting this principle, unconsciously
assumes an anterior principle, viz., that every one has an equal
right to happiness. Mr. Mill, in remarking upon this position
(in his Essay on Utilitarianism), admits that such a principle is in
fact assumed; and indeed, says that without it the principle of
utility would be "a mere form of words without rational signification." It is however certain that the principle of equality of right
is not implied in the terms in which the principle of utility, as
ordinarily stated, or as stated by Bentham, Austin or Mill, and it
is therefore unquestionably an independent principle. It may be
added that the principle assumed is itself altogether inconsistent
with the principle of private utility, and also with that of the
greatest happiness of the greatest number. For the only practical
expression of this principle is, that every man has an equal right to
the free use of his faculties, natural or acquired, in the pursuit of
happiness; which is, in effect, denied by the two theories referred
to; the former, in effect, denying that any man has such right,
and the latter denying such right in any of the minority.
Whether it is consistent with the theory of general utility can
not be either affirmed or denied, at least, until some definite expression is given to that theory.

can only be exceptional; and the general principle must always obtain that every man's life and faculties are his own, and can not, unless by virtue of some clearly defined right, be converted to the use of another man, or of any number of men. To assert that any innocent man's property or his person may be rightfully violated, or any hurt done to him, whenever advantage to an undefined majority of others can be secured thereby, or in other words, whenever it would be generally useful, is a proposition too absurd to require discussion; and assuming the proposition to be true, there would be no end to the startling consequences that might plausibly and perhaps legitimately, be drawn from it. Thus upon this hypothesis, it would be difficult to deny that the ancient custom of exposing children was right, or (in view of the modern doctrine of the survival of the fittest) to say that the processes of nature might not advantageously be applied by the state, by killing off a considerable portion of the population.[1] Nor would the custom of the Massagetæ (Herod, 1, 215) of fatting and eating their elderly relations appear to be altogether unreasonable. In short, as Bentham says of natural rights, "there is no reasoning with fanatics armed

---

[1] Accordingly Hæckel (History of Creation, Ch. vii,) refers with apparent approval to the Spartan law which provided for the inspection of newly born children, and the killing of the weak and sickly, and expressly recommends capital punishment for "incorrigible and degraded criminals," as "not only just, but also a benefit to the better portion of mankind." Upon the same principle castration might be recommended as equally efficacious and more humane.

with" utility, "which each one understands as he pleases, and applies as he sees fit."

§ 583. The utilitarians, however, apparently use the term "utility" in neither of the senses we have given, but in a sense based upon the apparent analogy existing between the state or community and the natural man. In other words, they conceive of the state as of an actual being, susceptible, like man, of pleasure or pain, and of being compensated for pain in one part by pleasure in another. "That which is conformable to the utility or the interest of an individual," says Bentham, "is that which tends to augment the total sum of his happiness. That which is conformable to the utility or the interest of the community is what tends to augment the total sum of happiness of individuals who compose it." Or, as Mr. Bain states it, he defines utility as "the tendency of actions to promote the happiness and prevent the misery of the party under consideration, which party is usually the community in which one's lot is cast." Bain's Moral Science, 245.

§ 584. Accordingly, Bentham gives us specific rules for calculating utility, which are the same in the case of the community as in that of the individual; the process being to calculate, by what he calls a process of moral arithmetic, on the one hand all the pleasures, and on the other all the pains, which a given act or class of acts may have a tendency to produce, and to strike a balance between them.

Accordingly, if all the pleasures were experienced

by one set of individuals and all the pains by another, the rule would still apply; and if the pleasures of the one set were greater than the pains of the other, the act or class of acts would be useful. Indeed, it might even happen, considering the difference of men in sensibility, that the pleasure experienced by a minority might in the aggregate be greater than the pains experienced by the majority; and in such case, the act or class of acts, according to the definition, would be useful. Manifestly, however, this is sheer nonsense; for there can not be such a thing as happiness, except as existing in actual sentient beings, and there can not, therefore, be a general utility distinct from the utility of individuals.

§ 585. As should be expected, therefore, this principle is by no means a sure guide in moral questions; for there is hardly a class of wrongs or injuries which does not present cases which, so far as human knowledge can judge, may be justified by it. If, for instance, a poor man should come into possession of property of a rich one, under such circumstances that it would be impossible for the owner or any one else to know of the fact, and if we suppose the loss of the property to be of but little moment to the latter, and its acquisition of great moment to the former, perhaps relieving him and his family from pressing distress, it seems obvious, viewing the question independently of any other moral principle than that of general utility, that the act of retaining the property, both in its particular and in its general consequences, would, at least in some cases, be useful; or in other words, that it would tend, in a greater degree than the opposite course of conduct, to produce the greatest aggregate of happiness; or, if this conclusion could be wrong, at least it may be asserted that the question, considered from the standpoint of utility alone, would in many cases be an extremely doubtful one, and that many fairly good men would decide it as we have indicated.

§ 586. Hence it is necessary for the utilitarian to assert another proposition, namely, that the judgment is to be made, not of the particular act, but of the general class of acts to which it belongs; or in other words, that utility requires of us that we should conform our conduct to general rules governing classes of cases. In the language of Austin: "According to that theory, our conduct would con form to rules inferred from the tendencies of actions, but would not be determined by a direct resort to the principle of general utility. Utility would be the test of our conduct ultimately, but not immediately; the immediate test of rules to which our conduct would conform, but not the immediate test of specific or individual actions. Our rules would be fashioned on utility, our conduct on our rules. . . . . If we would try the tendency of a specific or individual act, we must not contemplate the act as if it were single and insulated, but must look at the class of acts to which it belongs:" Austin's Jur. 6, 7.

§ 587. But the proposition thus modified is not altogether consistent with the proposition in the original form; for, admitting that in estimating the utility or inutility of a particular act, we must take into account its tendency to encourage the commission of similar acts, yet, in many cases, the balance of utility might still be in favor of the particular act, though belonging to a class generally pernicious; and such cases, therefore, present exceptions to the rule. Accordingly, Mr. Austin admits that when this is the case, the act, according to the theory of utility, is right. "There certainly are cases," he says, "of comparatively rare occurrence, wherein the specific considerations balance or outweigh the general. . . . . It would be mischievous to depart from the rule which regarded any of these cases, since every departure from a rule tends to weaken its authority; but so important are the specific consequences which would follow our resolves, that the evil of observing the rule might surpass the evil of breaking it. Looking at the reasons from which we inferred the rule, it were absurd to think it inflexible. We should therefore dismiss the rule, resort directly to the principle on which our rules were fashioned, and calculate specific consequences to the best of our knowledge and ability:" Id. 120, 121.

§ 588. But even with this modification, it is obvious that the utilitarian theory must in general be insufficient as a practical guide; for not only will the great mass of mankind always be incompetent to judge of all the consequences, immediate and general, of a particular class of acts, but the task is too much, perhaps, for human wisdom, and certainly for the wisdom of any one man, or even generation of men. And when we add to the task of framing general rules the further task of judging whether it will be useful or expedient to apply them, the difficulty of the problem becomes insuperable.

§ 589. Accordingly, as we have seen, utilitarians are obliged to supplement their theory still further, by asserting another proposition; namely, that utility requires that there should be a certain and definite guide, and that, as there is no other, the will of the government must be adopted as the ̗paramount standard of right and wrong—a principle, however, which they themselves admit is not universally true. "If," says Austin, "we take the principle of utility as our index to the divine commands, we must infer that obedience to established government is enjoined generally by the Deity. For without obedience to powers that be, there were little security and little enjoyment. The ground, however, of the inference is the utility of the government; and if the protection which it yields be too costly, or it vex us with needless restraints, and load us with needless exactions, the principle that points at submission as our general duty may counsel and justify resistance. . . . . Whether resistance to government be useful or pernicious, be consistent or inconsistent with divine pleasure, is therefore an anomalous question. We must try it by a direct resort to the ultimate or presiding principle, and not by the divine rule which the principle clearly indicates. To consult the rule were absurd. For the rule being general and applicable to ordinary cases, it ordains obedience to government, and excludes the question:" Id. 121. So Bentham tells us that in such a case "we ought to examine if it is

more dangerous to violate the law than to obey it;
we ought to consider whether the probable evils of
obedience are less or greater than the probable evils
of disobedience."

§ 590. Another obvious objection to the utilitarian theory is that it identifies right absolutely
with utility, and the latter principle is held to be
the only test in judging of the rectitude of human acts or conduct. It follows, therefore, that
those acts, or classes of acts, which are the most
useful are not only right, but they alone are right,
and all inconsistent acts or conduct wrong. Hence
it follows that no acts can be morally indifferent,
and that even in matters concerning ourselves alone,
the course of conduct which will conduce most to
our interest, or in other words, will give us the
most pleasure, is the only right one, and that all
others are wrong. Hence, to refer to an illustration
already given, where the question is as to how one
shall enjoy his holiday, to take the course least calculated to afford him enjoyment, is not only un-
wise, but wrong, and (if the word is to be admitted
in the vocabulary of the utilitarians) sinful. It is
obvious, however, as we have observed, that many
acts are morally indifferent, and that the term
"right," as applied to actions, usually means
nothing more than that the act is not wrong.

§ 591. The principle of utility should therefore
be stated merely as a limitation upon the principle
of liberty, so as to assert only that nothing can be
right which is hurtful (*nocens*), or opposed to utility,
and that all innocent or harmless acts fall within

the scope of man's rightful free agency. In this form alone, as we have elsewhere observed, can the principle be of any practical utility as a test or standard of right.[1]

[1] In conclusion, it may be remarked that the utilitarian theory, like the legal theory which it is supposed to support, and the prevailing theory of sovereignty, or, as it may be called, the theory of governmental absolutism, furnishes another striking illustration of the truth of Bacon's profound aphorism (cited *supra*, § 377, note), as to the power of words over the mind; and perhaps in the whole range of history no more striking instances of this tyranny can be found.

INDEX.

(383)

25

388 INDEX.

392 INDEX.

396　　　　　　　　INDEX.